AF335269

Momoyama Decorative Painting

Volume 14
THE HEIBONSHA SURVEY OF JAPANESE ART

For a list of the entire series see end of book

CONSULTING EDITORS

Katsuichiro Kamei, *art critic*
Seiichiro Takahashi, *Chairman, Japan Art Academy*
Ichimatsu Tanaka, *Chairman, Cultural Properties Protection Commission*

Momoyama Decorative Painting

by TSUGIYOSHI DOI

translated by Edna B. Crawford

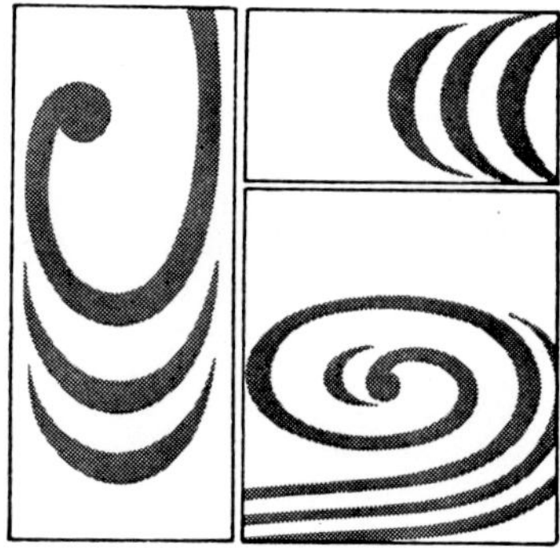

New York · WEATHERHILL / HEIBONSHA · Tokyo

This book was originally published in Japanese by Heibonsha under the title *Momoyama no Shoheki-ga* in the Nihon no Bijutsu series.

A full glossary-index covering the entire series will be published when the series is complete.

First English Edition, 1977

Jointly published by John Weatherhill, Inc., of New York and Tokyo, with editorial offices at 7-6-13 Roppongi, Minato-ku, Tokyo 106, Japan, and Heibonsha, Tokyo. Copyright © 1964, 1977, by Heibonsha; all rights reserved. Printed in Japan.

Library of Congress Cataloging in Publication Data: Doi, Tsugiyoshi, 1906–/ Momoyama decorative painting. / (The Heibonsha survey of Japanese art; v. 14)/ Translation of Momoyama no shōhekiga. / 1. Painting, Japanese— Kamakura, Momoyama periods, 1185–1600. 2. Screen painting, Japanese./ I. Title. II. Series./ND1053.4.D6413   1977 / 759.952 / 76-44338/ ISBN 0-8348-1024-7

Contents

Momoyama Decorative Painting

Preface

IN THIS BOOK the Momoyama period refers to the years between 1573, the year of the final collapse of the Ashikaga shogunate that ruled Japan during the Muromachi period (1336–1573), and 1614, the year before the Toyotomi clan was overthrown by the forces of Tokugawa Ieyasu,* founder of the Tokugawa shogunate. These four decades, called the Momoyama period in Japanese art history, are also known as the Azuchi-Momoyama period.

During the last century of the Muromachi period the Ashikaga shogunate became too weak to govern the country and Japan lapsed into a state of civil strife lasting about a hundred years. During this time authority in the country was divided among contesting feudal lords.

Late in the period Oda Nobunaga emerged as the most powerful of the feudal lords. He was well on his way to assuming control of the entire country when he was assassinated in 1582. Toyotomi Hideyoshi, one of Nobunaga's vassals and an outstanding military leader, succeeded him and completed the unification of Japan. During the Momoyama period Japan was predominantly under the control of Nobunaga and later the Toyotomi clan. The term Azuchi-Momoyama derives from Nobunaga's castle in Azuchi (present Shiga Prefecture) and Hideyoshi's Fushimi Castle, or Fushimi-Momoyama Castle, in Kyoto.

* The names of all premodern Japanese in this book are given, as in this case, in Japanese style (surname first); those of all modern (post-1868) Japanese are given in Western style (surname last).

Even though Oda Nobunaga and Toyotomi Hideyoshi built majestic castles to display their power, not one remains today. Nobunaga's Azuchi Castle was totally destroyed by fire during the fighting following his assassination. Similarly, Hideyoshi's Osaka Castle burned in 1615 during the fighting in which the Toyotomi clan collapsed, and his Fushimi Castle was dismantled by the Tokugawa shogunate in 1615.

Vigor and forcefulness distinguished the painting of this period, reflecting the outlook of the entire nation in a new era. This book also discusses decorative paintings produced immediately before and after the Momoyama period. These help to illustrate the special characteristics of the painting of the Momoyama period and the development of the art of decorative painting.

Because *shoheki-ga* are painted over several contiguous surfaces, most of the figures in this book show only portions of an entire work. Nevertheless, the captions indicate a detail only when less than a single *fusuma* (paper-covered sliding partition) or wall panel is shown. The dimensions of the pictures as given in the captions indicate the measurements of a single *fusuma* or wall panel.

Many of the *shoheki-ga* discussed in this book are located in minor temples within a larger temple compound. When the painting is in a minor temple, the name of the main temple is also given in the caption: for example, Juko-in, Daitoku-ji, or Shinju-an, Daitoku-ji.

CHAPTER ONE

The Meaning and Characteristics of Shoheki-ga

TRADITIONAL FORMS OF PAINTING

Japanese paintings are seen in a variety of formats. Hanging scrolls and framed pictures are seen in most homes, but there are many other types, as well. One is the hand scroll, or picture scroll. Originally introduced from China, it developed its own colorful history as a form of Japanese painting. Picture scrolls in the *yamato-e* style, which flourished during the Heian (794–1185) and Kamakura (1185–1336) periods, occupy a unique place among the fine arts of the world.

Another art form, that of painting on folding screens, was introduced from China but developed most distinctively in Japan. It began at least as early as the Nara period (646–794). Of one hundred folding screens listed in the *Todai-ji Kemmotsu-cho,* an inventory of items belonging to the Emperor Shomu (r. 724–49) and donated to the Todai-ji temple in Nara, twenty-one were painted. Later, folding screens were painted by artists of many traditions, including *yamato-e* and the Chinese-style *kara-e,* and assumed an important place in Japanese painting.

In addition to picture scrolls and screens, pictures were also painted on smaller surfaces, such as fans, picture books, and small squares and rectangles of stiffened paper. Of these, the fans are the most decorative and elegant. Many excellent fan paintings survive.

However, there are still other important forms of Japanese painting. One is wall paintings, or murals, the oldest form of painting both East and West. In Japan as elsewhere, wall paintings have been discovered in ancient tombs. Wall paintings in Buddhist temples developed when Buddhism was introduced to Japan in the sixth century. Representative examples include paintings on plaster walls like those of the Golden Hall of the Horyu-ji temple in Nara and the Amida Hall of the Hokai-ji temple in Kyoto, as well as paintings on wood-paneled walls or wooden doors like those of the Golden Hall of the Muro-ji in Nara, the five-storied pagoda of Kyoto's Daigo-ji, and the Phoenix Hall of the Byodo-in near Kyoto. In later centuries, pictures were painted on paper mounted on walls. At first Shinto shrines did not use wall paintings for ornamentation, but partly as a result of the influence of wall paintings in Buddhist temples, a number of later Shinto shrines adopted this type of decoration.

Ceiling painting is another form intimately related to wall painting. Ceiling paintings are also closely related to *shoheki-ga* and were used in both religious and residential architecture. Interesting works of both types survive.

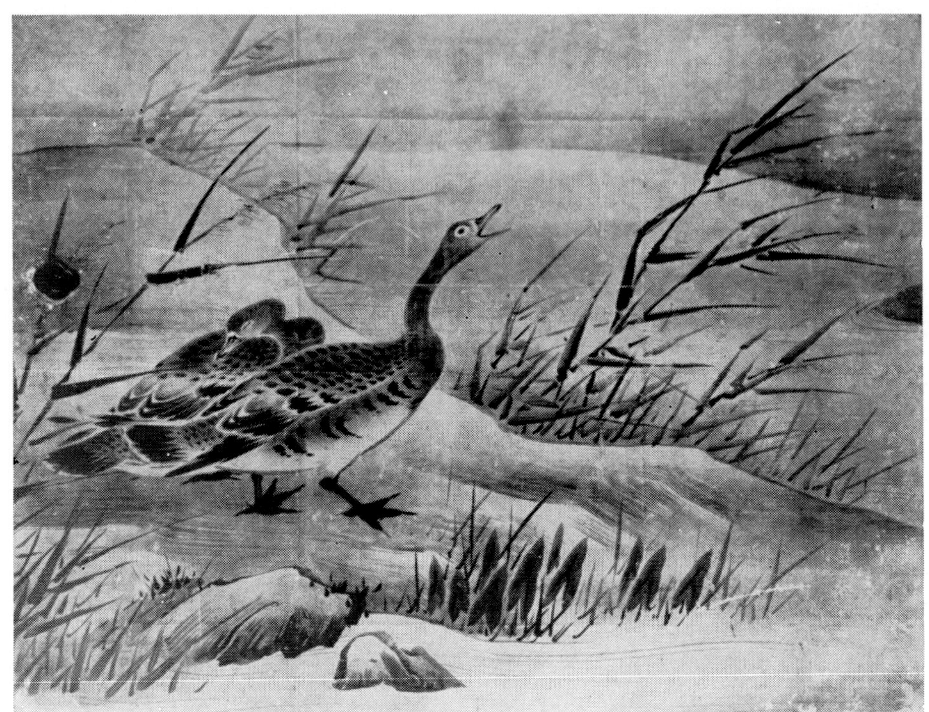

1. *Kano Eitoku: detail from* Flowers and Birds. Fusuma, *ink on paper; 177 × 143.5 cm. 1566.* *Main hall, Juko-in, Daitoku-ji, Kyoto.*

SHOJI AND SHOJI-E   The *shoheki-ga* discussed in this book are representative of one of the most important forms of Japanese painting. The *sho* of *shoheki-ga* refers to *shoji; shoheki-ga* is a general term for paintings on *shoji,* which are also called *shoji-e,* or paintings on paper mounted on a wall. The character *sho* means "to separate, block, shut out, or screen," and *shoji* are partitions used to divide the interior space of a house. Originally the term *shoji* was used for a screen, but today it refers to sliding panels consisting of a wooden lattice with white paper pasted on one side. These were first called *akari-shoji, akari* meaning "transmitting light." This form developed later than the sliding partitions called *fusuma-shoji,* which will be discussed below.

Single-panel screens called *tsuitate-shoji* have the longest history as interior partitions. They were used in palaces, temples, and the mansions of the nobility, and sometimes were decorated with paintings. Examples appeared at least as early as the Nara period, and it is known that the Yakushi-ji in Nara contained screens portraying a Chinese Buddhist priest, Hsuan-chuang San-tsang, and the Miroku (Maitreya) Paradise. It is also known that Nara's Saidai-ji had screens depicting the Fudaraku Paradise of Kannon (Avalokitesvara) and the Yakushi (Bhaisajyaguru) Paradise. Screen painting continued over a long period. The famous screen with the scene of the K'un-ming Pond in China and another with a scene of rough seas were placed in the Seiryoden of the imperial palace in Kyoto during the Heian period. *Tsuitate-shoji* were named among the "fixtures and furnishings of homes" listed in the *Makura no Soshi* (Pillow Book) by the Heian court lady Sei Shonagon.

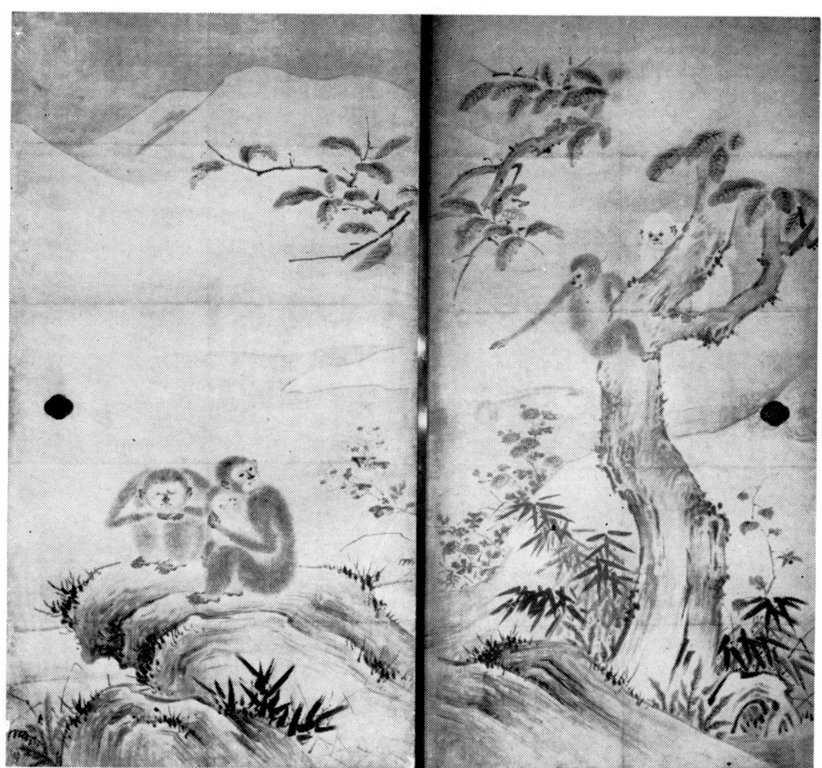

2. Kano Shoei: Monkeys. Fusuma, *ink on paper; 177 × 94 cm. 1566. Main hall, Juko-in, Daitoku-ji, Kyoto.*

In the early Heian period (794–897) the sliding partitions that today are generally called *fusuma* were invented, although they too were called *shoji* at that time. These *fusuma-shoji* were constructed by covering a fine wooden lattice with silk, some other fabric, or paper pasted on both sides of the frame. *Fusuma* are used to separate rooms. Usually they rest in tracks cut in the floor and lintel and can be opened or closed as needed by means of recessed hand grips. However, some *fusuma* are not meant to be moved, such as the *Kenjo Shoji,* bearing portraits of thirty-two Chinese sages, in the Shi-shinden of the Kyoto Imperial Palace.

Traditionally there were two types of interior partitions, screens and sliding partitions, both of which were used as painting surfaces. In time *sugi-shoji, tobusuma,* and *akari-shoji* were created. All these are classified as *shoji. Sugi-shoji,* now generally called *sugido,* are partitions of cedar wood that usually slide open and shut. Pictures are painted directly on the wood. *Tobusuma* refers to *fusuma-shoji* with a wooden board attached to the frame on one side and paper pasted on the other. Pictures are painted on the paper-covered side. As mentioned earlier, *akari-shoji* are the sliding panels that are simply called *shoji* now. The white paper of *shoji* is not used for painting. A variant of *akari-shoji* called *koshi-shoji* has a wainscot on the lower part. (When the wainscot is high, it is called a *koshidaka-shoji.*) Pictures on the wainscot may be painted either directly on the wood or on paper pasted on the wainscot. Both forms of picture are called *koshi-shoji-e.*

Thus there are many varieties of *shoji-e,* or paintings on partitions. Of these *fusuma-e,* or sliding-partition paintings, are the most important form

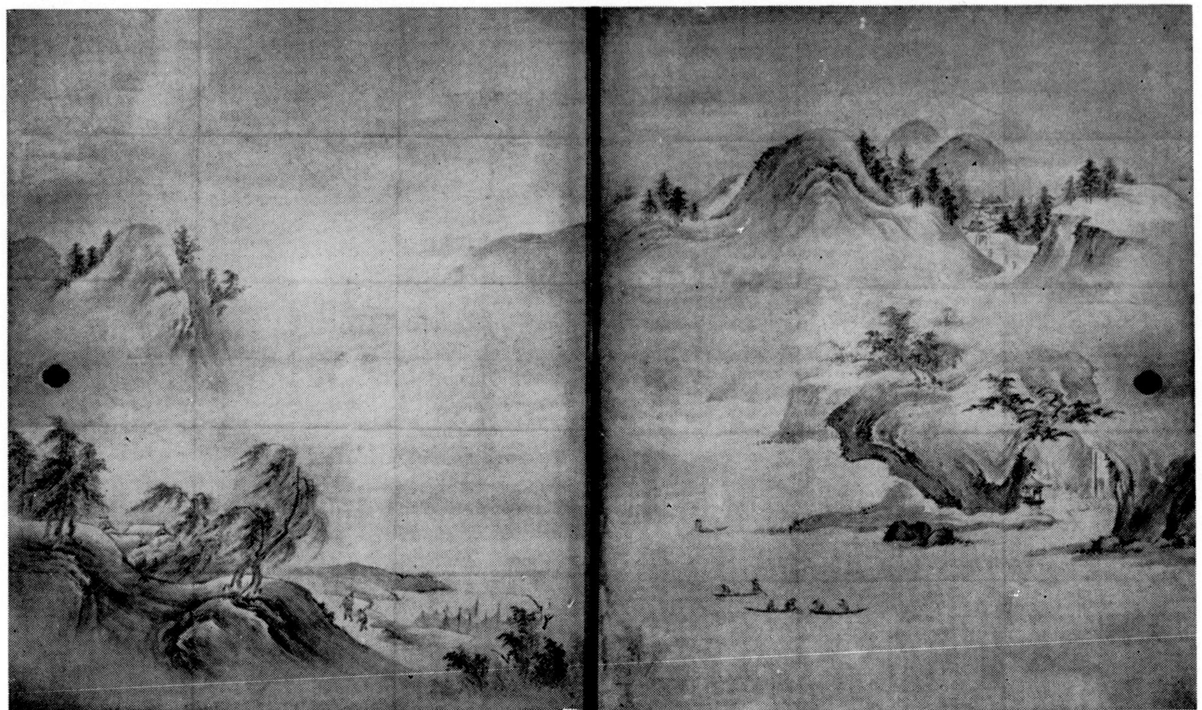

3. *Kano Shoei:* Landscape. Fusuma, *ink on paper; 177 × 143.5 cm. 1566. Main hall, Juko-in, Daitoku-ji, Kyoto.*

and have the most colorful history. Pictures painted on paper mounted on a wall are closely related to *fusuma-e.* As we have noted, this type of wall painting was used to some extent in religious architecture, and together with *fusuma-e* it played a significant role in interior decoration. The entire genre of wall and partition paintings is included in *shoheki-ga.*

The term *shohei-ga* is similar to *shoheki-ga.* However, the subject matter of *shohei-ga* is broader than that of *shoheki-ga* and includes folding-screen paintings. Often *shoheki-ga* and screen paintings are treated as one genre because they are closely related and developed together, but this book, focusing on decorative painting directly related to architecture, will discuss only *shoheki-ga.*

Shoheki-ga differ in many ways from other forms of painting. In viewing and studying them, it is important to understand their unique nature and limitations.

FUSUMA PAINTING AND RESIDENTIAL ARCHITECTURE

As pointed out above, *fusuma* painting plays a leading role in *shoheki-ga.* Unlike plaster walls, *fusuma* have no structural function. They can be removed from a building at any time. Yet when they are in the closed position, *fusuma* function as walls, dividing the interior space. In this sense *fusuma* have the same quality as walls, and *fusuma* painting can be considered a form of wall painting. Since *fusuma* were invented in Japan, *fusuma*

4. *Hasegawa Tohaku: detail from* Pine Tree and Flowers. *One of a pair of twofold screens; colors and gold on paper; each* ▷
panel 226.5 × 165.5 cm. 1592. Chishaku-in, Kyoto.

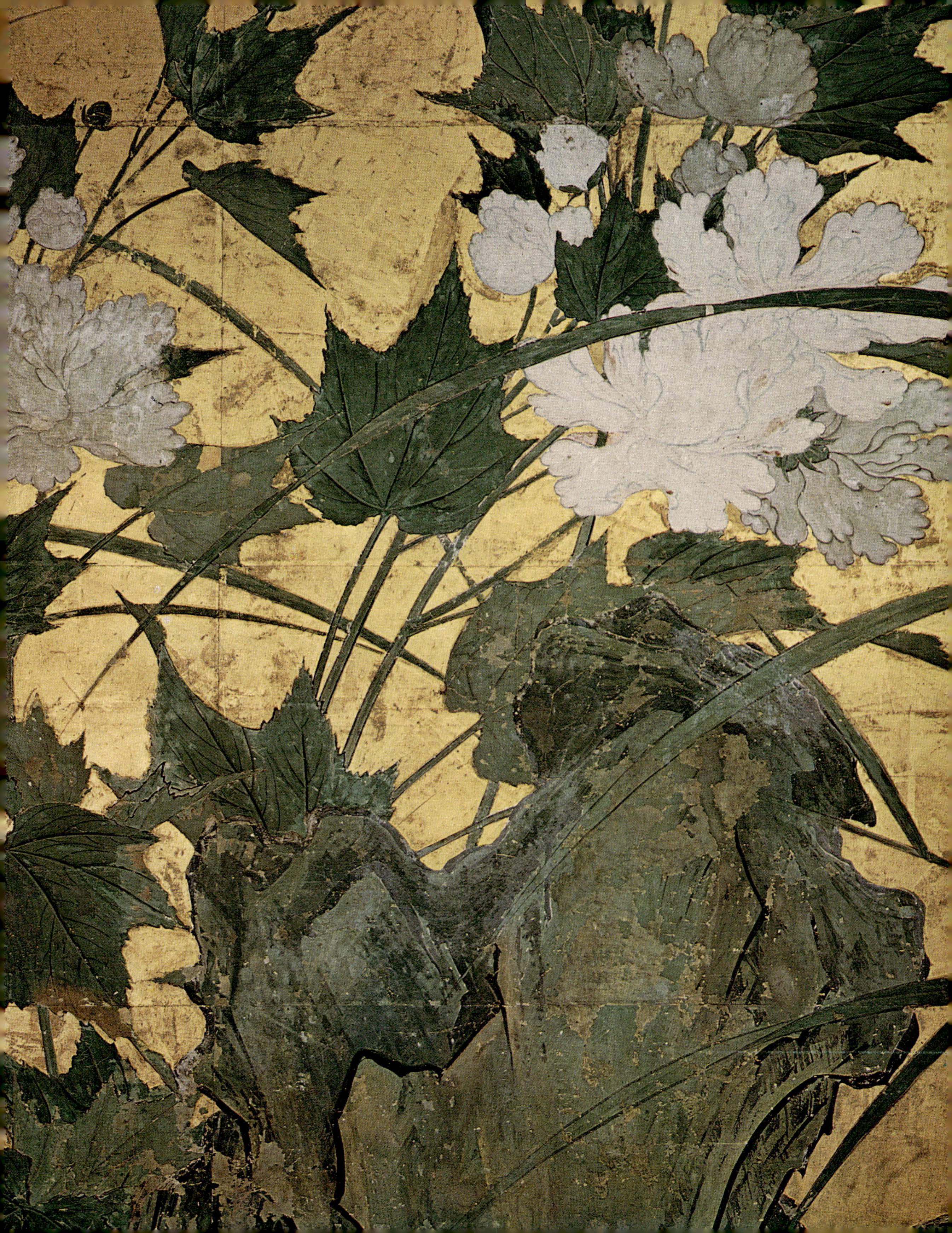

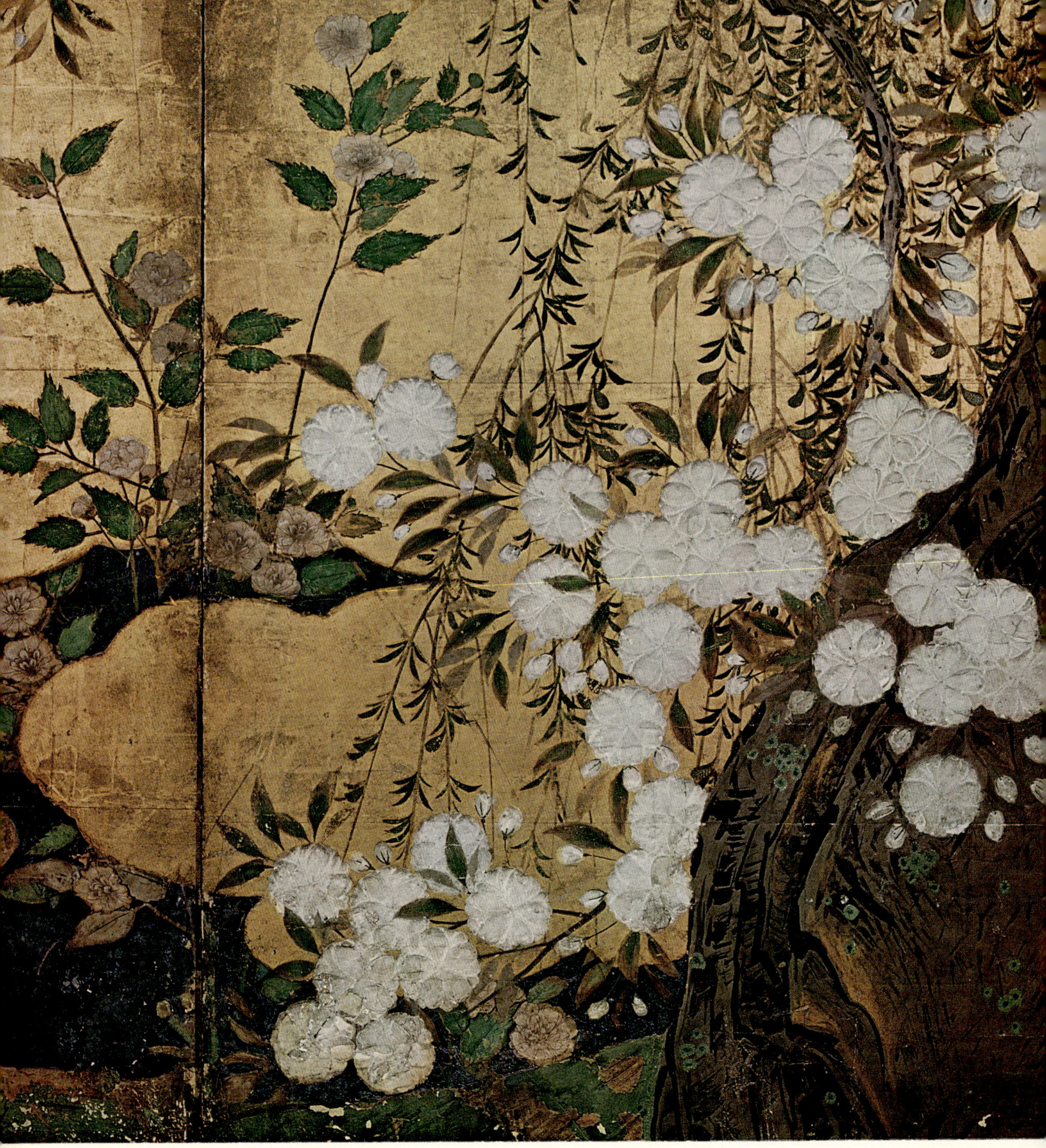

5. *Hasegawa Kyuzo: detail from* Cherry Tree. *Colors and gold on paper mounted on a wall; 172.5 × 139.5 cm. 1592. Chishaku-in, Kyoto. (See also Figures 90, 91.)*

6. *Hasegawa Tohaku: detail from* Maple Tree. *Colors and gold on paper mounted on a wall;* ▷
172.5 × 138.5 cm. 1592. Chishaku-in, Kyoto. (See also Figure 79.)

7 *(overleaf).* Kano Sanraku: Peonies. Fusuma, *colors and gold on paper;* ▷
184.5 × 99 cm. Early seventeenth century. Shinden, Daikaku-ji, Kyoto.

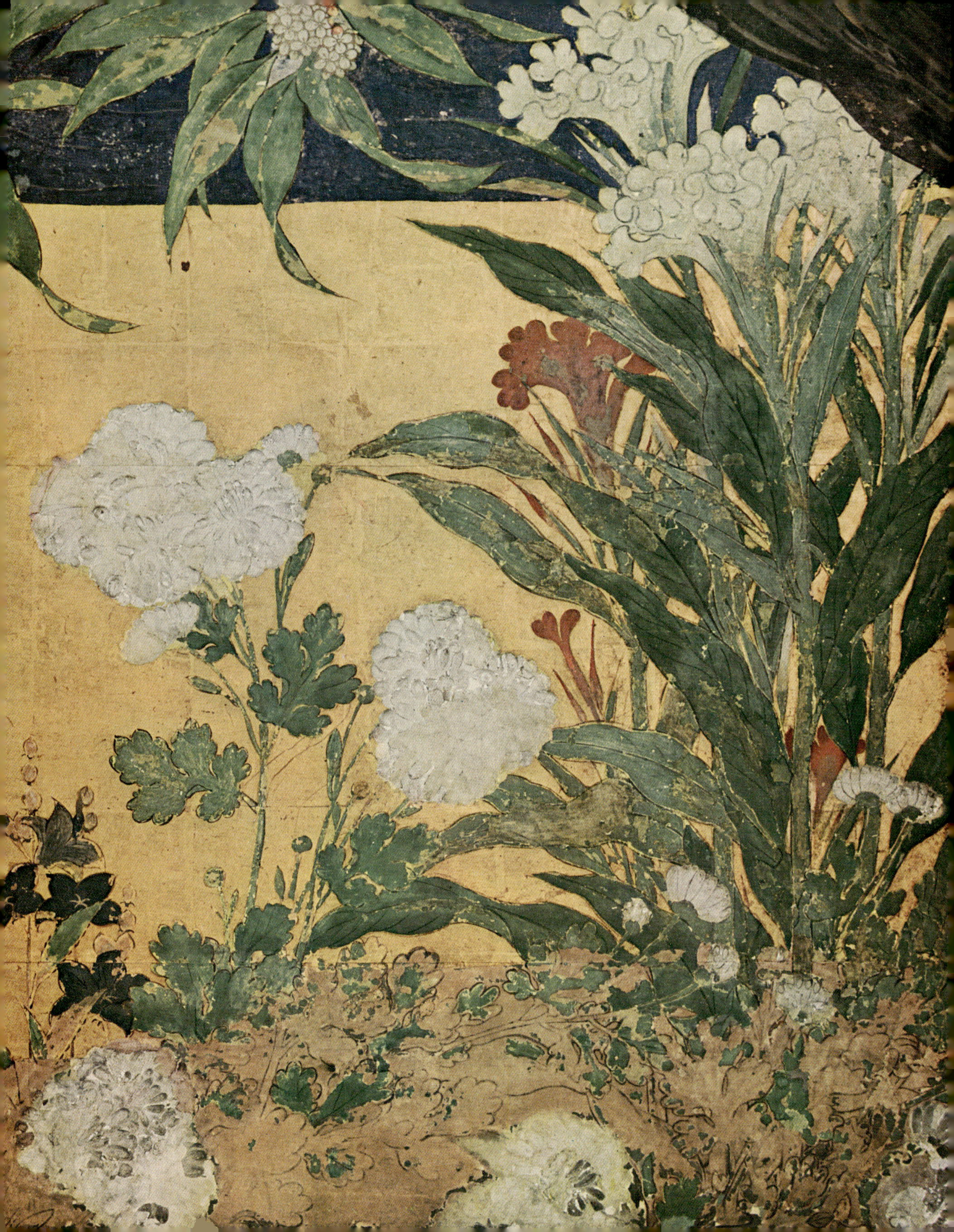

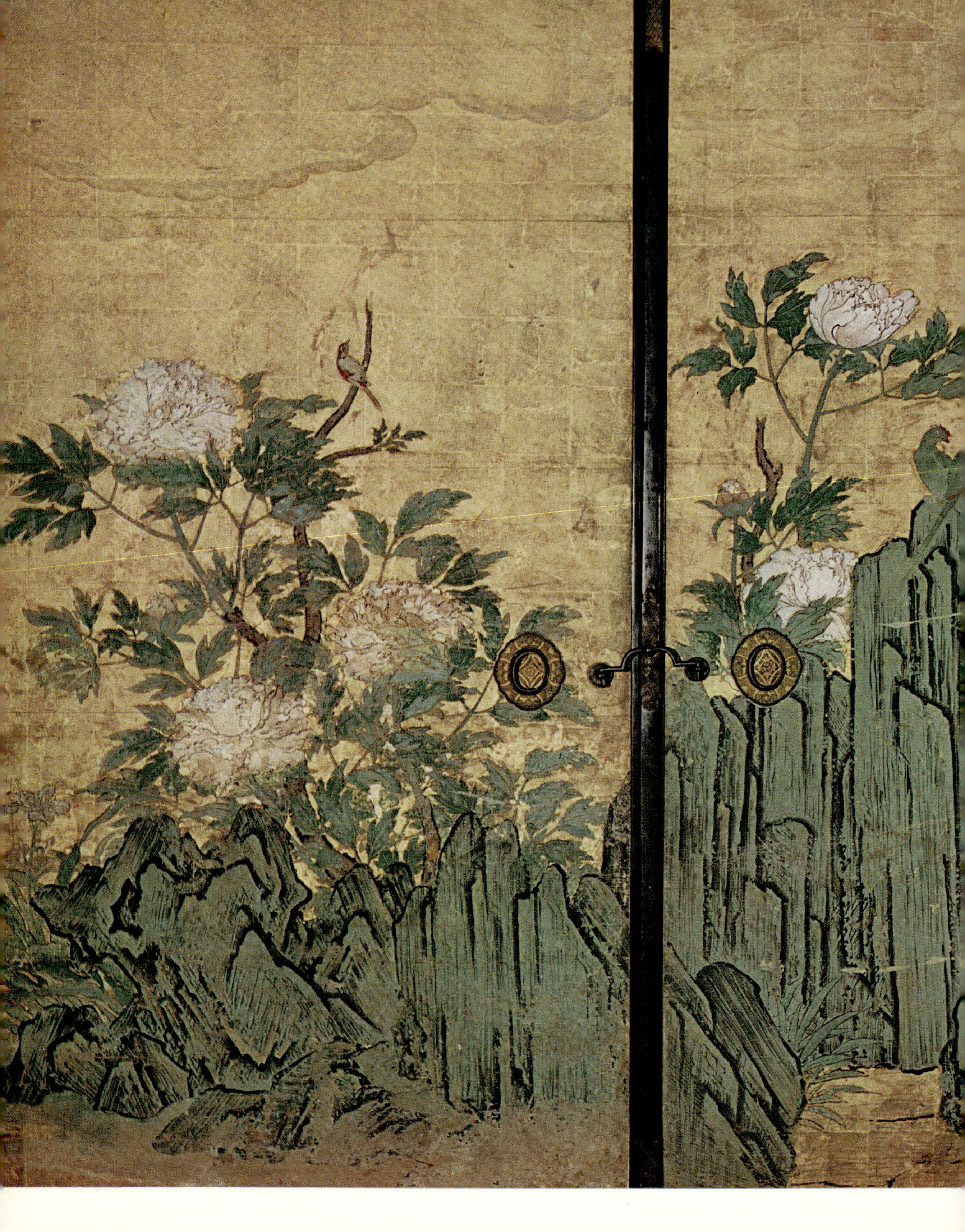

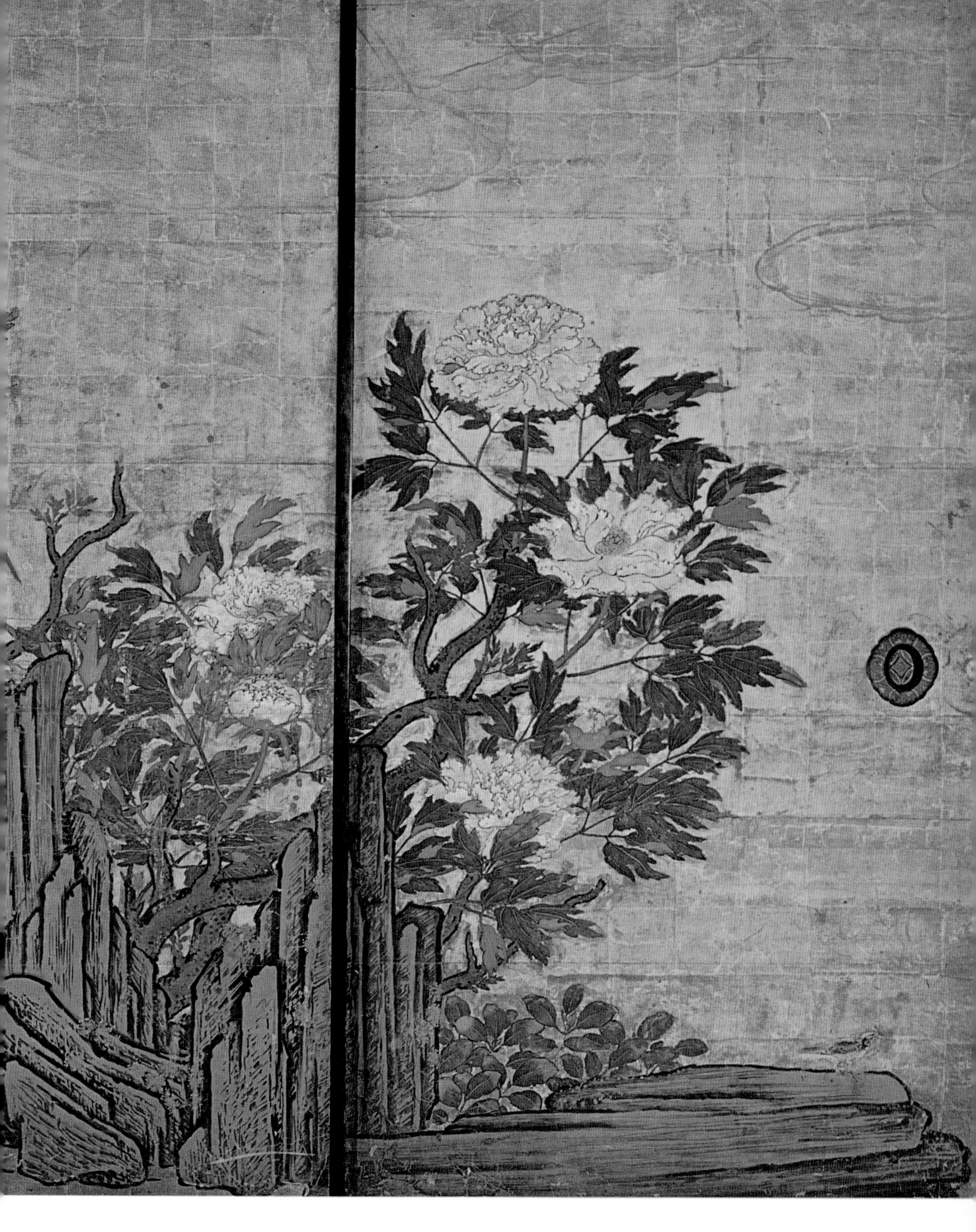

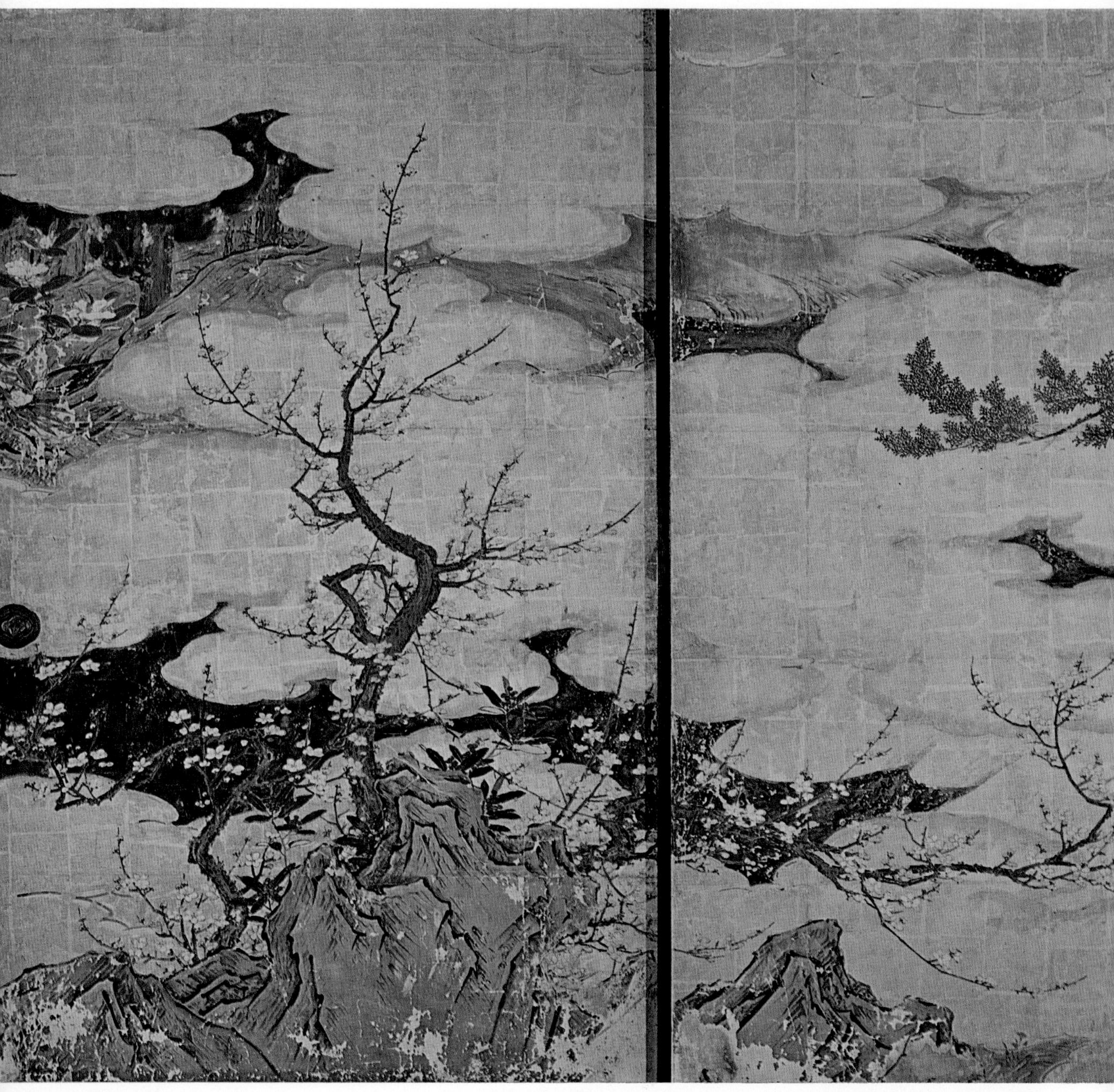

8. *Kano Mitsunobu:* Flowers and Birds. Fusuma, *colors and gold on paper; 177 × 117 cm. 1600. Reception hall, Kangaku-in,* *Onjo-ji, Shiga Prefecture. (See also Figure 23.)*

9. *Attributed to Kano Eitoku: detail from* Japanese Cypress. *Eightfold screen, colors and gold* ▷ *on paper; 170 × 462.5 cm. Late sixteenth century. Tokyo National Museum.*

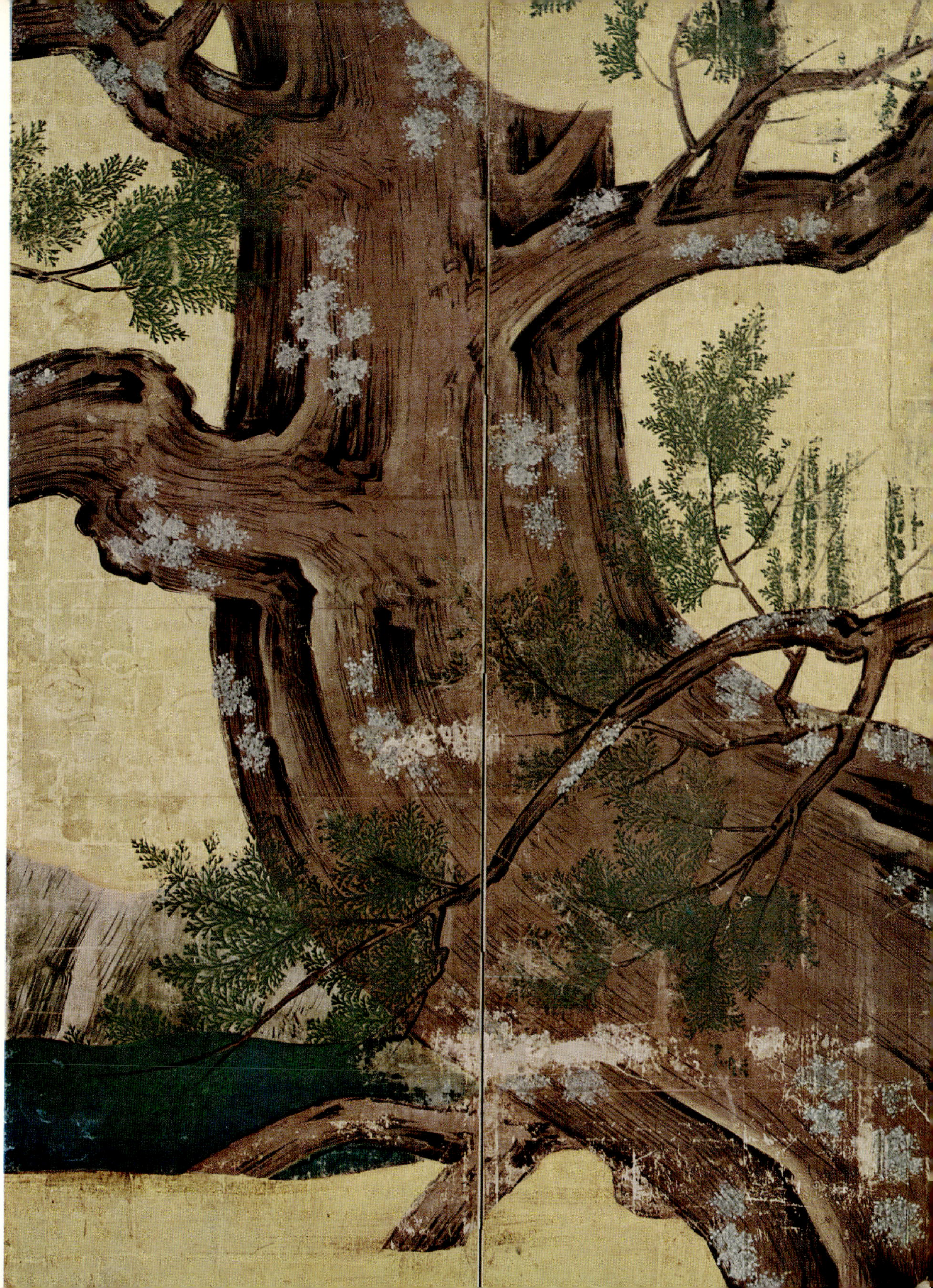

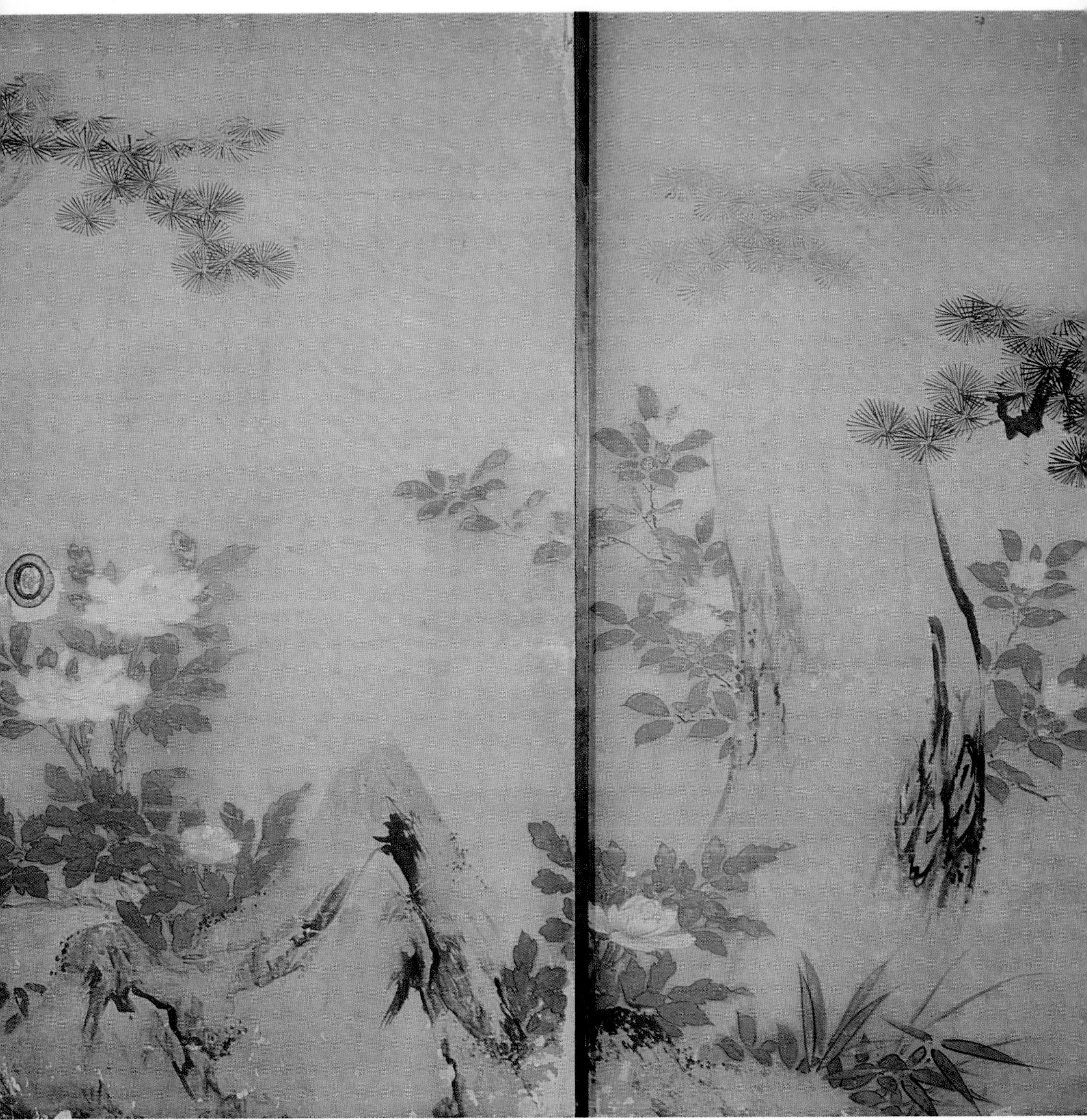

10. Kaiho Yusho: Flowers and Birds. Fusuma, *colors on paper; 167 × 93 cm. Late sixteenth century.* Shoin, *Reito-in, Kennin-ji, Kyoto. (See also Figure 64.)*

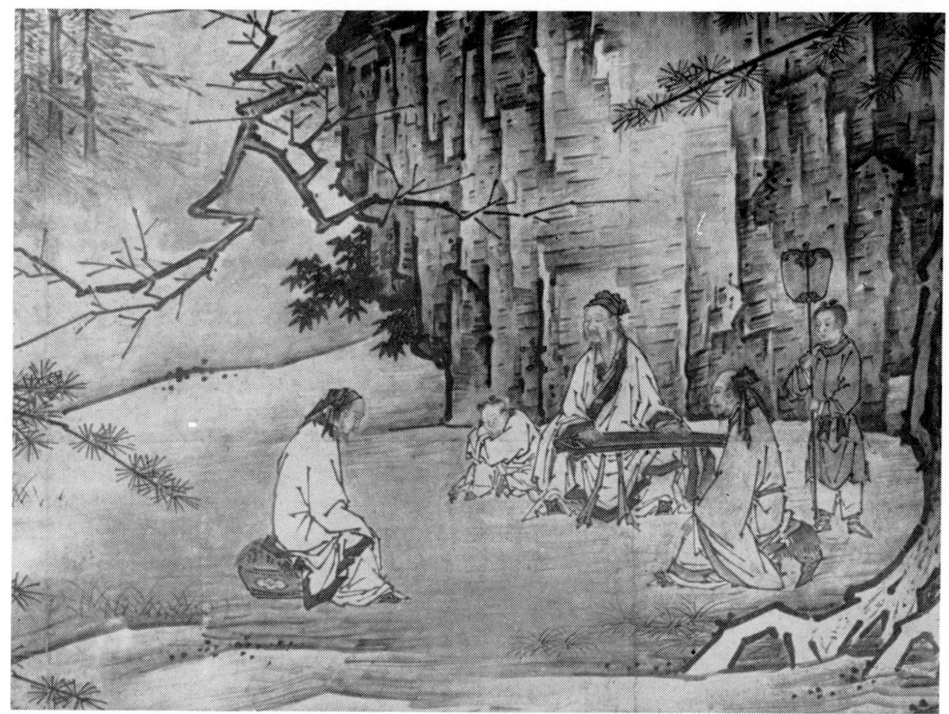

11. *Kano Eitoku: detail from* Landscape and Figures, *illustrating the four gentlemanly accomplishments.* Fusuma, *ink and light colors on paper; 177 × 143.5 cm. 1566. Main hall, Juko-in, Daitoku-ji, Kyoto.*

painting is a form of wall painting unique to Japan.

Notwithstanding the fact that *fusuma* painting was occasionally used in the religious architecture of Shinto shrines and Buddhist temples, it found its main use in residential architecture. As a part of this architecture, *fusuma* painting underwent a colorful development. In shrines and temples, *fusuma* paintings were used mainly in the residences of the priests rather than in the buildings used for religious purposes. Wall paintings in the residential architecture of Japan, including *fusuma* paintings, are synonymous with *shoheki-ga.* Paintings of religious subjects are seen in *shoheki-ga,* but because *shoheki-ga* were used mainly in residences, the paintings more often depict themes characteristic of decorative art.

ARCHITECTURE AND DECORATIVE PAINTING

Unlike independent paintings, *shoheki-ga* are decorative paintings incidental to architecture and subordinate to it. They play a supporting role to enhance architecture, which plays the leading part. And this is why the paintings must harmonize with the architecture. It is important that the artist have a deep understanding not only of the aesthetic character of the architecture but also of its function. Then a subject and style of painting appropriate to the architecture must be selected. Nijo Castle in Kyoto, built in 1602, contains *shoheki-ga* painted in the early part of the Kan'ei era (1624–44). *Shoheki-ga* of grand and showy design and style were painted in the rooms for official use, such as the *tozamurai,*

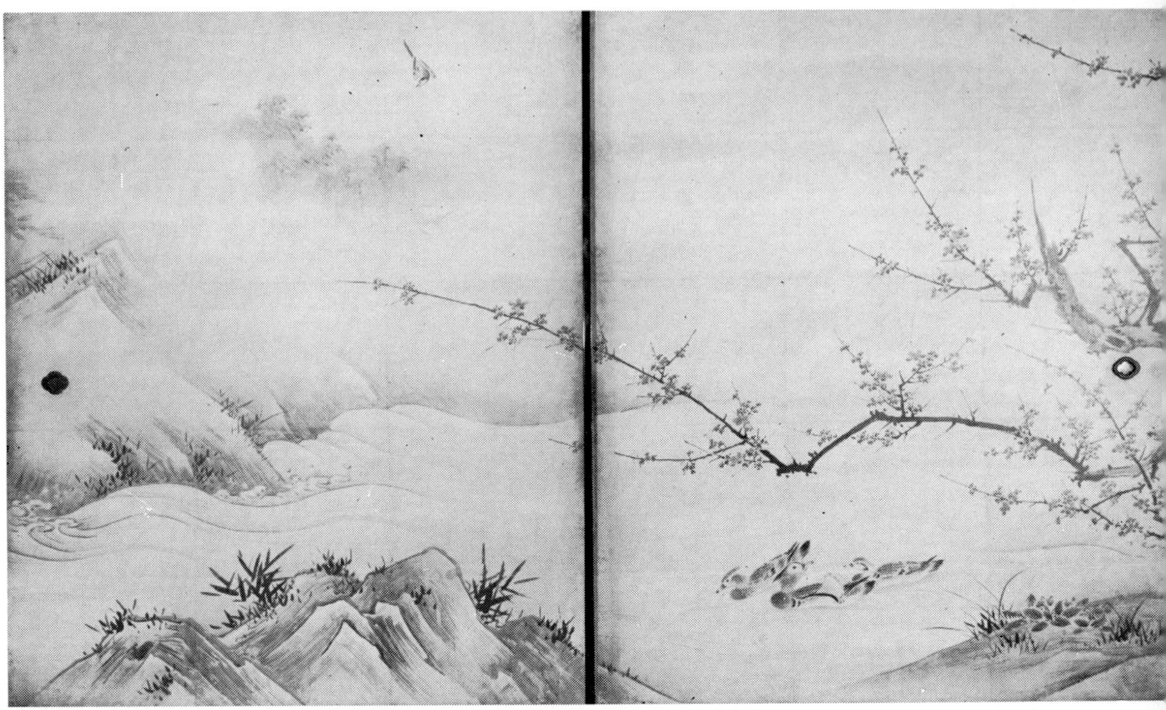

an anteroom for visiting daimyo; the *shikidai,* where the daimyo reported the reason for his visit and handed over his presents to the shogun; and the *ohiroma,* where the shogun formally received the daimyo. On the other hand, the *shoheki-ga* in the *shiroshoin,* the shogun's informal living and sleeping quarters in the residential wing, were quiet, unpretentious landscapes. These are examples of decorative art produced with a clear understanding of the nature and function of the architecture itself.

Because *shoheki-ga* are subordinate to architecture, both the size and the shape of painting surfaces and their locations are regulated by the scale and framework of the building. The artist has no choice but to accept these limitations, which are intrinsic to *shoheki-ga.* Yet the work of excellent *shoheki-ga* artists does not suffer because of such limitations. These master artists have yielded to the restrictions placed on them but have not been discouraged or intimidated by them. In their creative work, they have handled the given situation in a positive way and made the most of it. Their

works of art, painted in the space assigned, fully satisfy the decorative needs of the architecture.

PAINTING SURFACE AND SURROUNDING SPACE

One characteristic of *shoheki-ga,* as of other forms of wall painting, is the large painting surface compared to other types of painting, together with the fixed nature of the size, shape, and location of the painting surface. When the painting of *shoheki-ga* in castles began in the mid-sixteenth century, huge painting surfaces appeared for the first time in the history of Japanese art. This characteristic expansiveness became even more marked later in the century.

In addition to their total size, *shoheki-ga* are distinguished by their extensive horizontal painting surface. Of course this characteristic, a long continuation of the painting surface from right to left, is also seen in hand scrolls. A pair of folding screens also presents a rather long continuous painting surface. However, a long horizontal painting surface

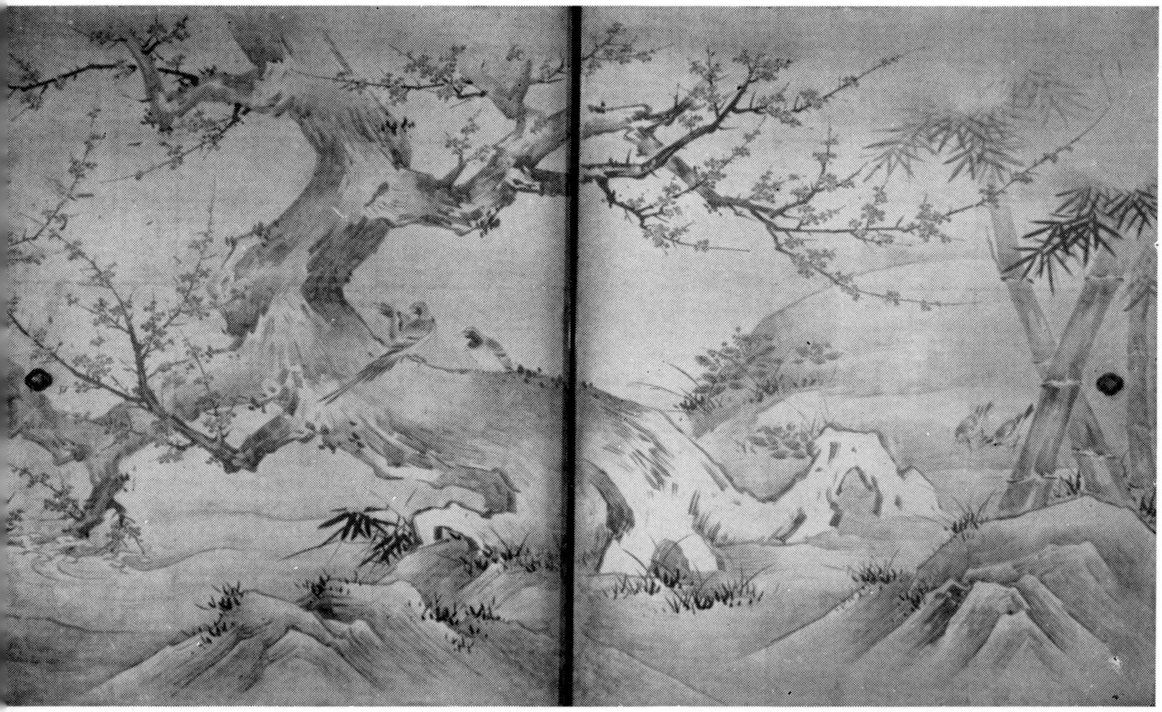

12 (above). *Kano Eitoku:* Flowers and Birds. Fusuma, *ink on paper; 177 × 143.5 cm. 1566. Main hall, Juko-in, Daitoku-ji, Kyoto. (See also Figure 14.)*

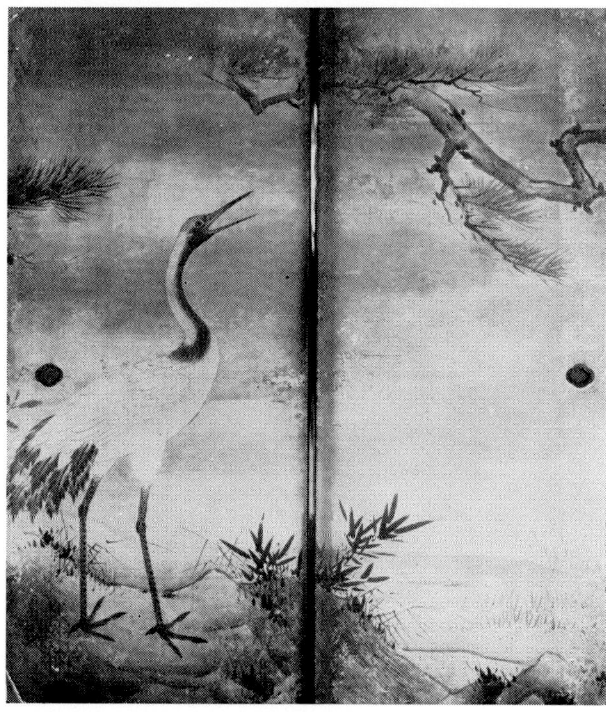

13. *Kano Eitoku:* Flowers and Birds. Fusuma, *ink on paper; 177 × 74 cm. 1566. Main hall, Juko-in, Daitoku-ji, Kyoto.*

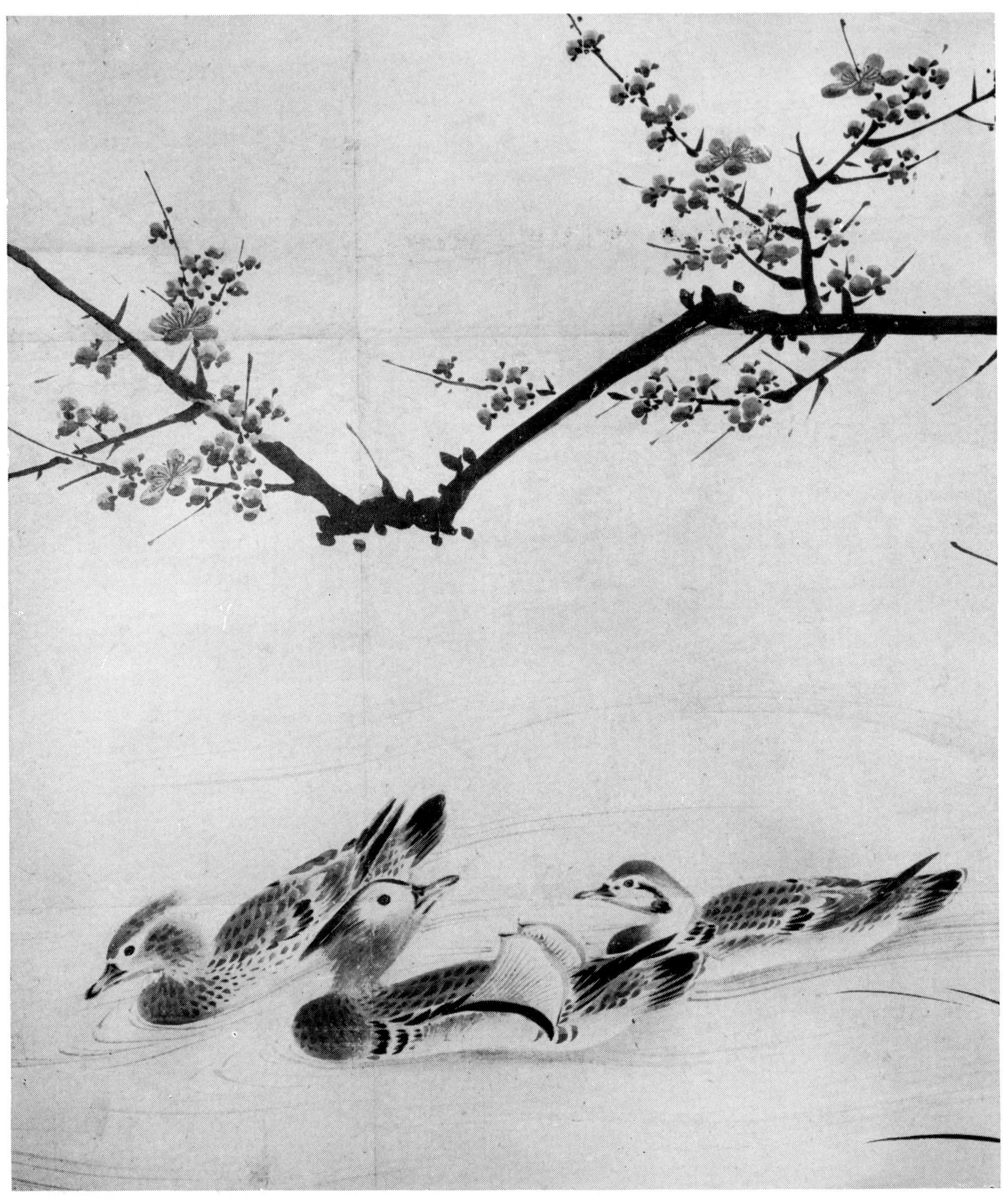

14. Kano Eitoku: detail from Flowers and Birds. Fusuma, *ink on paper; 177 × 143.5 cm. 1566. Main hall, Juko-in, Dai-toku-ji, Kyoto. (See also Figure 12.)*

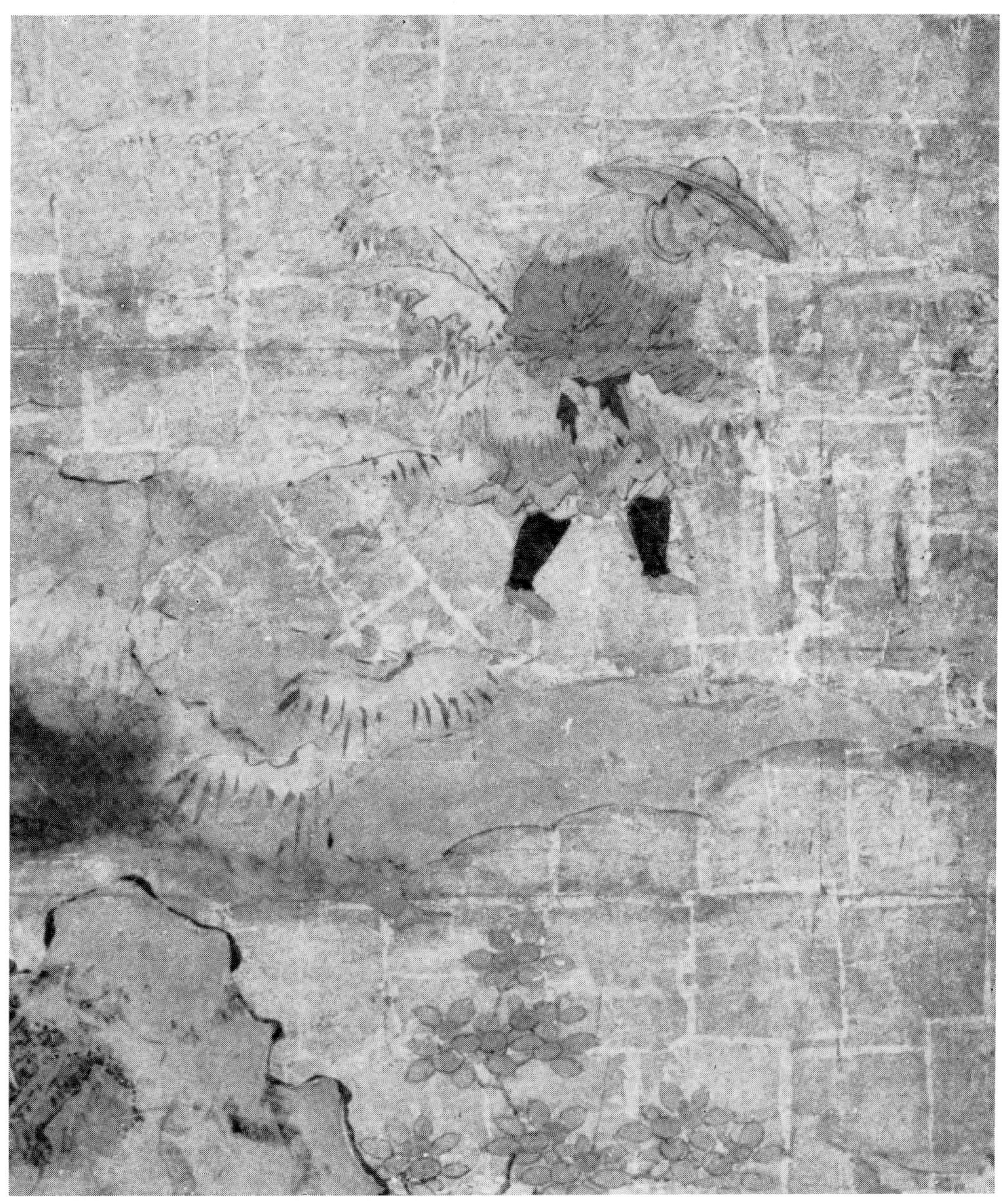

15. Attributed to Kano Eitoku: detail from Twenty-four Paragons of Filial Piety, *showing Meng Tsung.* Fusuma, *colors and gold on paper; 184 × 98 cm. Late sixteenth century.* Ohojo, *Nanzen-ji, Kyoto. (See also Figure 40.)*

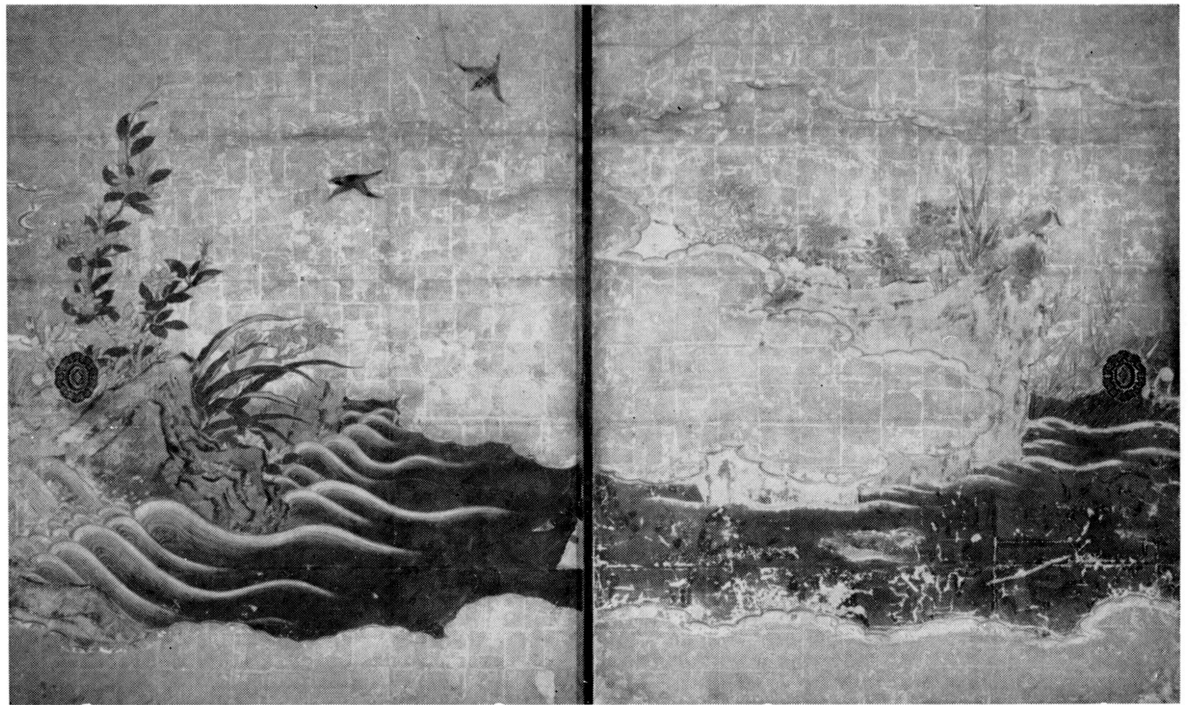

16. *Attributed to Kano Eitoku:* Flowers and Birds. Fusuma, *colors and gold on paper; 177 × 143 cm. Late sixteenth century.* Shinden, Emman-in, Shiga Prefecture.

in combination with a large total area is unique to *shoheki-ga.* The painting surface of *fusuma* paintings, which comprise the majority of *shoheki-ga,* is usually made up of many *fusuma* lined up side by side (Figs. 98, 99). The larger the room, the greater the number of *fusuma* used, which naturally increases the extent of the painting surface in the horizontal direction. The special characteristics of a horizontally long painting surface become especially noticeable when all four sides of a huge room consist of *fusuma.* As the artists of picture scrolls exerted their ingenuity in composing paintings to meet the challenge of a horizontally long painting surface, *shoheki-ga* artists also devised various ways of handling this characteristic. Of course, the painting surface of *shoheki-ga* not only extends horizontally but sometimes continues from one wall of a room to the next. Let us consider the diagram of a room

shown opposite. If *fusuma* paintings are to be placed on walls A and B of the same room, it is necessary for the paintings on both A and B to form a harmonious whole and for the compositions of A and B to be linked as if they formed a continuous painting. At the same time, care must be taken to avoid monotony, by varying the design and composition. The treatment of the design and composition of *shoheki-ga* can become very complicated because there are times when *fusuma* paintings are desired not only on walls A and B but on all four walls of the room.

During the Edo period (1615–1868), some artists designed witty compositions utilizing the three-dimensional space created by the *fusuma* surfaces extending from wall A to wall B, including the angle of the corner. One example is a composition in which a figure on painting surface A is gazing

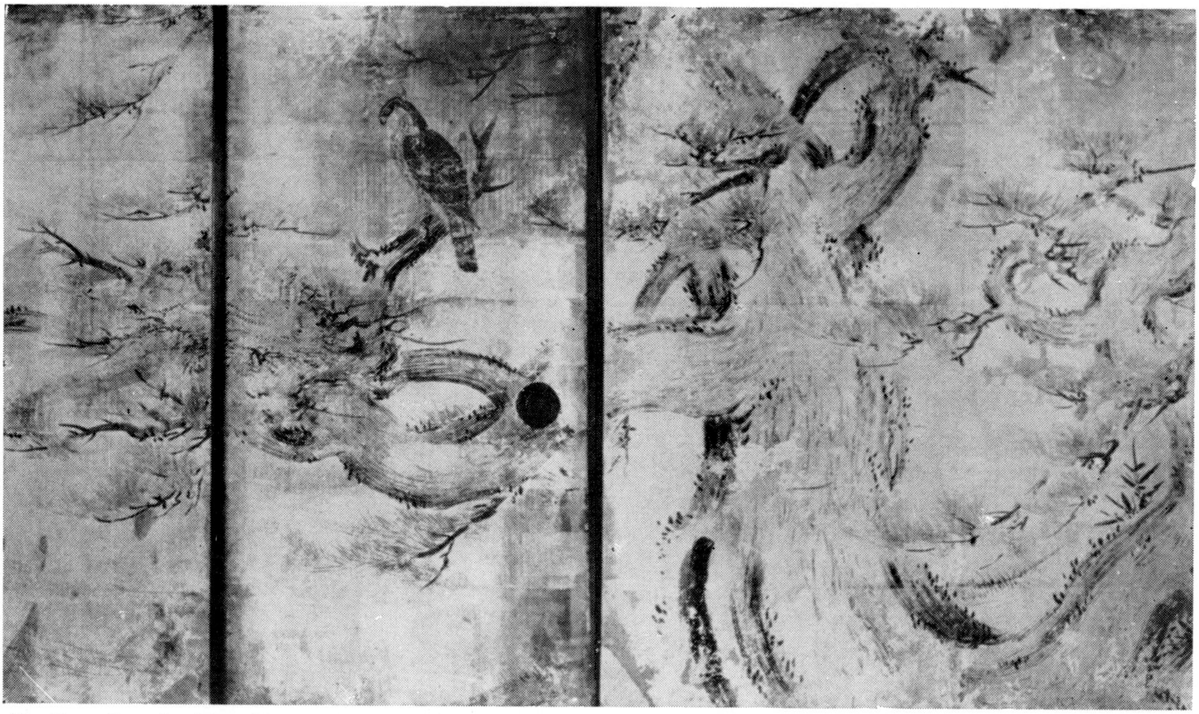

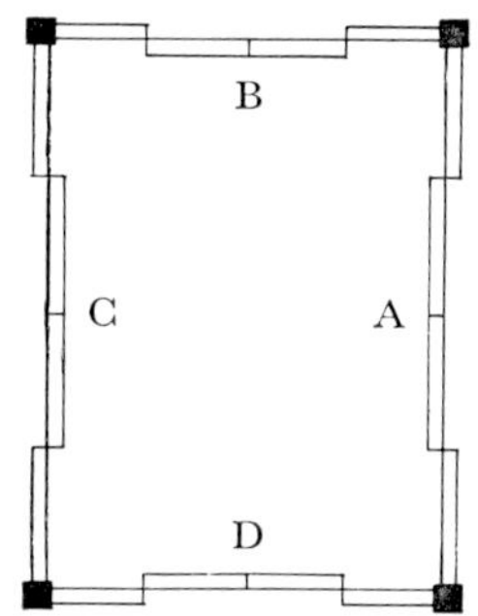

17. *Kano Sanraku:* Pine Tree and Hawk. Fusuma *and paper mounted on a wall;* fusuma *179.5 × 93.5 cm., wall painting 183.5 × 179.5 cm. Shoshinden, Daikaku-ji, Kyoto.*

at a figure on painting surface B. Maruyama Okyo (1733–95), one of the most famous Japanese artists of the Edo period, attempted this in the Kakushigi-no-ma in the reception hall (*kyakuden*) of the Daijo-ji in Hyogo Prefecture. Ikeno Taiga (1723–76) frequently used a similar type of composition.

FACTORS IN PAINTING SHOHEKI-GA

Usually *shoheki-ga* are painted in many rooms of a building; it is rare to find *shoheki-ga* in only one room. The imperial palaces and the castles of feudal lords contained a great many rooms, and frequently all contained *shoheki-ga*. Sometimes the task of painting was assigned entirely to one artist, while in other cases the rooms were distributed among several artists. In either case, when *shoheki-ga* were required in many rooms, selecting the subject matter

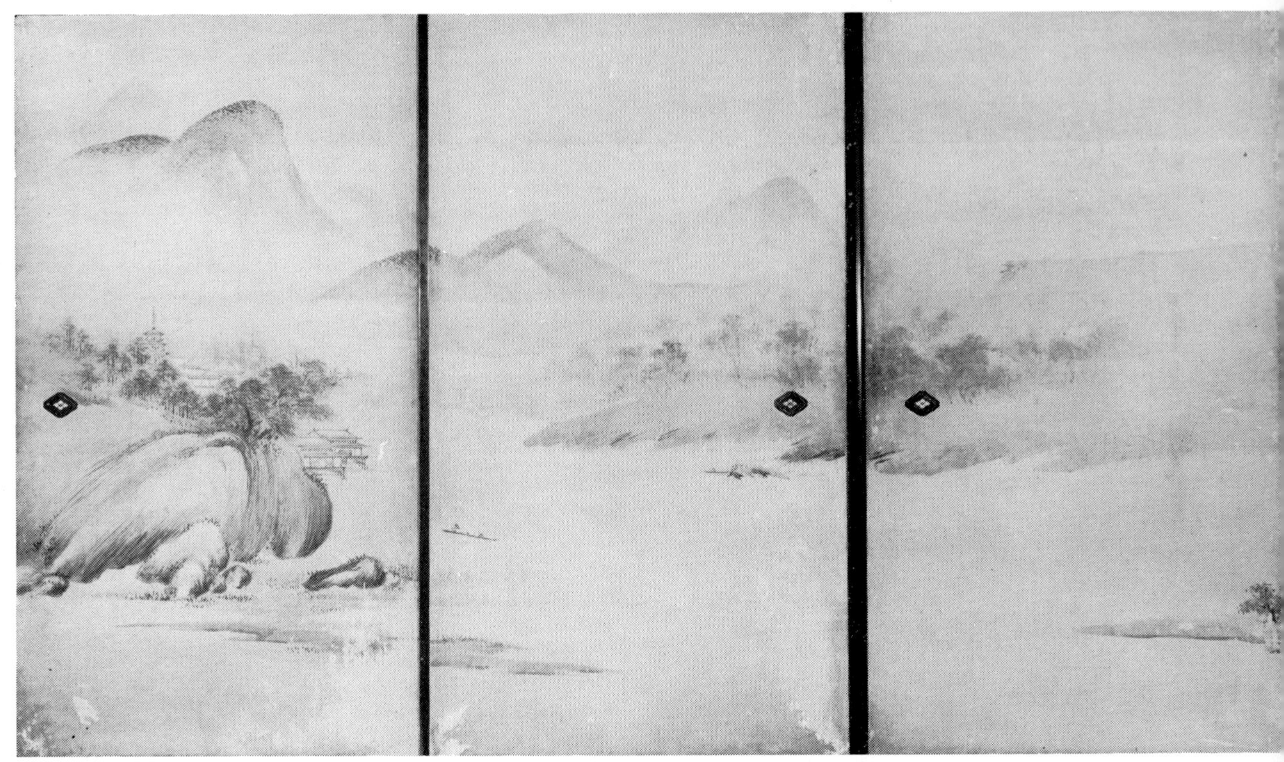

for the paintings in each room became a problem. Although no sweeping statement can be made, because *shoheki-ga* themes changed with the times, we can say that in the Momoyama period the subject matter available was varied. In some instances the selection was mixed, with an appropriate assortment of landscapes, paintings of flowers and birds (*kachoga*), and representations of human figures. In other cases, only two of these subjects were allotted, and in some instances only one—only landscapes, or only flowers and birds.

Kano Eino (1631–97), writing on "methods of painting on walls and partitions" in the *Honcho Gashi,* an art history of Japan, gives these guidelines: "Paint landscapes in the *jodan* [the raised area of a palace room, used by nobles and lords], figures in the *chudan* [the area between *jodan* and *gedan*], and flowers and birds in the *gedan* [the lower part of the room, used by vassals]. In the rooms under the eaves, paint animals. In a magnificent palace, the various pictures should be done in rich colors throughout. It is in accordance with the rules to paint what is suitable to the given circumstances and the request of the client." However, in reality, most *shoheki-ga* did not follow the rule of landscapes in the *jodan,* figures in the *chudan,* and flowers and birds in the *gedan;* instead, subjects were chosen according to the request of the client and the specific circumstances. *Shoheki-ga* presented additional complications not seen in other forms of painting. Because *shoheki-ga* were frequently executed in many rooms at the same time, it required ingenuity to vary not only the subjects of the paintings in each room but also the styles.

18. *Kano Sanraku:* Landscape. Fusuma, *ink on paper; 172 × 92 cm. Early seventeenth century.* Shoin, *Daitsu-ji, Shiga Prefecture.*

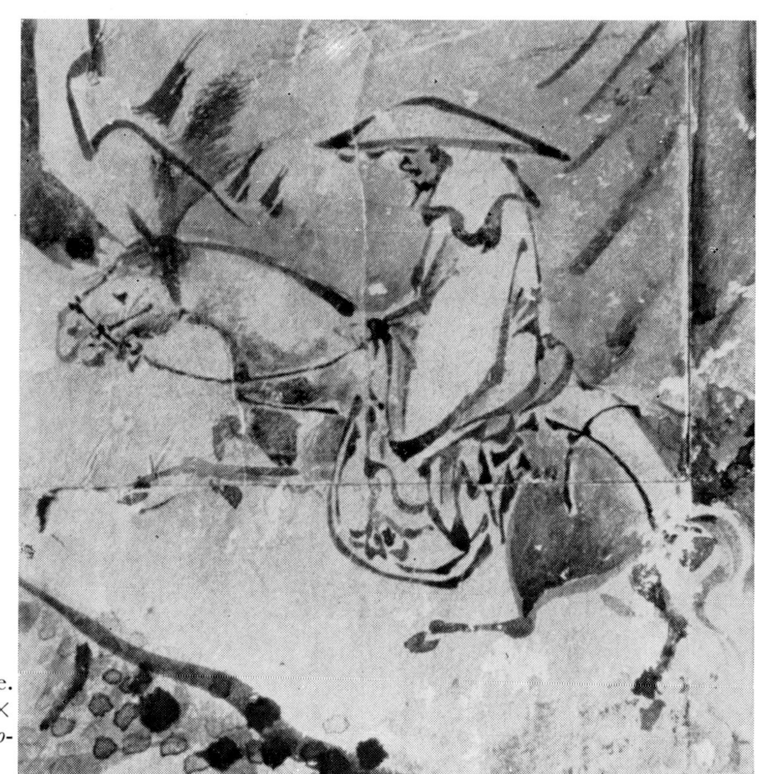

19. *Kano Sanraku: detail from* Landscape. Fusuma, *ink and light colors on paper; 185.5 × 116 cm. Early seventeenth century.* Hojo, *Sho-den-ji, Kyoto. (See also Figure 48.)*

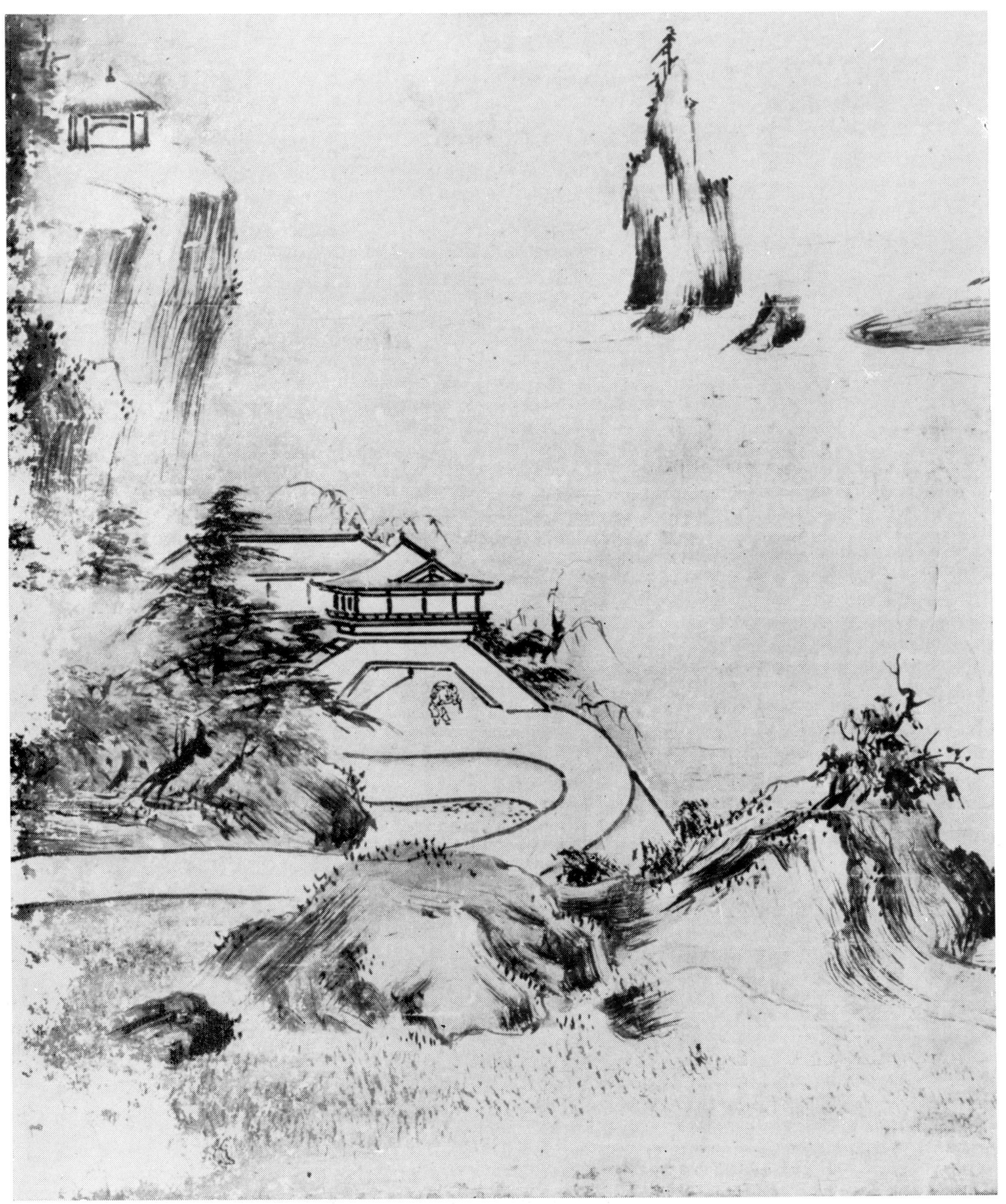

20. *Kano Sanraku: detail from* Landscape. *Ink on paper mounted on* chodai, *a decorative partition; 134 × 92.5 cm. Early seventeenth century. Shoshinden, Daikaku-ji, Kyoto.*

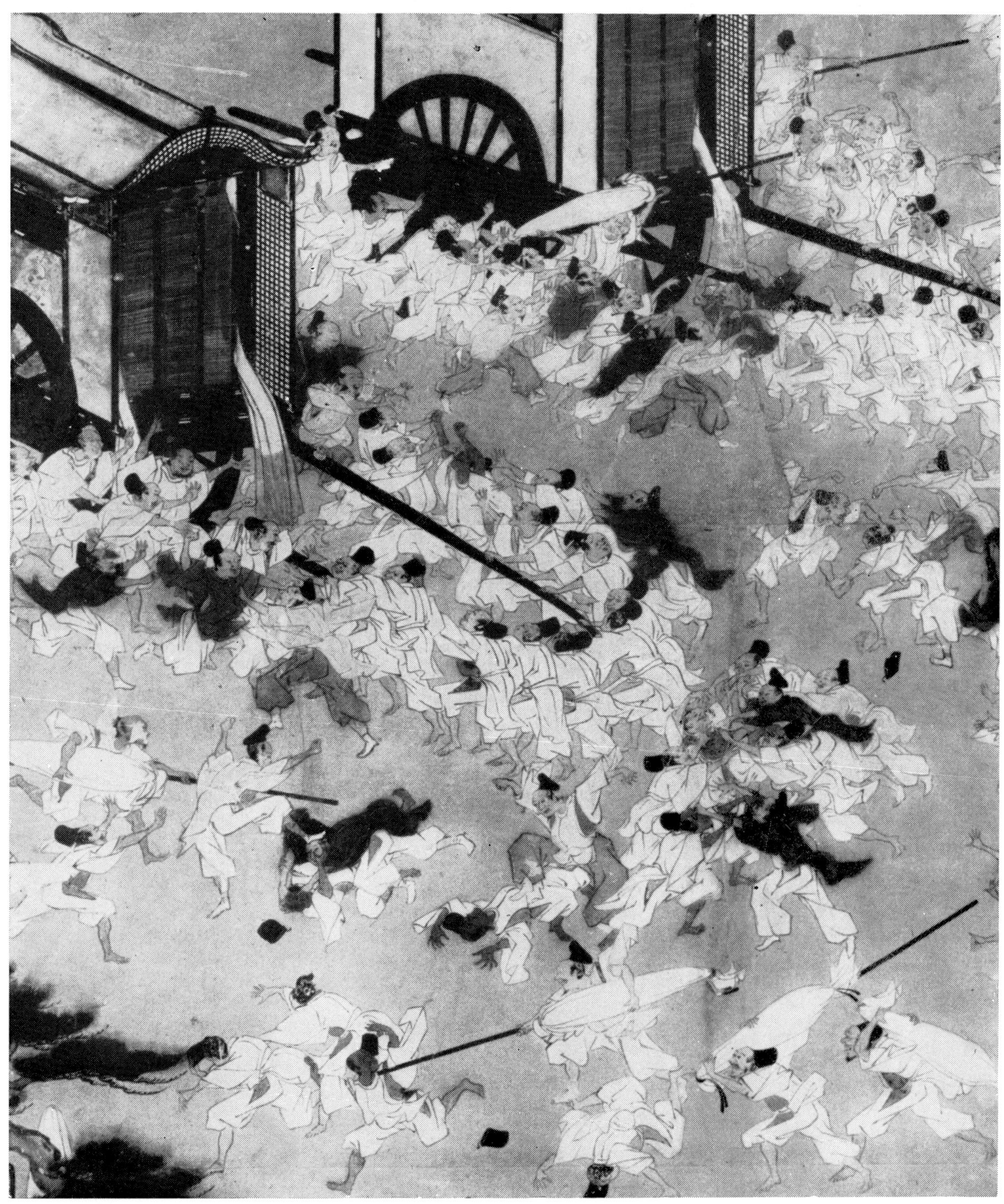

21. Kano Sanraku: detail from **Battle of the Carriages,** *a scene from the* **Genji Monogatari** *(Tale of Genji). One panel of a fourfold screen, colors on paper; 174 × 399.5 cm. Early seventeenth century. Tokyo National Museum.*

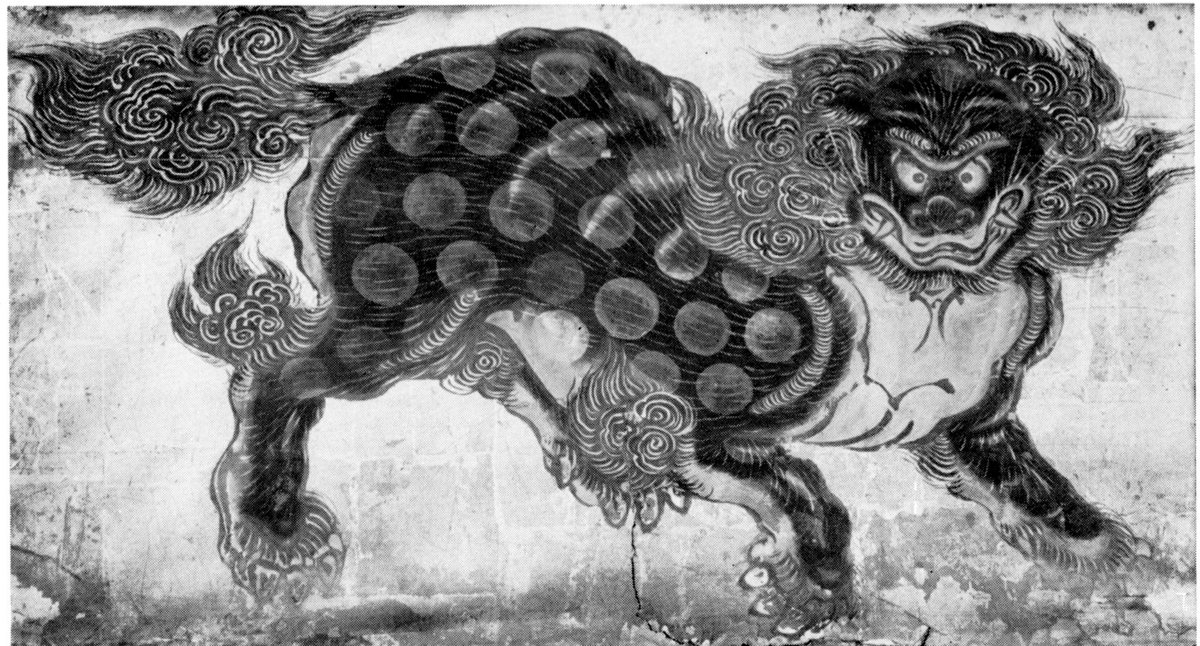

22. Kano Sanraku: section of Chinese Lions. *Colors and gold on paper mounted on wood panel; 44.5 × 198.5 cm. 1621.* Hondo, *Yogen-in, Kyoto. (See also Figure 49.)*

When an artist was requested to paint *shoheki-ga,* he first made a detailed examination of the building itself, considering the architectural factors, then ascertained the wishes and ideas of the client. Only then did the artist formulate a plan for the subjects, compositions, and styles of the paintings. He first drew a small rough sketch and showed it to the client. After approval, the artist started to paint. Figures 100 and 101 show the sketch and the finished painting, respectively, of part of *Plum Tree and Bamboo,* a *shoheki-ga* in the Goedo of the Nishi Hongan-ji temple, Kyoto. This work was executed in 1810 by Yoshimura Kokei (1769–1836) of the Maruyama school. Though it was painted after the Momoyama period, it shows clearly the process of painting *shoheki-ga.*

CHAPTER TWO

The Yamato-e and Kanga Styles

WHEN SHOHEKI-GA ARE MENTIONED, the magnificent paintings of the Momoyama period come to mind immediately. However, these Momoyama *shoheki-ga* did not emerge full-blown. *Shoheki-ga* painting had a long history and tradition preceding the Momoyama period.

There were three traditions of *shoheki-ga* painting before the Momoyama period: the *kara-e, yamato-e,* and *kanga* styles. The *kara-e* style, which flourished during the early Heian period, represents the dawn of *shoheki-ga*. The *yamato-e* style reached its zenith during the time of the Fujiwara clan's ascendancy (967–1068). This style continued in use through the Kamakura period and into the Muromachi period (1336–1573). In the history of *shoheki-ga,* the *yamato-e* style is considered classic. The *kanga* style emerged in the latter part of the Kamakura period. Its influence grew with time, and it flourished in the Muromachi period.

KARA-E–STYLE SHOHEKI-GA   As mentioned earlier, it is clear that paintings on screens existed at least as early as the Nara period, but *shoheki-ga,* centered on *fusuma* painting, began in the early Heian period. The wall painting of a landscape executed during the reign of Emperor Saga (r. 809–23) in the Seiryoden of the Kyoto Imperial Palace is recognized as an early example of *shoheki-ga*. This painting no longer exists, but it is the subject of a poem by Emperor Saga. This and the responding poems by Sugawara Kiyogimi, Miyako Haraka, and Shigeno Sadanushi are helpful in inferring the design and style of the wall painting. According to these verses, which are included in a collection of prose and poetry called the *Keikoku-shu,* the landscape painting on the wall of the Seiryoden was a vast panorama painted in some detail. It is assumed that the painting was in the *kara-e* style, which deals with Chinese genre and landscape subjects. It is believed that this landscape painting not only depicted Chinese subjects but also was painted in the Chinese style using Chinese techniques.

Shoheki-ga in the *kara-e* style came into use in the architecture of the Japanese imperial court due to the influence of the murals in the palaces of T'ang-dynasty (618–906) China. Murals had existed there during the Han dynasty (c. 206 B.C.–A.D. 220). During the Six Dynasties (c. 220–589), religious murals in Buddhist and Taoist temples and murals in palaces became increasingly fashionable. Wall painting reached its peak in China during the T'ang dynasty, when many master painters strove to outdo one another in this form. T'ang-dynasty murals presented a grand spectacle unprecedented in the history of Chinese fine arts. There is no question that the wall paintings in the Golden Hall of the Horyu-ji and other such works in Japan were produced under the influence of the flourishing tide of mural painting in China. From the Nara period to the early Heian period official embassies were sent to China, and Buddhist priests also went

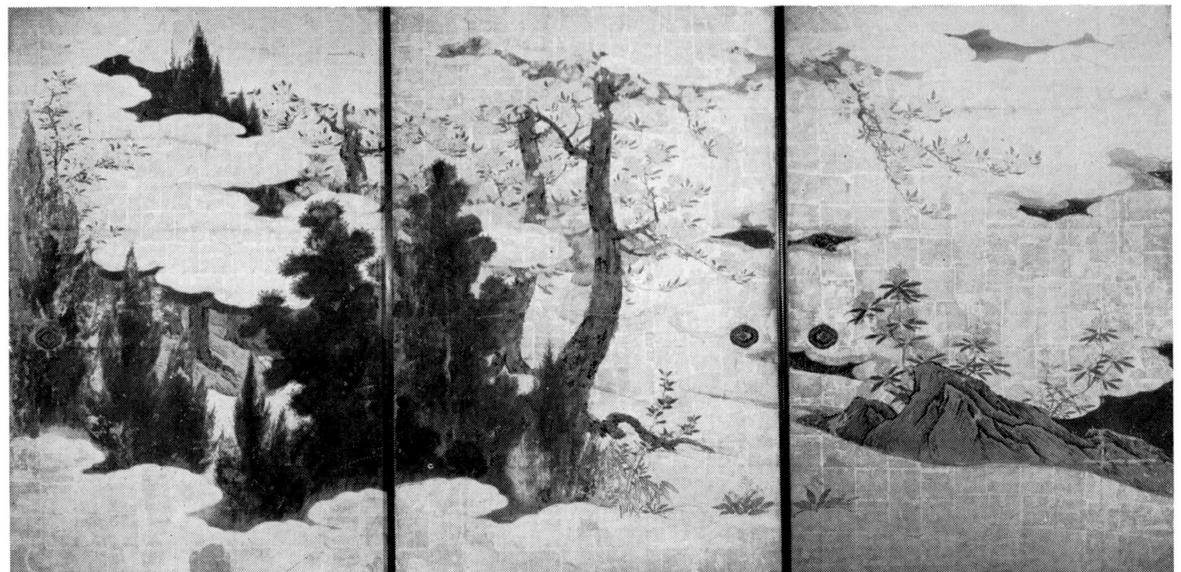

23. *Kano Mitsunobu:* Flowers and Birds. Fusuma, *colors and gold on paper; 177 × 117 cm. 1600. Reception hall, Kangaku-in, Onjo-ji, Shiga Prefecture. (See also Figure 8.)*

there to study. The T'ang dynasty had a great influence on Japan in every area, and there is little doubt that the custom of using decorated walls and partitions in Japanese court architecture was learned from the decoration of the Chinese courts. Consequently the *shoheki-ga* of the early Heian period were modeled after the paintings of China not only in subject but also in style and technique.

YAMATO-E–STYLE SHOHEKI-GA
In the early Heian period, wall paintings in the *kara-e* style were used mainly in the architecture of the imperial palaces, but they also appeared in the living quarters of Buddhist priests, who were exposed to the new ideas of the time. As the life style of the nobility became increasingly luxurious, more and more *shoheki-ga* were painted to decorate their residences. The years of the Fujiwara clan's ascendancy became a golden age of *shoheki-ga*. The typical style of the

shoheki-ga of this time was *yamato-e,* which had developed from *kara-e* but treated Japanese subjects in a Japanese manner. A Heian-period landscape screen formerly owned by the To-ji in Kyoto and now in the Kyoto National Museum (Figs. 108, 109) is *kara-e* in subject but *yamato-e* in style. The wall paintings of the Phoenix Hall of the Byodo-in, done about the same time, deal with religious subjects, but they show the influence of the *yamato-e shoheki-ga* being painted in residences at that time.

Sweeping landscapes predominated as subjects of *yamato-e shoheki-ga* in the Heian period. Paintings expressing what the *Genji Monogatari,* or *Tale of Genji,* calls "the disposition of the rich landscape" best suited the current taste. Large numbers of folding screens were also painted, especially for happy occasions. Naturally screen painting was important in the *yamato-e* tradition. Some of these *shoheki-ga* and screen paintings added human interest by including genre elements, while others

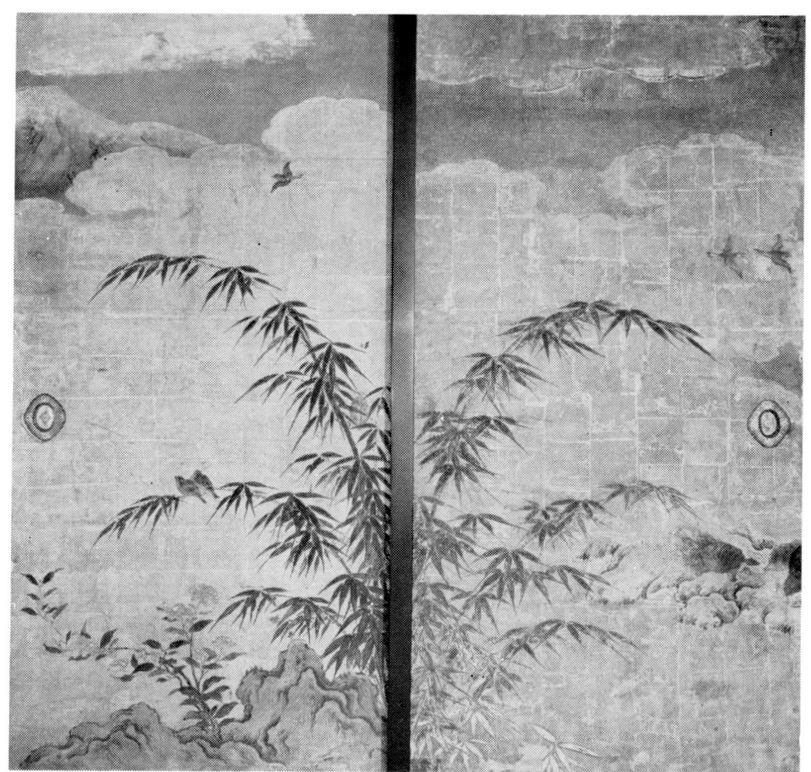

24. *Kano Mitsunobu:* Sparrows and Bamboo. Fusuma, *colors and gold on paper; 169 × 84.5 cm. Early seventeenth century.* Hojo, *Honen-in, Kyoto.*

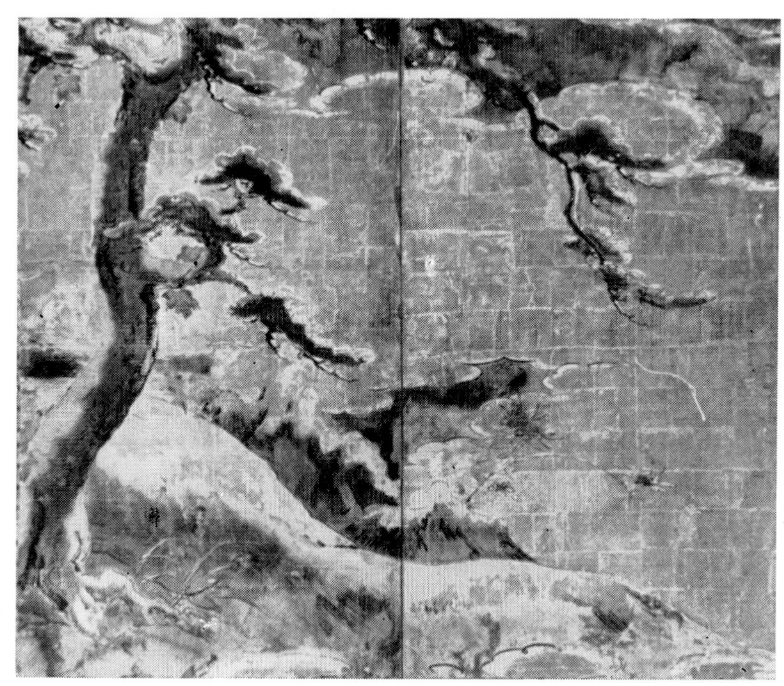

25. *Kano Mitsunobu:* Pine Tree in the Snow. *Colors and gold on paper; one of a pair of twofold screens; 153.5 × 172 cm.* Hojo, *Honen-in, Kyoto.*

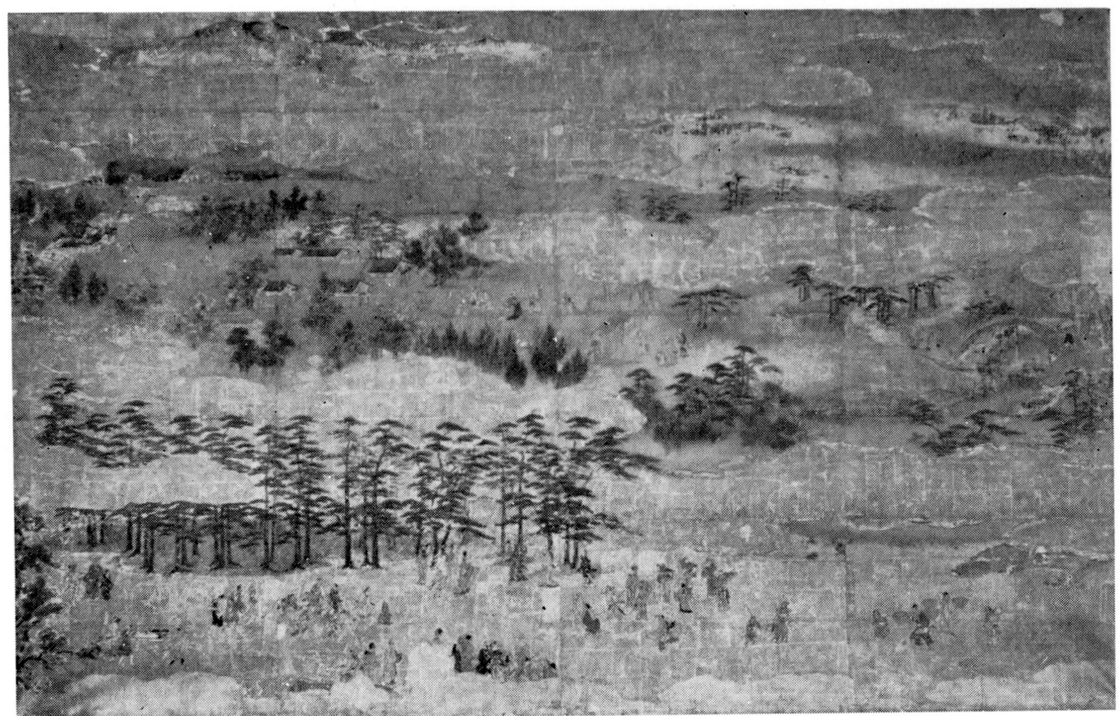

26. *Kano school: genre painting. Colors and gold on paper mounted in tokonoma; 249 × 378 cm. Early seventeenth century. Kyoto National Museum. (See also Figures 27, 86.)*

depicted famous locales. They were richly decorative in color and composition, the latter characterized by detailed painting using a very delicate touch.

The sole surviving such work may be the *Shotoku Taishi Eden* (Pictorial Biography of Prince Shotoku) from the Edono, or Portrait Hall, of the Horyu-ji (now in the Tokyo National Museum), painted in 1069 and recently remounted as ten separate panels. The To-ji landscape screen and the wall paintings of the Phoenix Hall of the Byodo-in are other important reference materials. In addition, *yamato-e* picture scrolls, such as the *Genji Monogatari Emaki* (Tale of Genji Picture Scroll; Fig. 106) and the *Ban Dainagon Ekotoba* (Story of the Courtier Ban Dainagon Picture Scroll), a three-scroll set painted in the late Heian period, furnish considerable information concerning the *shoheki-ga* and the folding-screen paintings of the period because *shoheki-ga* and folding screens are illustrated in these scrolls.

KANGA-STYLE SHOHEKI-GA   By the Kamakura period, *shoheki-ga* in the *yamato-e* style had lost their grandeur, but the tradition remained and was carried on into the Muromachi period. The changes that took place in the *yamato-e* style of *shoheki-ga* during this time are noteworthy. However, the typical *shoheki-ga* of the Muromachi period were done not in the *yamato-e* but in the *kanga* style. *Kanga* was a type of painting that developed in connection with the Zen Buddhist sects introduced to Japan from China during the Kamakura period. This style derived from the Chinese painting of the Sung (960–1279) and Yuan (1279–1368) dynasties. Ink paint-

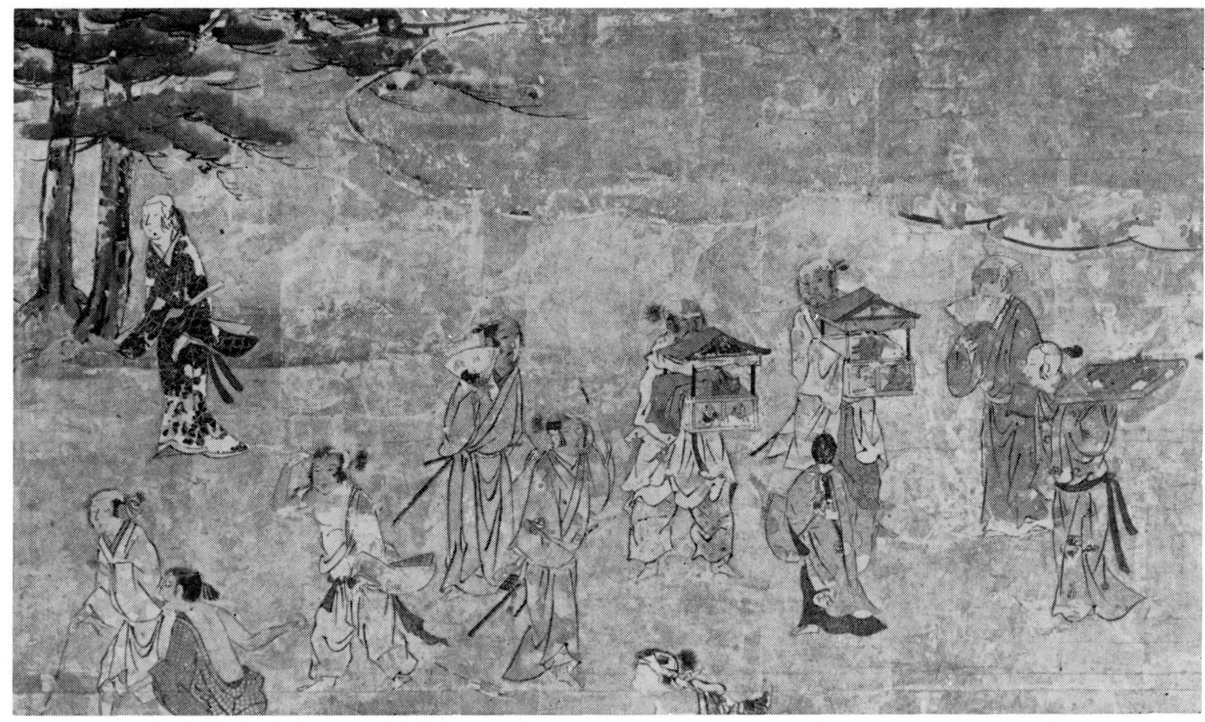

27. *Kano school: detail from genre painting. (See also Figures 26, 86.)*

ing was the core of the *kanga* style, which was gradually adopted for *shoheki-ga,* becoming the origin of a new tradition opposed to the old *yamato-e* style. *Kanga*-style painting began in the latter part of the Kamakura period, probably in the living quarters of Zen priests, and gradually spread to the mansions of the nobility and warrior aristocracy and to the living quarters of priests of other Buddhist sects.

Picture scrolls in the *yamato-e* style from the late Kamakura period enable us to glimpse how *shoheki-ga* in the *kanga* style were used. Among these picture scrolls are the *Kasuga Gongen Reigen-ki* (The Kasuga Gongen Miracles), a rich and beautiful twenty-scroll set depicting the origin and miraculous virtues of the Kasuga Shrine in Nara, and the *Honen Shonin Eden* (Pictorial Biography of Saint Honen; Fig. 104). The pictorial biography of

Hsuan-chuang San-tsang and the *Tosei Eden,* a pictorial record of the arrival from China of Chien-chen, founder of the Toshodai-ji in Nara, and his missionary work to spread the Kairitsu (Vinaya) sect of Buddhism, show the use of the *kanga* style in decorative paintings to enhance an exotic atmosphere.

At first the subject matter of many *kanga*-style *shoheki-ga* was landscapes painted in ink, but later, flower-and-bird themes were added. From the fifteenth-century *Kammon Gyoki,* a diary of Prince Gosukoin, we know that Shubun, a priest who was a leading *kanga* artist of the early Muromachi period, painted on *fusuma* in 1438. He painted flowers and birds as well as landscapes, and is thought to have executed many *shoheki-ga* for distinguished families. A comment on Shubun made by the Zen priest Kisei Reigen (1403–88), a contemporary of

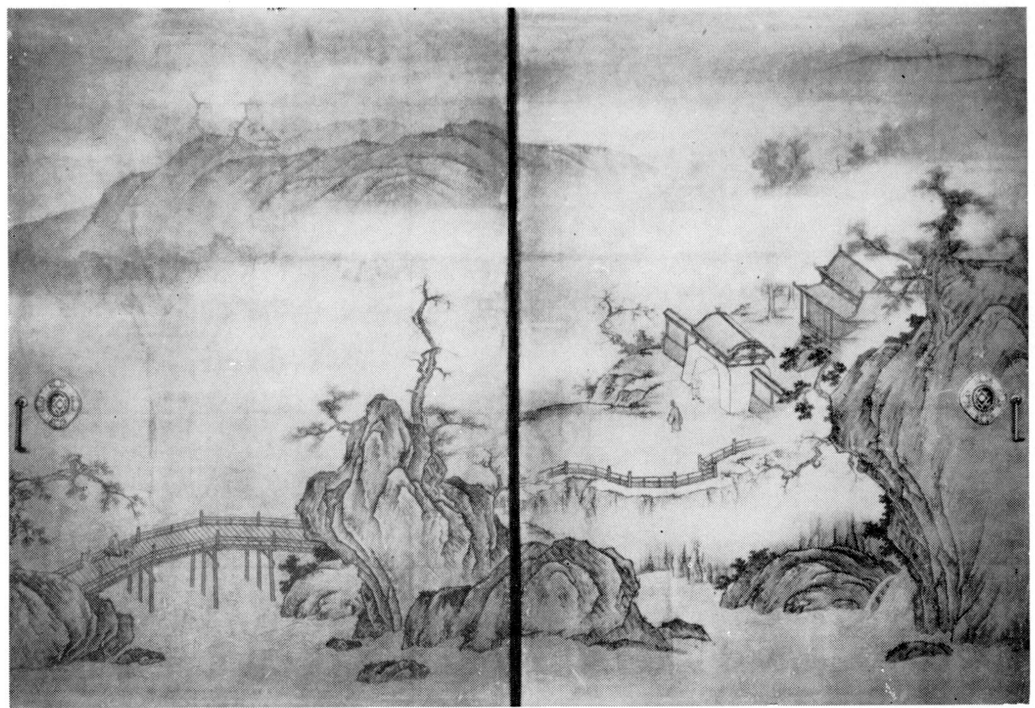

28. *Kano Koi:* Landscape. Fusuma, *ink and light colors on paper; 208.5 × 140 cm. Early seventeenth century.* Shiroshoin, *Nijo Castle, Kyoto.*

Shubun, supports this. Kisei Reigen wrote in the *Son'an Shoko* that Shubun's "paintings of landscapes, flowers, and birds in the mansions of the royalty and nobility brought splendor to the walls and partitions."

Shubun's *shoheki-ga* drew praise from his contemporaries as the best of the orthodox *kanga*-style *shoheki-ga* of the early Muromachi period. Regrettably, none of his works exist today, but there are a few surviving indications of the great influence his style of painting had. One is the *Konda Sobyo Engi* (Fig. 105). This picture scroll detailing the origin of the Konda Hachiman Shrine, Osaka Prefecture, was dedicated to the shrine by the shogun Ashikaga Yoshinori in 1433, during the period that Shubun was active. The detail in Figure 105 shows a landscape painted in ink, in the style of Shubun, on sliding cedar doors.

The wall paintings in the five-story pagoda at the Itsukushima Shrine in Miyajima, Hiroshima Prefecture, also give us a glimpse of what *kanga*-style *shoheki-ga* looked like in the early Muromachi period. The pagoda, built in 1407, contains the *kanga* painting *White-robed Kannon* on the wood-paneled wall behind a dais for a Buddhist image. Also noteworthy are the *Portraits of the Eight Patriarchs of the Shingon Sect* (Fig. 102) mounted on wood panels; the *kanga* landscape painted in ink behind each patriarch is reminiscent of Shubun's painting style. Naturally, all the paintings in the pagoda are of religious subjects, but they are valuable as surviving sources showing the nature of the *kanga*-style *shoheki-ga* being produced at that time.

As the Muromachi period advanced, *shoheki-ga* in the *kanga* style spread with the growing popularity of the *kanga* tradition itself. A remarkable

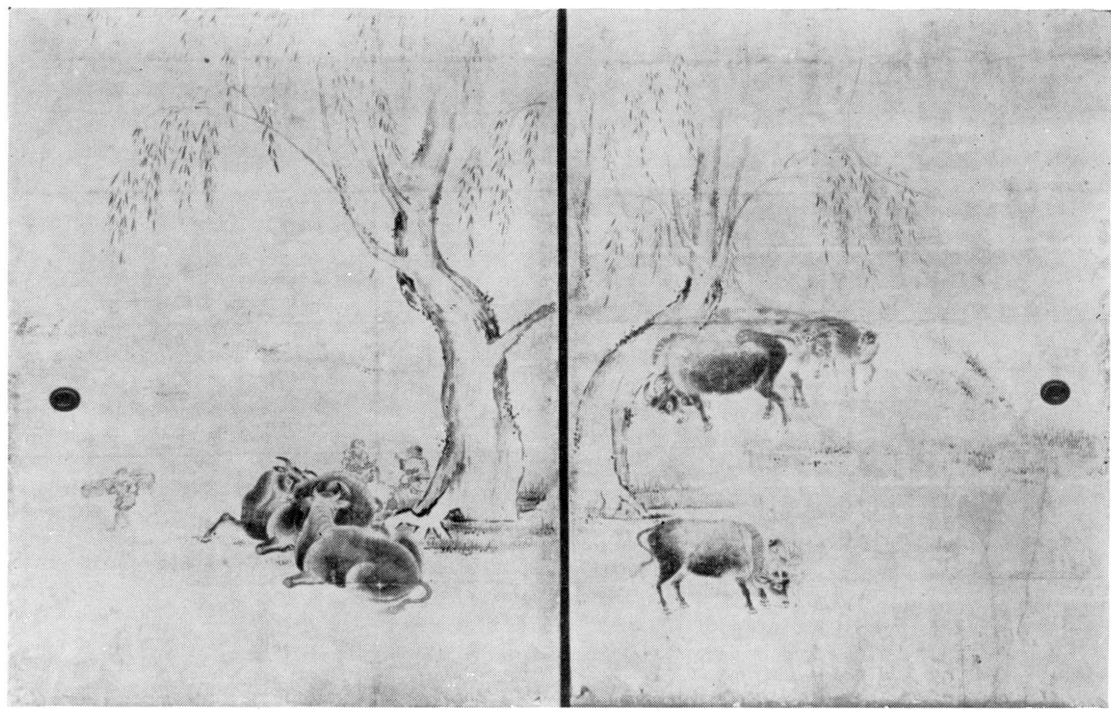

29. *Kano Koi:* Cattle in a Pasture. Fusuma, *ink on paper; 188 × 142 cm. 1616.* Hojo, *Toji-in, Kyoto.*

development ensued, especially during the time when Ashikaga Yoshimasa was shogun (1443–73). Following Shubun, Sotan (1413–81), a master artist in the *kanga* tradition, painted *shoheki-ga.* Sotan's son Sokei also merits attention as a *shoheki-ga* artist. The *fusuma* paintings that were formerly in the Yotoku-in of the Daitoku-ji, Kyoto, and are now in the custody of the Kyoto National Museum are by Sokei.

Other extant *kanga*-style *shoheki-ga* of the Muromachi period include the flower-and-bird and landscape paintings in ink, said to be by Soga Jasoku, in the reception hall of the Shinju-an, Daitoku-ji. These are representative of *shoheki-ga* in the *kanga* style painted in the late fifteenth century, at about the same time as the Yotoku-in *fusuma* paintings by Sokei. The ink *fusuma* landscape recently discovered in the Shinju-an and placed in the *shoin*

of the Tsusen-in, Daitoku-ji, was painted around the same time as the *shoheki-ga* in the Shinju-an reception hall and by an artist of the same school. It is another important surviving *kanga*-style *shoheki-ga* of this period.

JAPANIZATION OF KANGA Shortly after the time at which the Shinju-an and Yotoku-in *shoheki-ga* were painted, a brilliant *shoheki-ga* artist, Kano Motonobu (1476–1559), appeared. Fortunately his *shoheki-ga* in the Daisen-in of the Daitoku-ji and the Reiun-in of the Myoshin-ji, Kyoto, are extant, so that it is possible to define clearly the characteristics of his work. The works in the Daisen-in, *Flowers and Birds* (Fig. 110), *Zen Patriarchs,* and *Chinese Landscape and Figures,* were painted around 1513. *Zen Patriarchs* and *Chinese Landscape and Figures* came into the possession

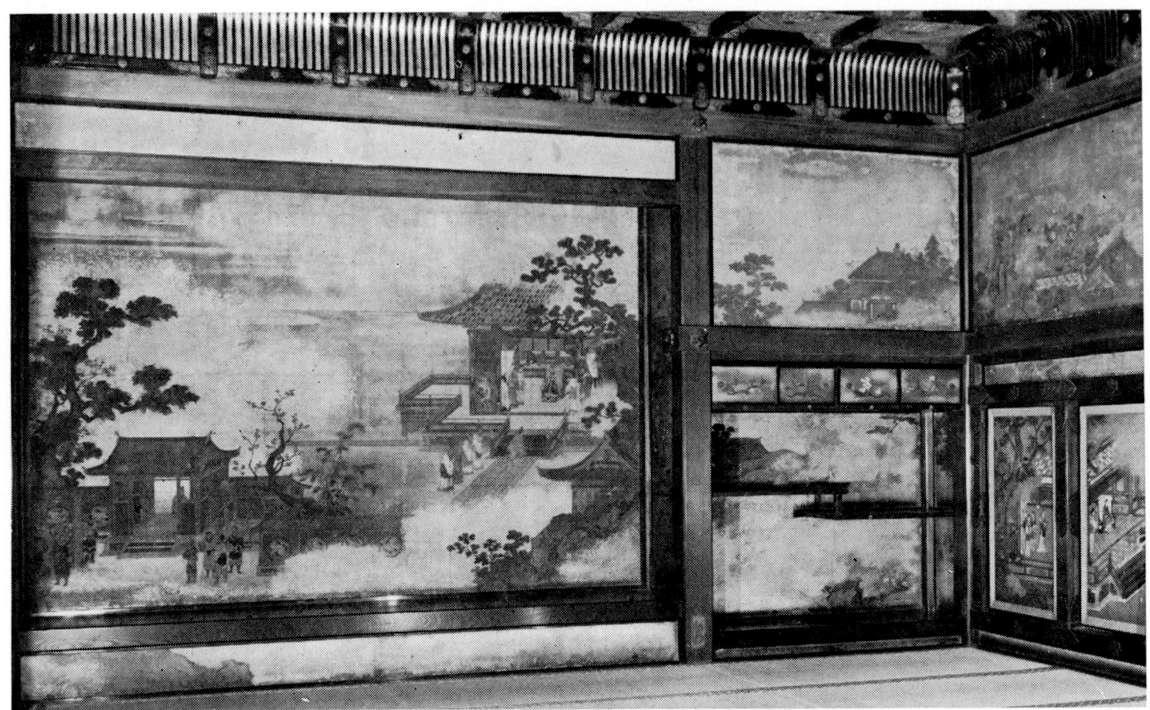

30. *Watanabe Ryokei:* Teikan, *a scene from a Chinese illustrated book on things emperors should guard against. Wall painting, colors and gold on paper. Early seventeenth century.* Shiroshoin, *Nishi Hongan-ji, Kyoto.*

of the Tokyo Imperial Museum (presently the Tokyo National Museum) during the Meiji era (1868–1912). The most interesting of these three *shoheki-ga* is *Flowers and Birds,* which features a decorative sense of beauty that had not been obvious in earlier *shoheki-ga* in the *kanga* style. The birds and flowers are beautifully painted in rich colors. In addition, the overall composition of the picture is simplified and unified around a large pine tree and waterfall. This painting shows a much stronger decorative intent than the *Flowers and Birds* in the Shinju-an. *Kanga*-style painting, mainly using ink and characterized by a quiet spirituality, originally developed in the ambiance of Zen Buddhism. However, with changing trends and tastes the style began to alter. A clearly defined decorative tend-

ency is seen for the first time in Motonobu's work. This new trend is most obvious in the *shoheki-ga* used to decorate residences.

The *shoheki-ga* in the Reiun-in are thought to have been painted about 1543, after those in the Daisen-in. Executed in either ink or ink and light colors, their subjects include flowers and birds, landscapes, and landscapes with figures. Some are rendered in a precise and detailed style, some in a simplified flowing style, and some in a style intermediate between the two. Of all these Reiun-in paintings, those of flowers and birds are the most refreshing, and though they are executed in ink alone, their composition is highly decorative. While the decorative trend seen in Motonobu's *shoheki-ga* is an indication of the Japanization of the *kanga*

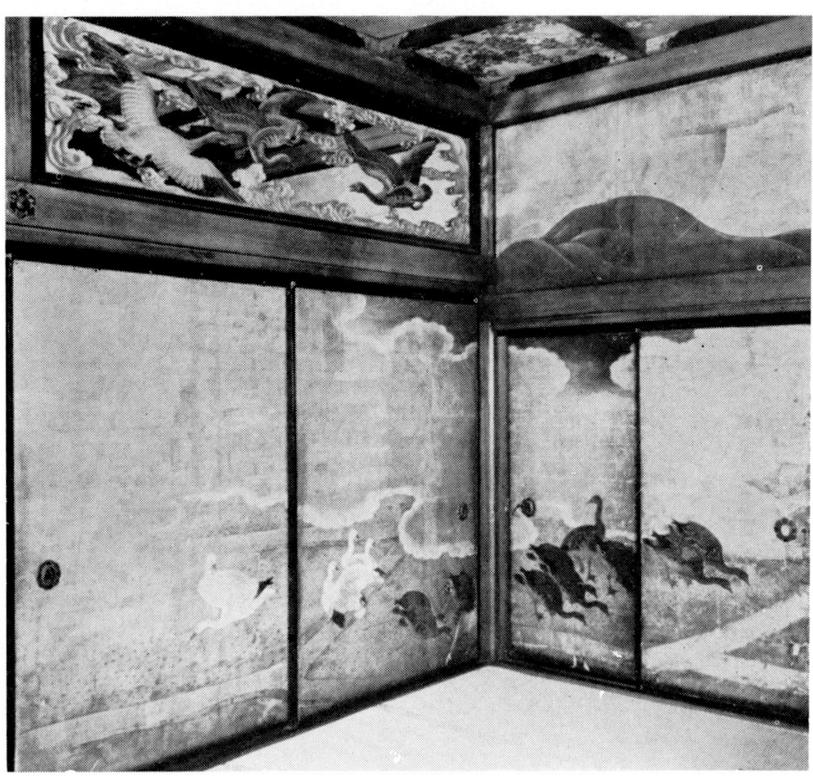

31. Watanabe Ryokei: Wild Geese. Fusuma, *colors and gold on paper. Early seventeenth century. Gan-no-ma, Nishi Hongan-ji, Kyoto.*

32 (below). Watanabe Ryokei: Landscape. Fusuma, *ink on paper; 183 × 118 cm. Early seventeenth century.* Hojo, Taizo-in, Myoshin-ji, Kyoto.

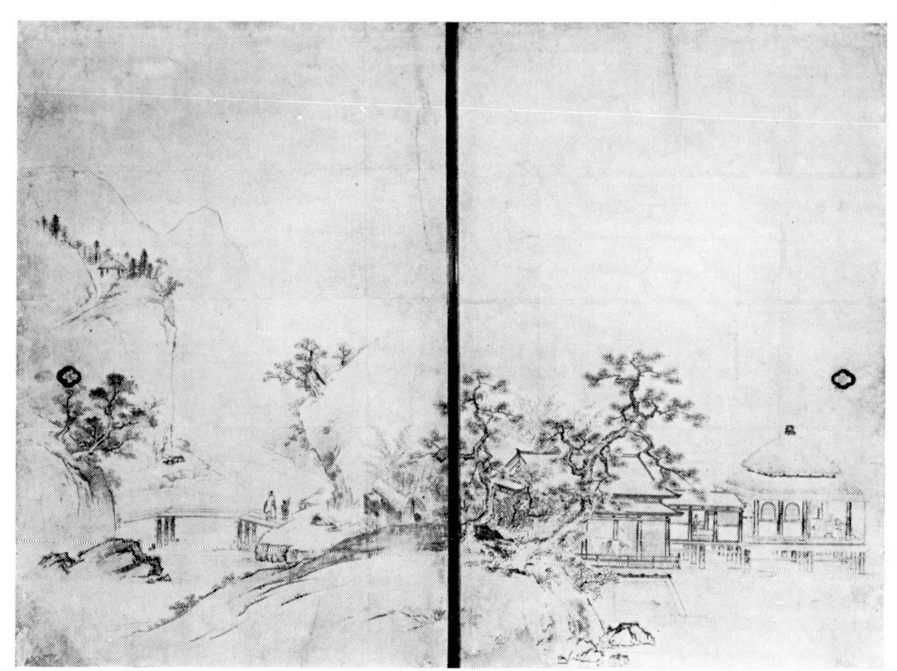

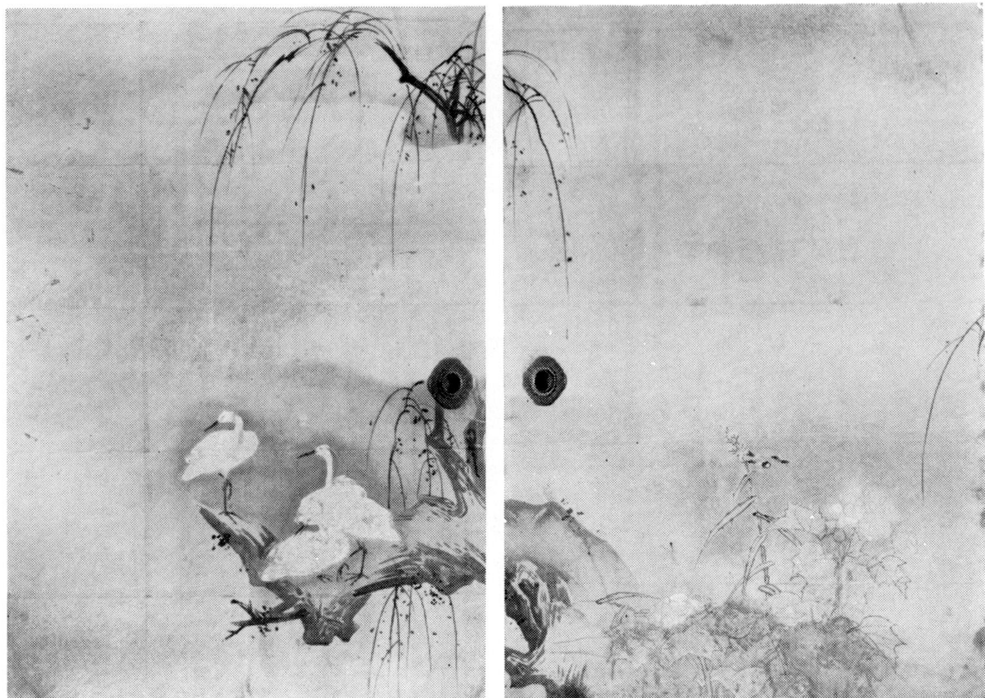

33. *Kano Tan'yu:* Willows and Herons. Fusuma, *ink and light colors on paper; 174 × 141 cm. 1634.* *Nagoya Castle, Aichi Prefecture.*

style, it also signifies that the *kanga* style had begun to move closer to the *yamato-e* style of the classic tradition.

MAGNIFIED, CLOSE-UP COMPOSITION

Although the *yamato-e* style of *shoheki-ga* appeared to have lost much of its vitality during the Muromachi period, overshadowed by the burgeoning *kanga* style, it is also true that several noteworthy developments in *yamato-e* painting occurred at that time. One was the realization of the "magnified, close-up" method of composition in *shoheki-ga*, especially those with flower-and-bird themes, in the latter half of the Kamakura period and the early Muromachi period. A composition method magnifying such subjects as flowers and birds is seen in *yamato-e* works painted at least as early as the early Kamakura period. It is clearly illustrated in the background of the *Portrait of Cloistered Emperor Goshirakawa,* belonging to the Myoho-in, Kyoto. Later in the Kamakura period this method of composition developed into close-up views on a larger scale, and by the early Muromachi period a large-scale type of composition that might be mistaken for *kanga*-style *shoheki-ga* had appeared. The painting on one of the cedar doors of the *hondo* (main hall) of the Kakurin-ji in Hyogo Prefecture (Fig. 103) is a rare surviving work showing this characteristic.

The Kakurin-ji *hondo* is said to have been built in 1397. A set of four large cedar sliding doors is placed between the sanctuary and the area to the east, and another set of doors is found between the sanctuary and the area to the west. One set depicts willows, reeds, and a flock of white geese. The other set shows pine and plum trees and two

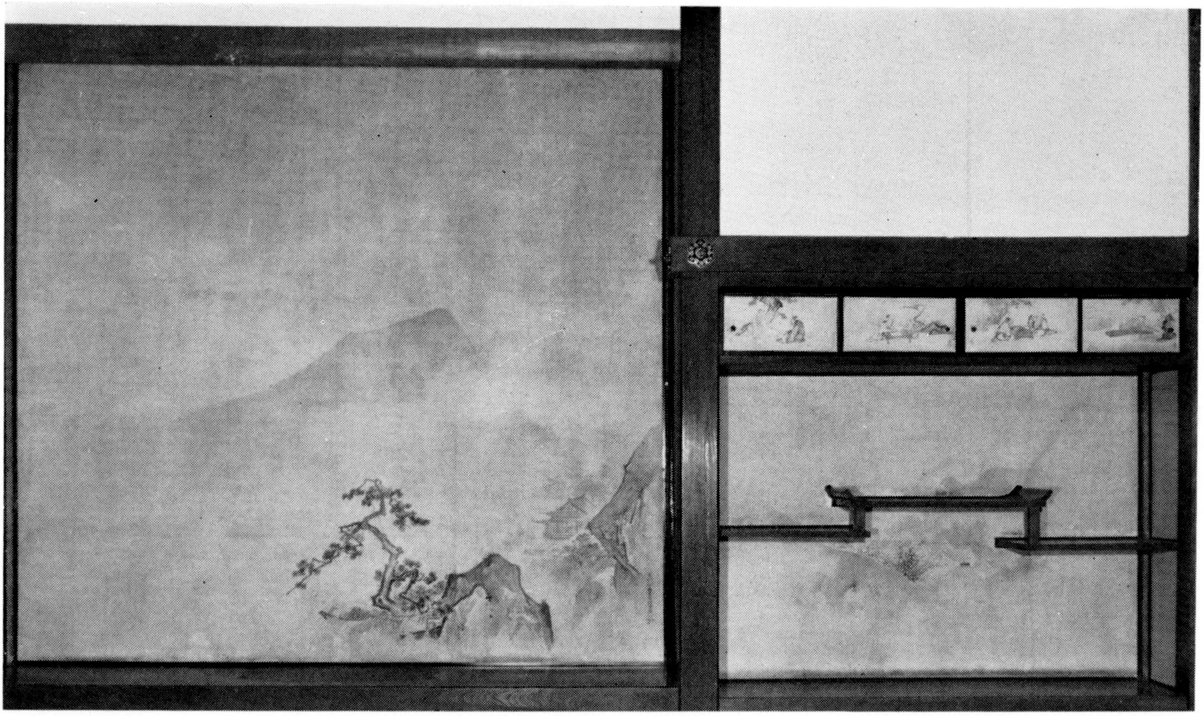

34. *Kano Tan'yu:* Landscape. *Ink on paper mounted in tokonoma; left panel 265 × 277 cm. 1642. Reception hall, Shojuraigo-ji, Shiga Prefecture.*

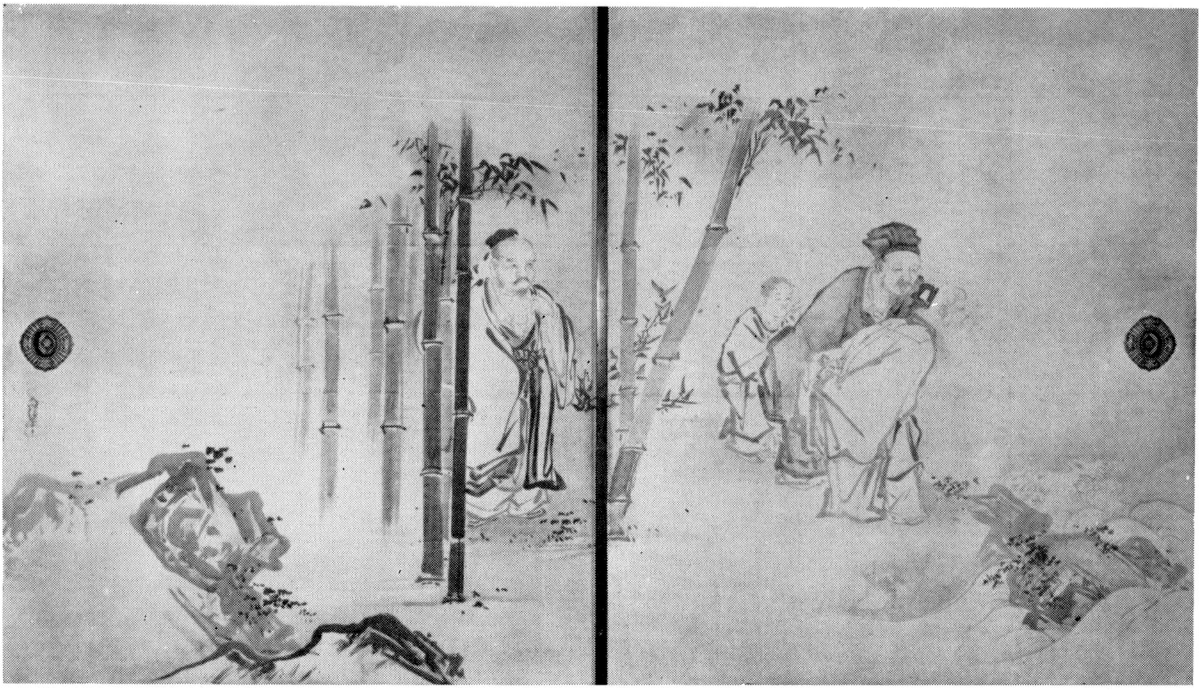

35. *Kano Naonobu:* The Seven Sages of the Bamboo Grove. Fusuma, *ink on paper; 176 × 150 cm. 1642. Reception hall, Shojuraigo-ji, Shiga Prefecture.*

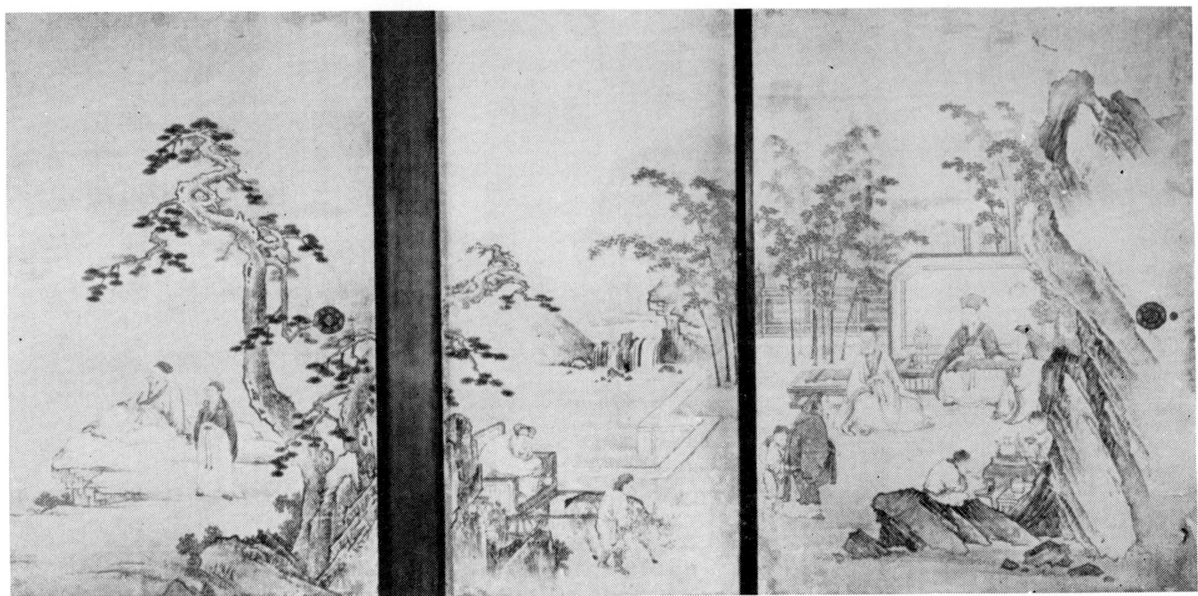

36. *Kano Sansetsu:* Landscape and Figures. *Ink on* fusuma *and paper mounted on a wall; left panel 185 × 113 cm., center panel* 185 × 95.5 cm., right panel 185 × 122.5 cm. 1631. Hojo, Tenkyu-in, Myoshin-ji, Kyoto.

cranes. Considerable peeling and other damage to the two sets of doors has occurred, but they are still major works in color. The scale of the compositions is very large. The date equivalent to 1577 is written in ink on the back of one door, but the style of the pictures indicates they were painted long before that time. It is reasonable to assume that they were painted when the *hondo* was built. Furthermore, because of the horizontal lines used to render low-lying mist, a convention frequently used in *yamato-e* painting, there is no question that the artist belonged to the *yamato-e* tradition. Cedar doors painted with flowers are frequently depicted in *yamato-e* picture scrolls of the late Kamakura and early Muromachi periods, but the Kakurin-ji doors are the only ones of that time still in existence. It is noteworthy that these paintings show the influence of the *kanga* style in their brushwork and in the delineation of the subjects of the painting.

The fact that *kanga* influences are seen in tradiional *yamato-e shoheki-ga* like these is an indication of the power of the *kanga* style itself, which soon was to prevail. It is also felt that the trend toward a magnified, close-up method of composition seen in the *yamato-e shoheki-ga* of this period was largely stimulated by the emerging *kanga* style of *shoheki-ga.*

BEGINNINGS OF THE KIMPEKI STYLE

Another important element in *yamato-e shoheki-ga* of the Muromachi period is the beginning of the elegant, sumptuous *kimpeki* (or *kompeki*) style, which combines the use of gold and rich colors on paper. As we will see, this is the style characterizing Momoyama *shoheki-ga.*

37. *Attributed to Kano Motonobu:* Flowers and Birds. Fusuma, *colors on paper; 184 × 98 cm. Late sixteenth century.* Ohojo, ▷
Nanzen-ji, Kyoto.

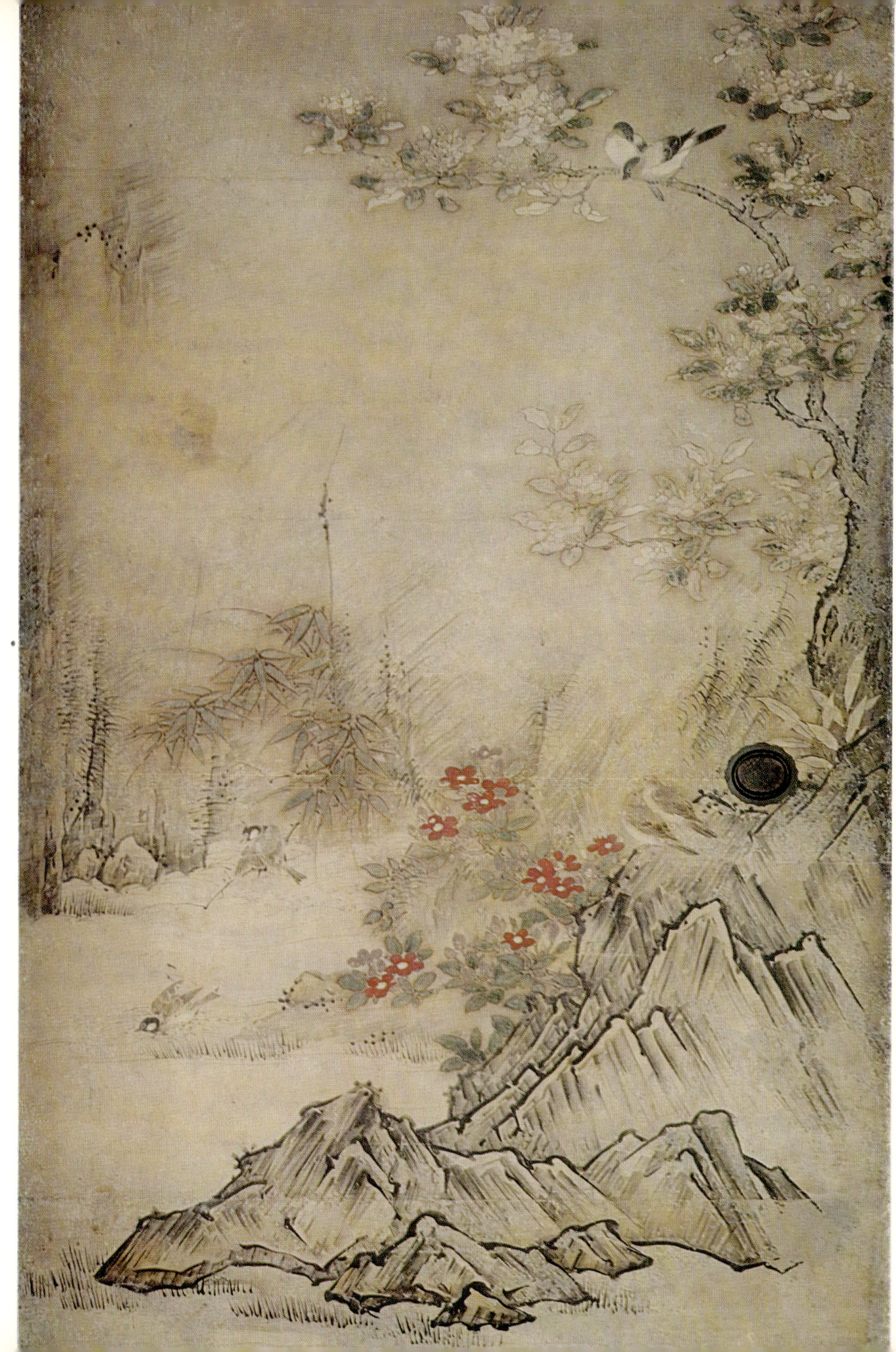

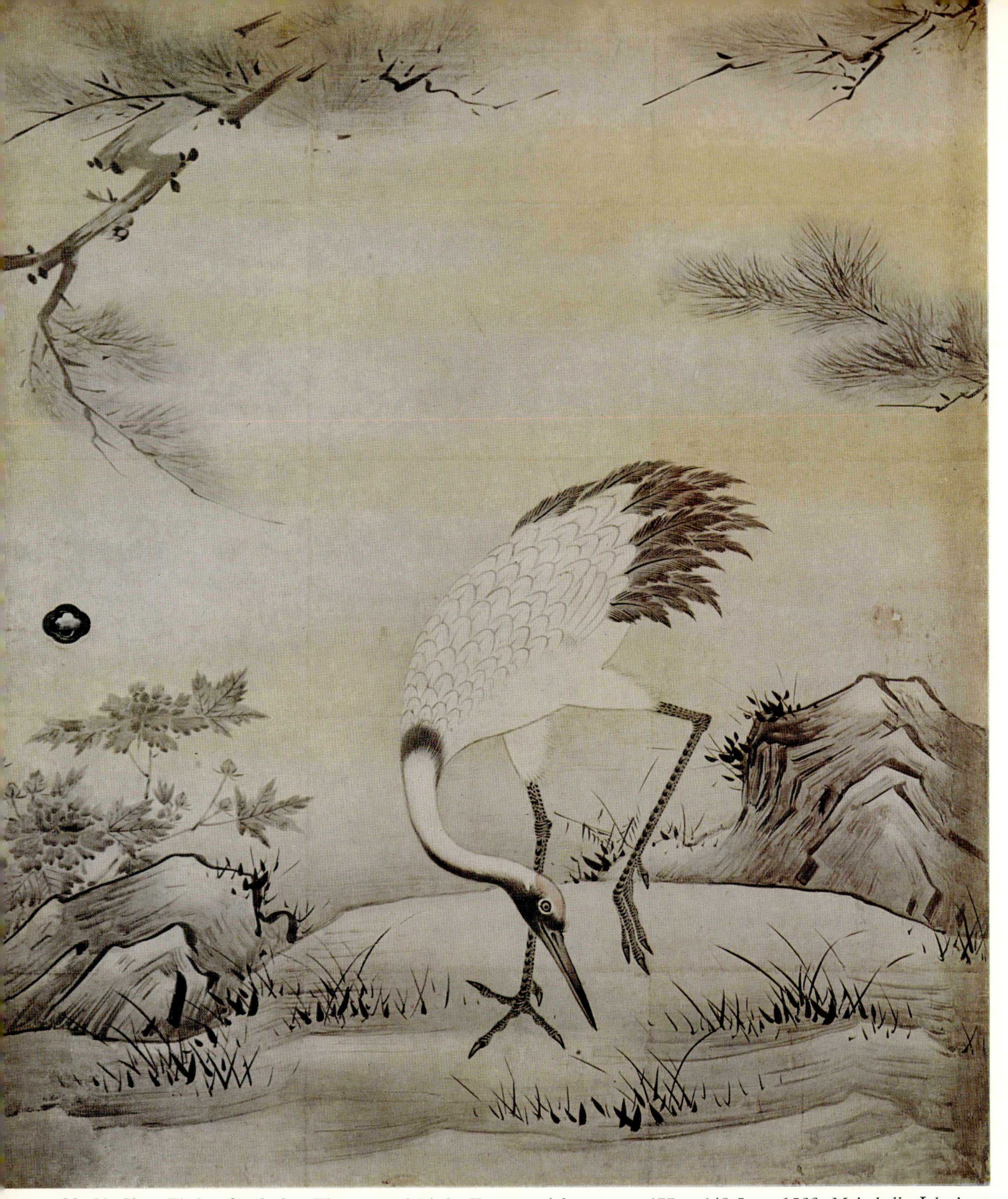

38, 39. *Kano Eitoku: details from* Flowers and Birds. Fusuma, *ink on paper; 177 × 143.5 cm. 1566. Main hall, Juko-in, Daitoku-ji, Kyoto. (See also Figure 12.)

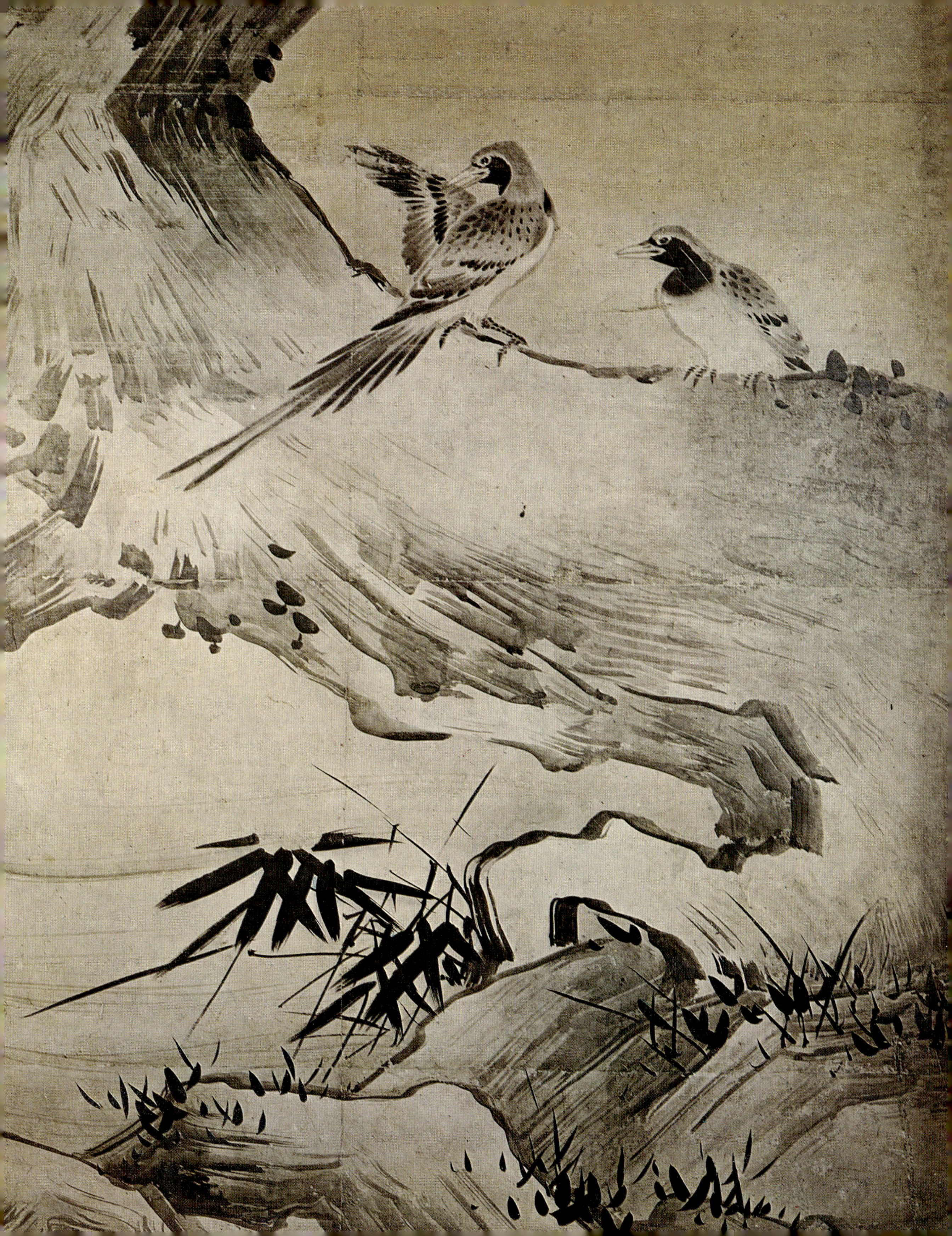

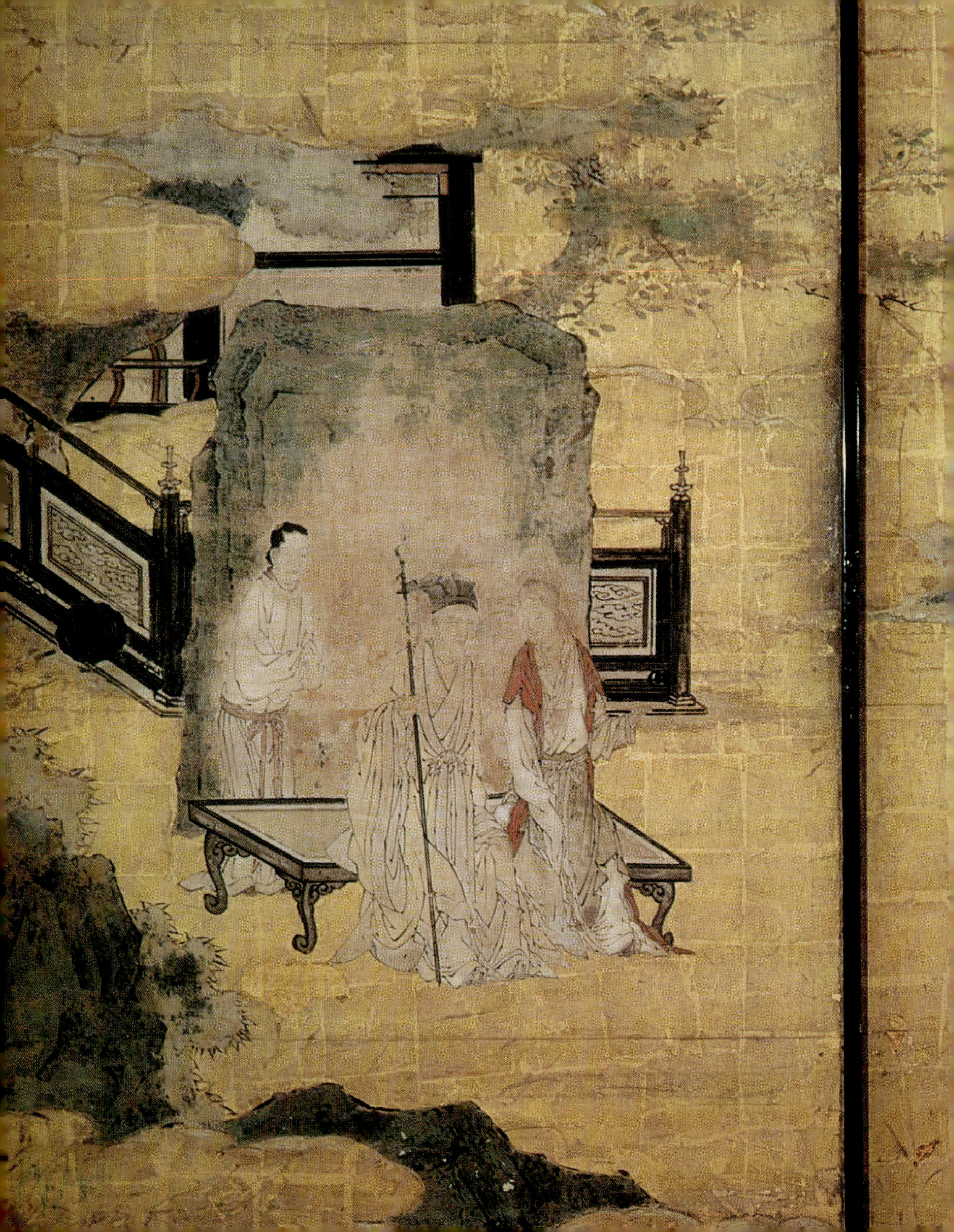

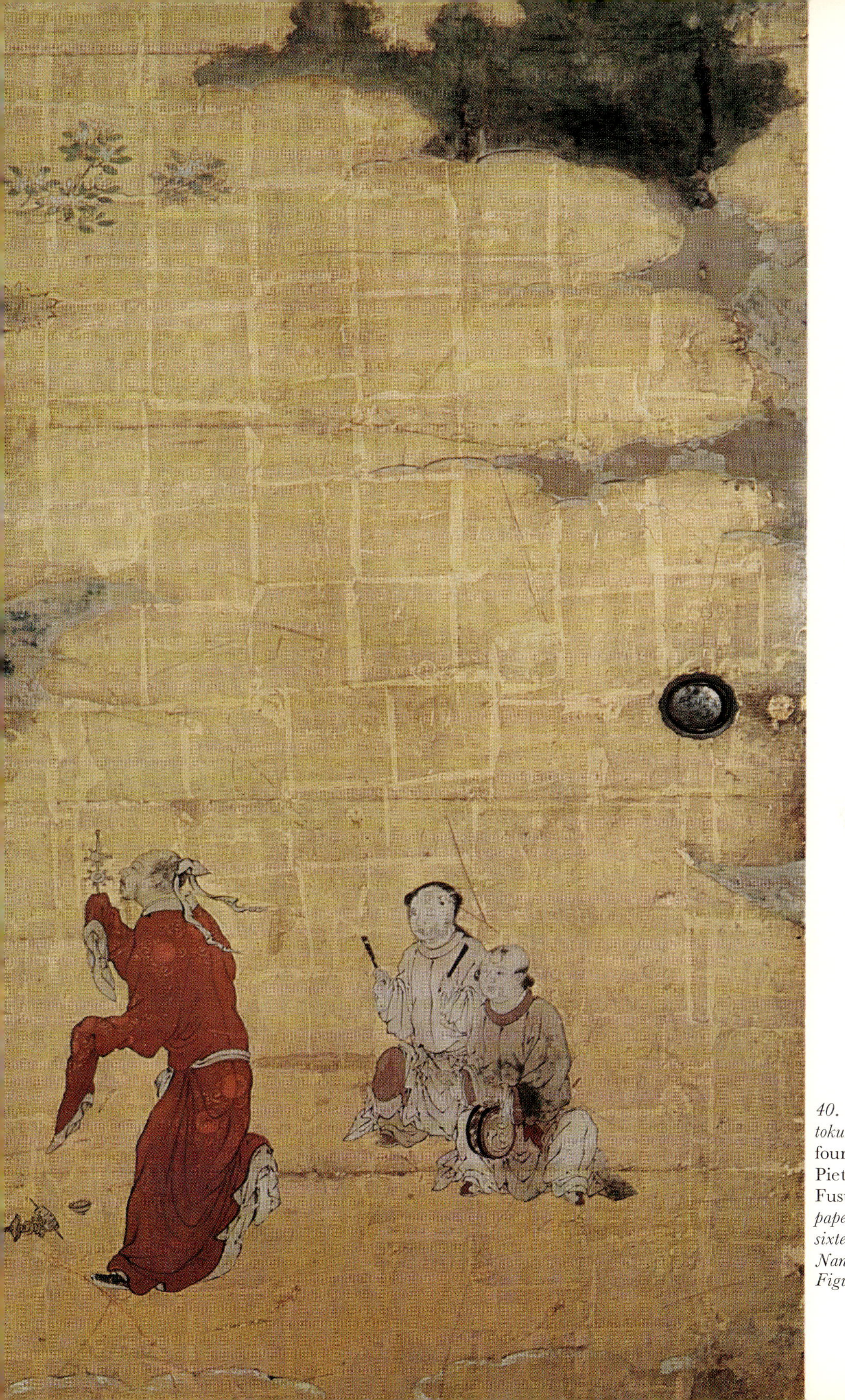

40. *Attributed to Kano Ei-toku: detail from* Twenty-four Paragons of Filial Piety *showing Lao Lai-tzu.* Fusuma, *colors and gold on paper; 184 × 98 cm. Late sixteenth century. Ohojo, Nanzen-ji, Kyoto. (See also Figure 15.)*

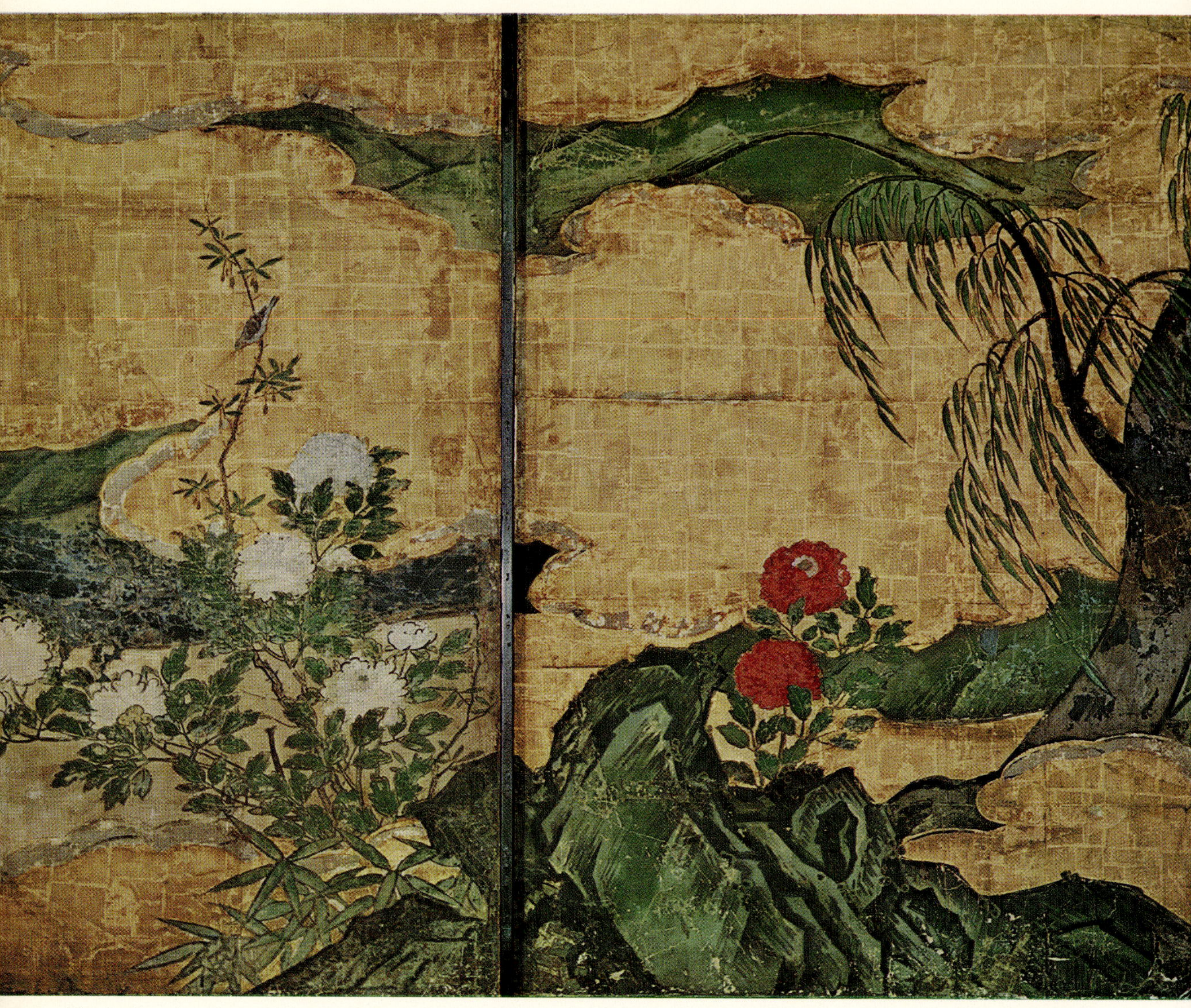

41. *Attributed to Kano Eitoku:* Flowers and Birds. Fusuma, *colors and gold on paper; 170 × 140 cm. Early seventeenth century.* Daishoin, *Myoho-in, Kyoto.*

42. *Attributed to Kano Eitoku: detail from* Pine Trees and Mountain Birds. *Colors and gold* ▷ *on paper mounted on a wall; 180 × 281 cm. Late sixteenth century.* Genkan, *Daikaku-ji, Kyoto.*

43 *(overleaf). Attributed to Kano Eitoku:* Flowers and Birds. ▷ Fusuma, *colors and gold on paper; 177 × 138 cm. Late sixteenth century.* Shinden, Emman-in, Shiga Prefecture.

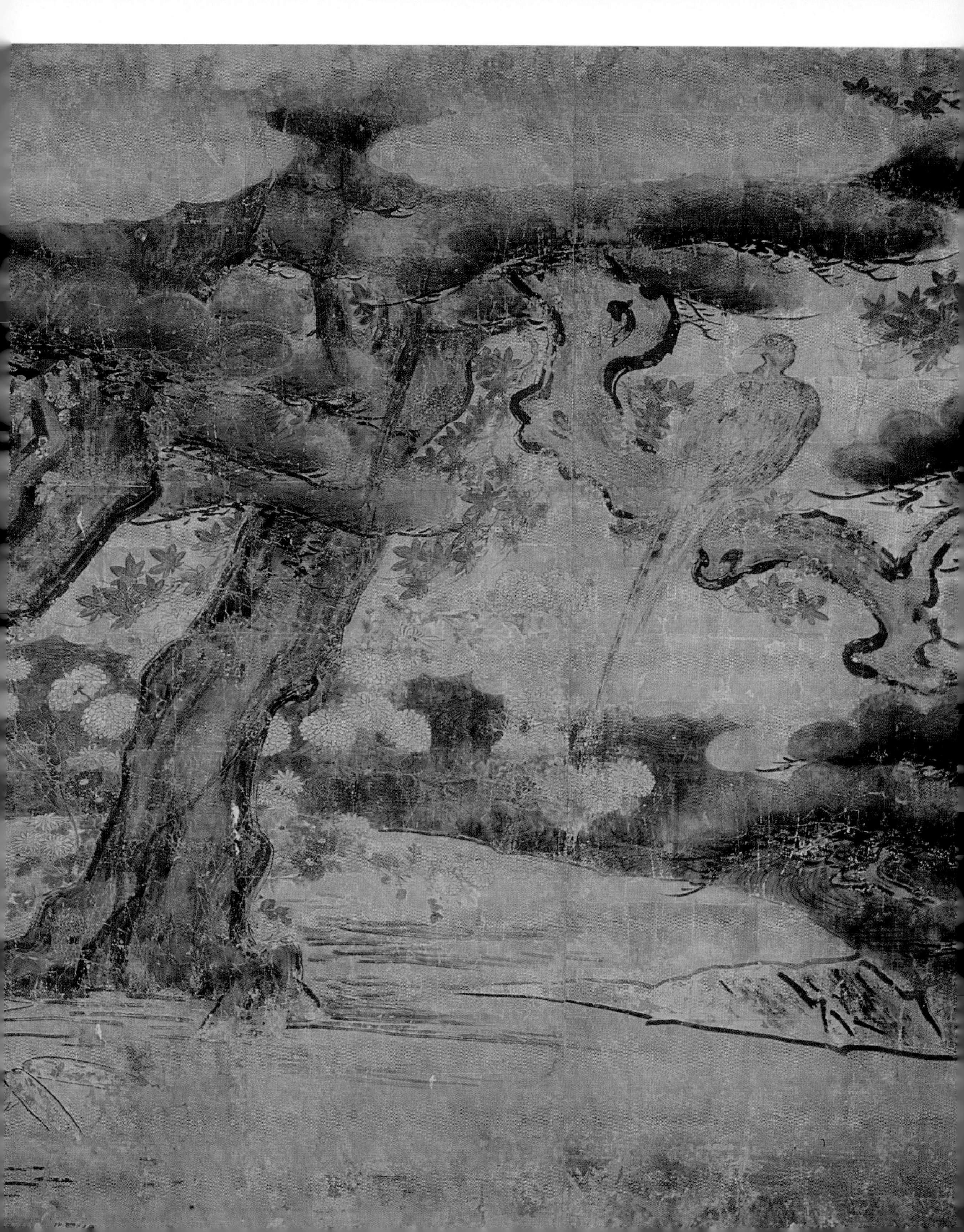

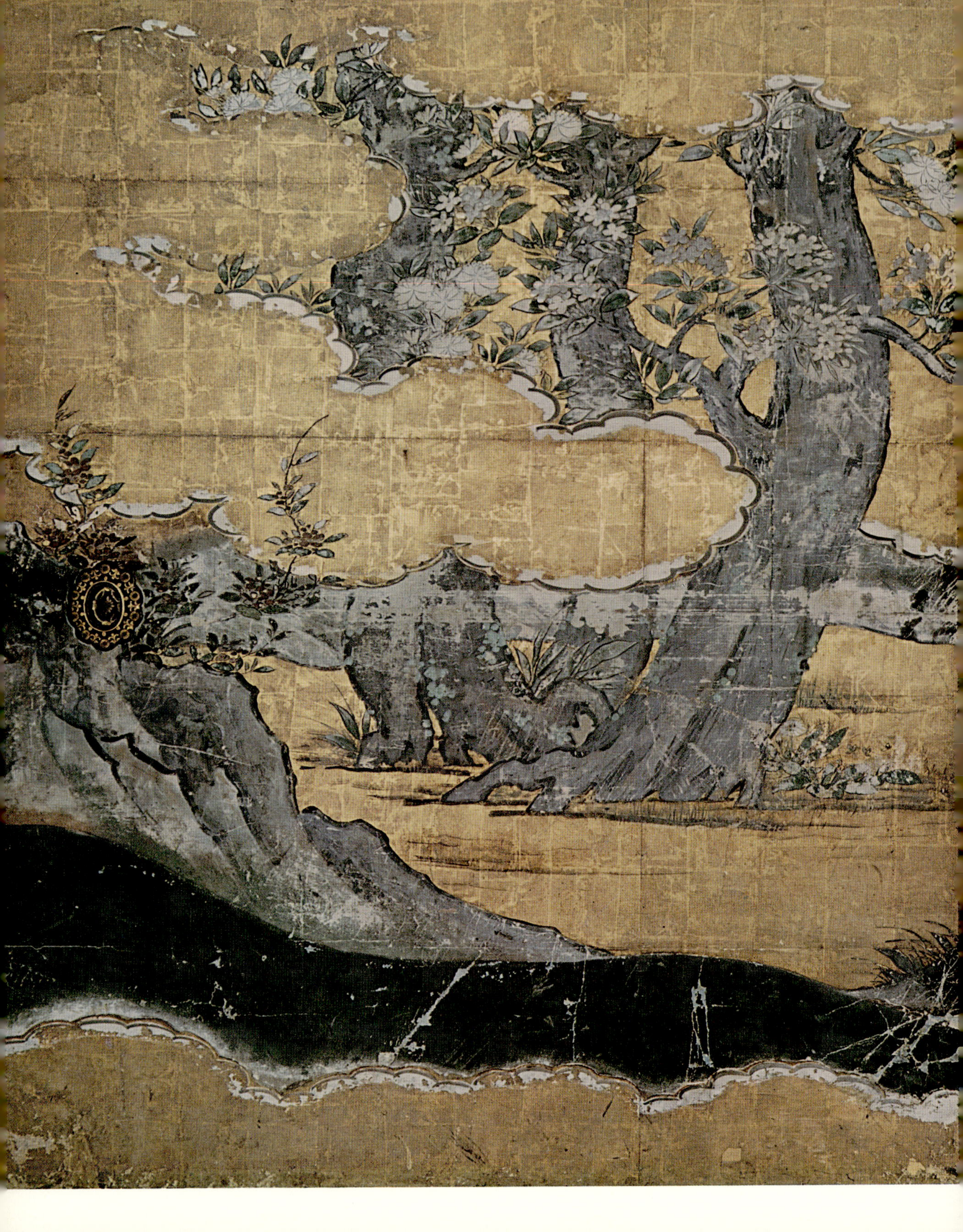

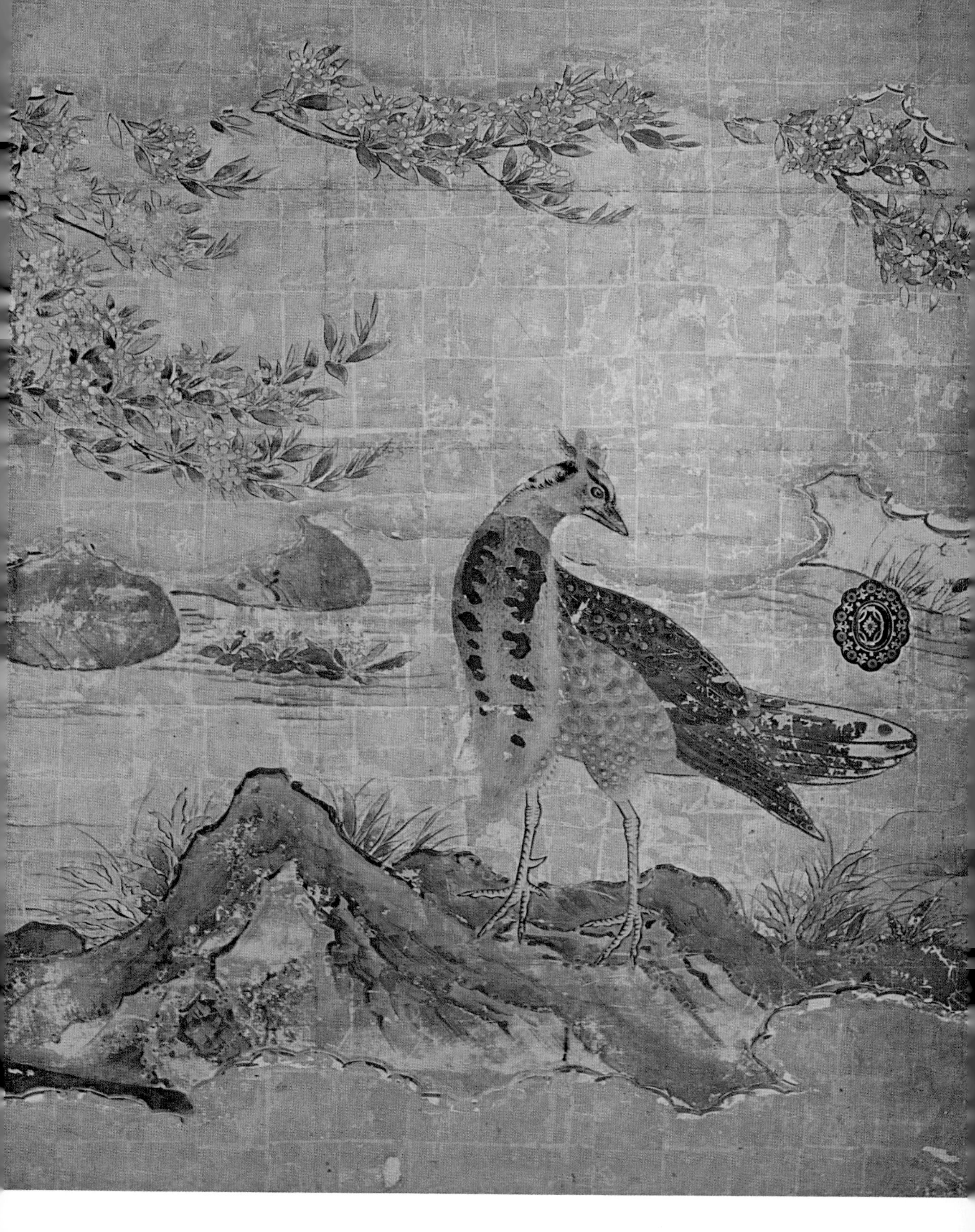

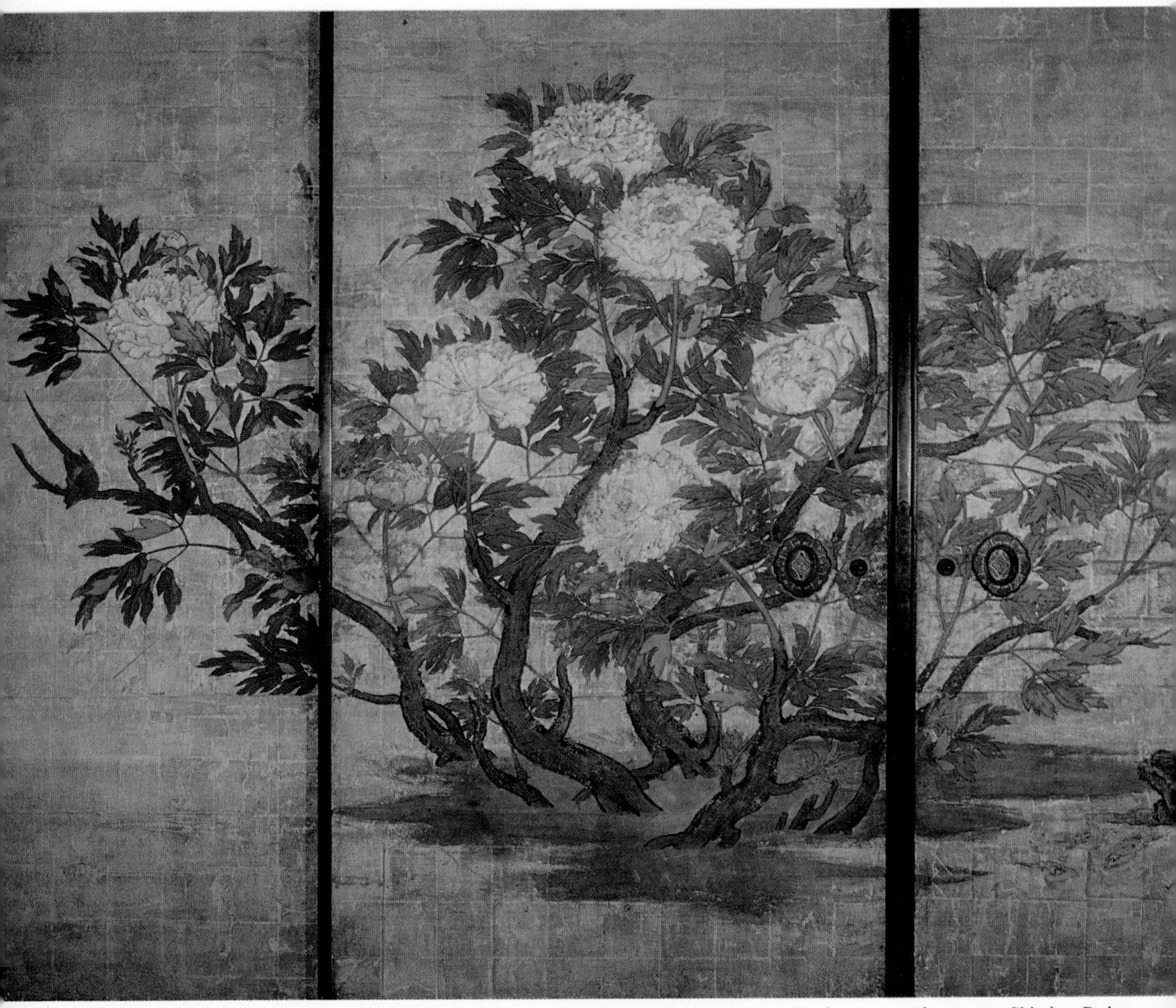

44, 45. Kano Sanraku: Peonies. Fusuma, *colors and gold on paper; 184.5 × 99 cm. Early seventeenth century. Shinden, Dai-kaku-ji, Kyoto.*

46 (overleaf). Kano Sanraku: Red Plum Blossoms. Fusuma, *colors and gold on paper; 184.5 ×* ▷
99 cm. Early seventeenth century. Shinden, Daikaku-ji, Kyoto. (See also Figure 47.)

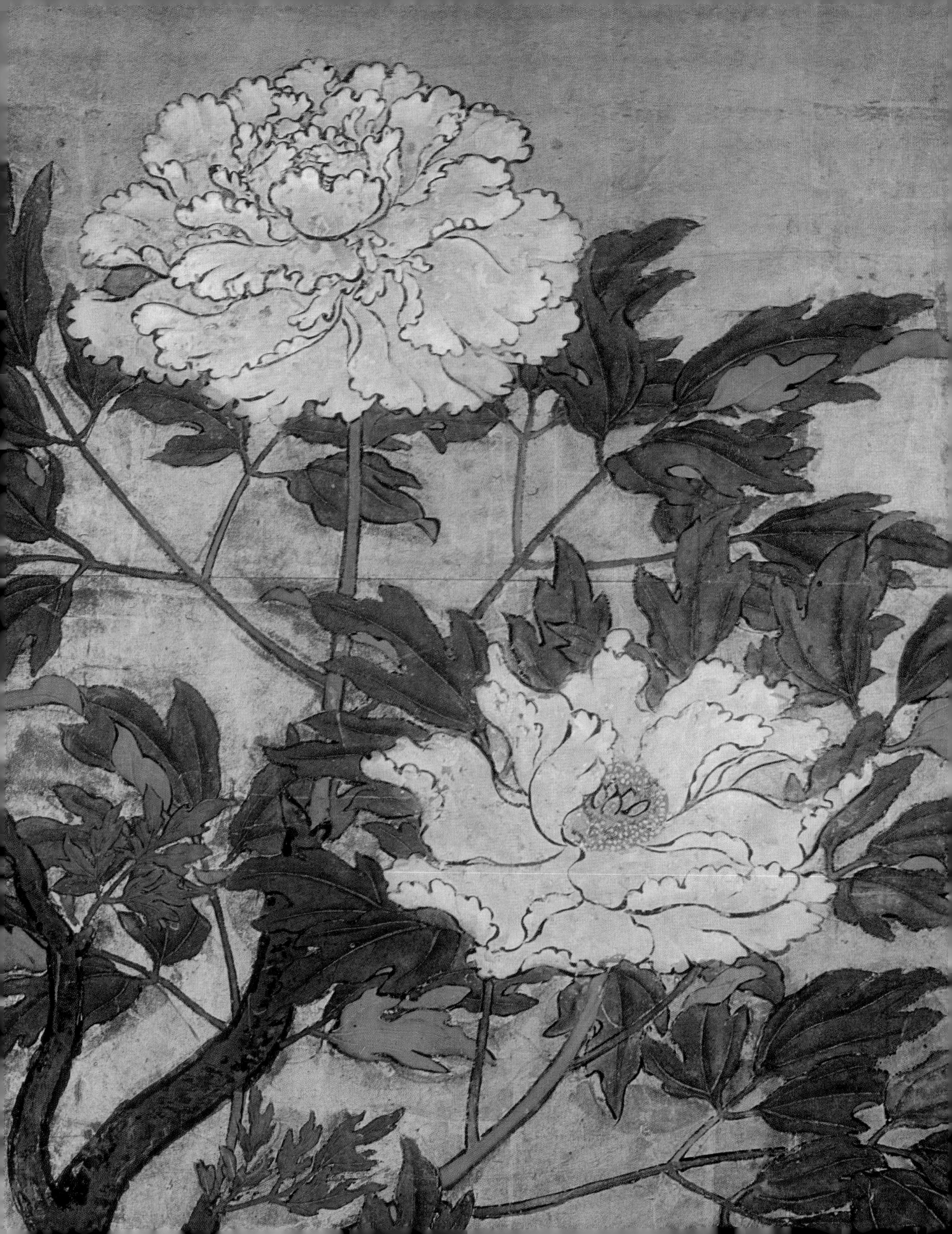

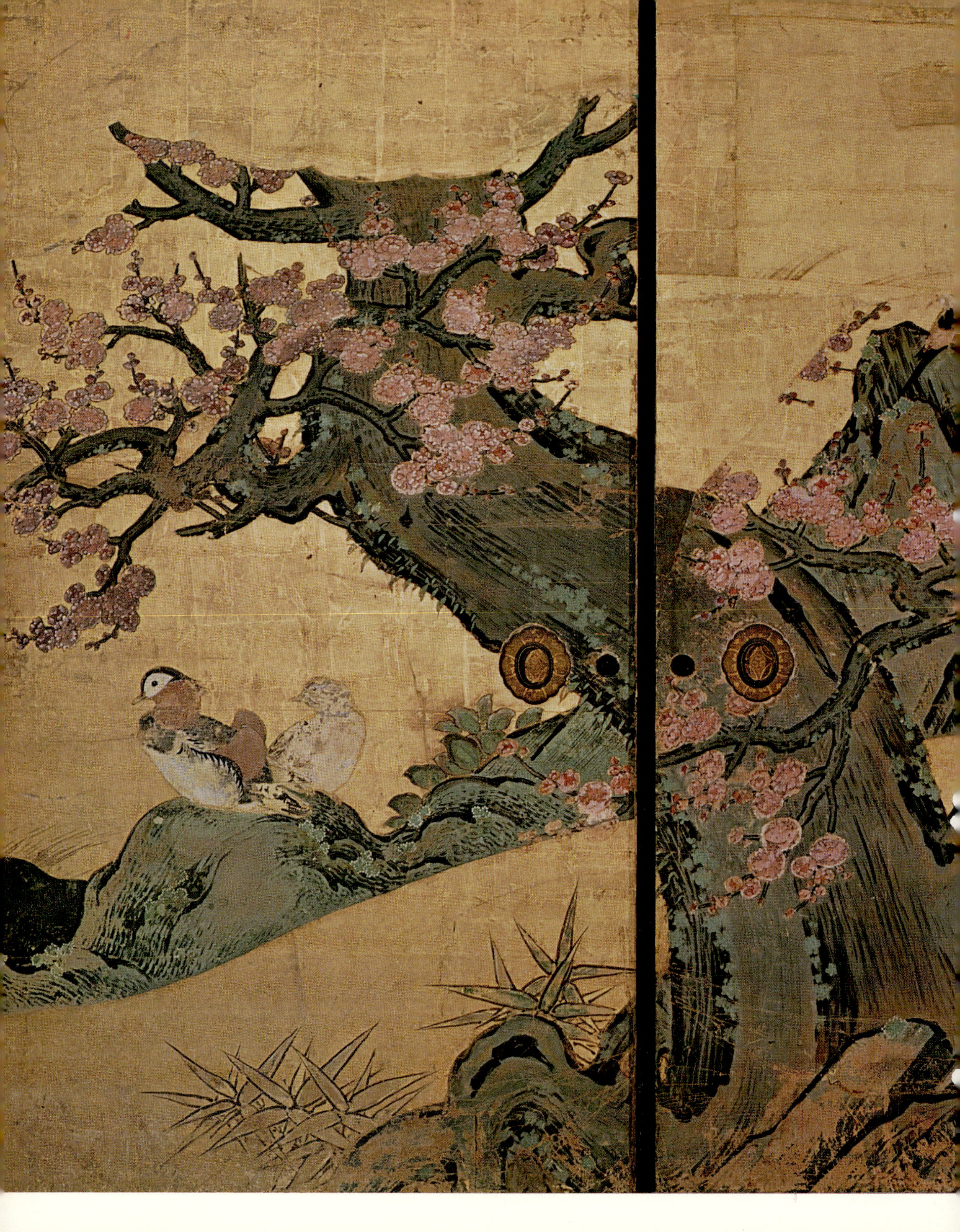

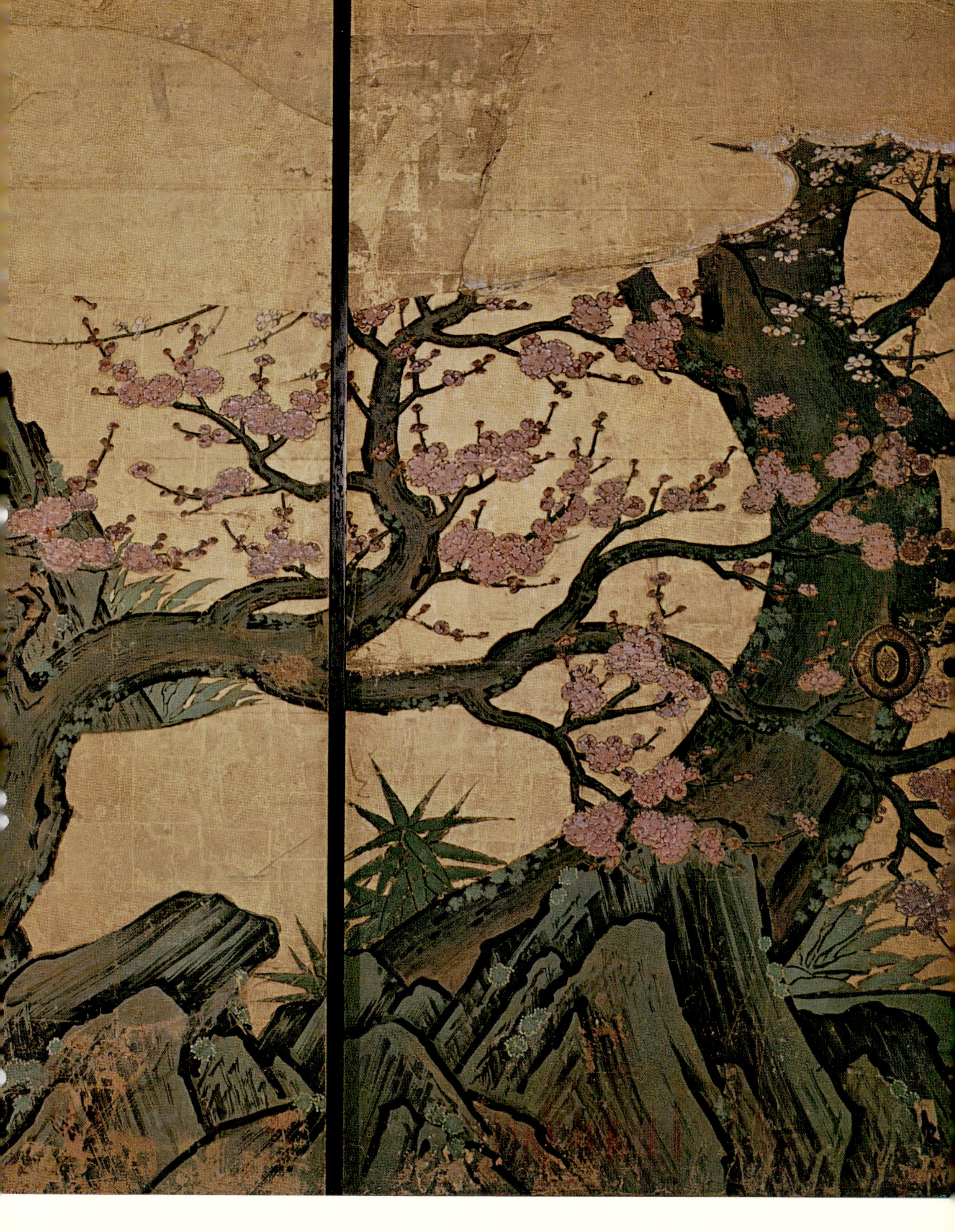

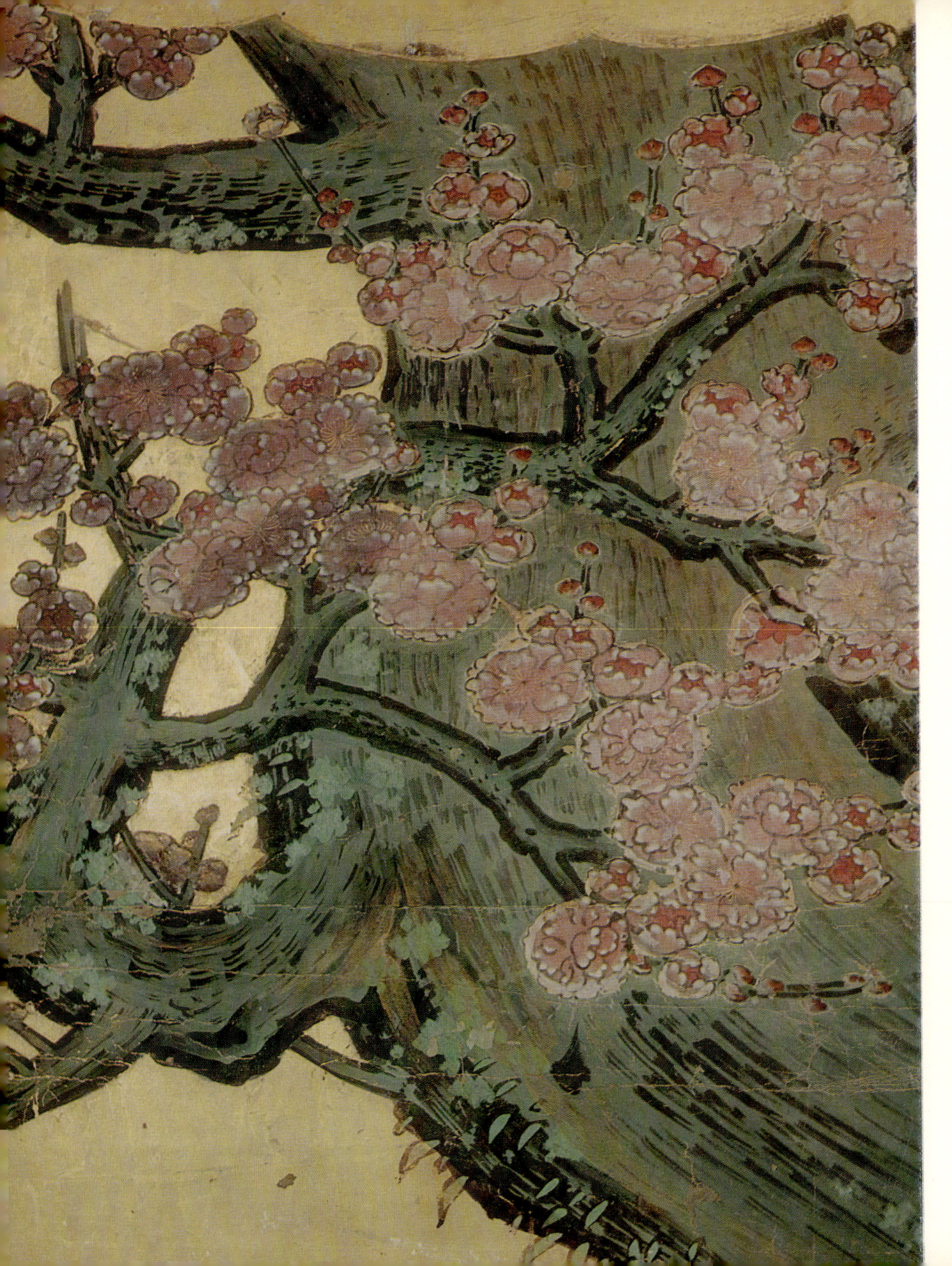

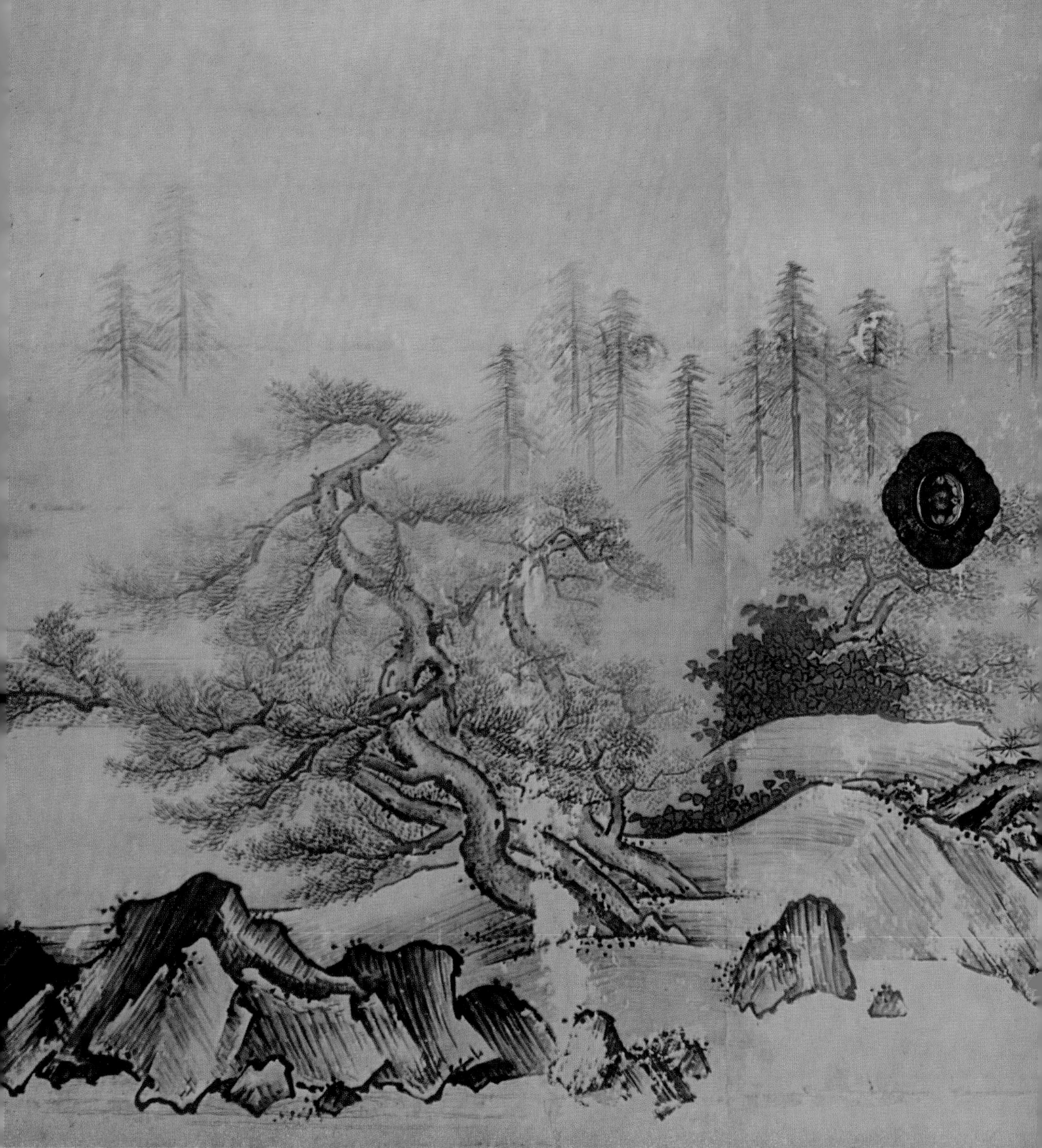

48. *Kano Sanraku: detail from* Landscape. Fusuma, *ink and light colors on paper; 185.5 × 116 cm. Early seventeenth century.* Hojo, *Shoden-ji, Kyoto. (See also Figure 19.)*

◁ 47. *Kano Sanraku: detail from* Red Plum Blossoms. *(See also Figure 46.)*

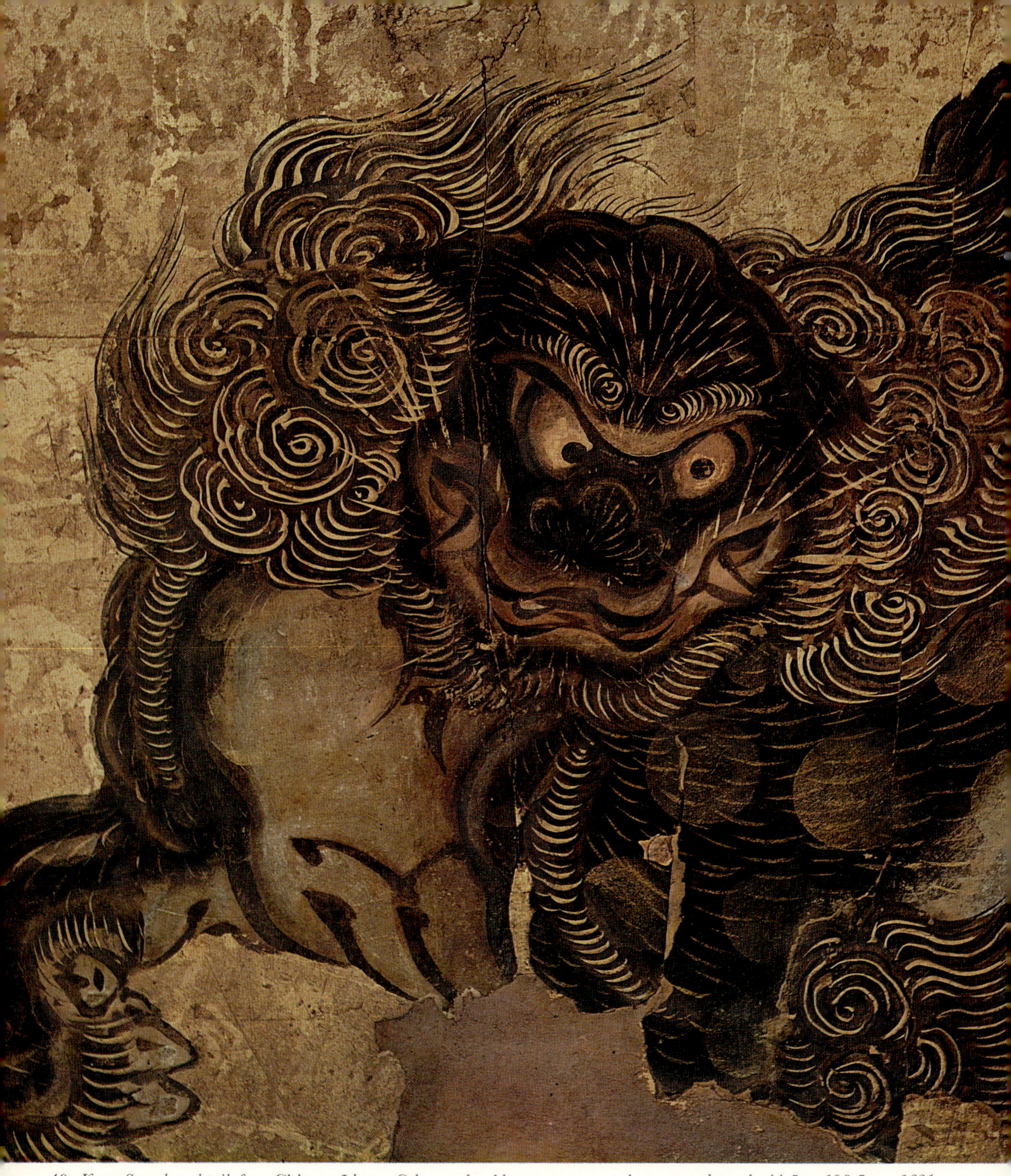

49. *Kano Sanraku: detail from* Chinese Lions. *Colors and gold on paper mounted on a wood panel; 44.5 × 198.5 cm. 1621.* Hondo, *Yogen-in, Kyoto. (See also Figure 22.)*

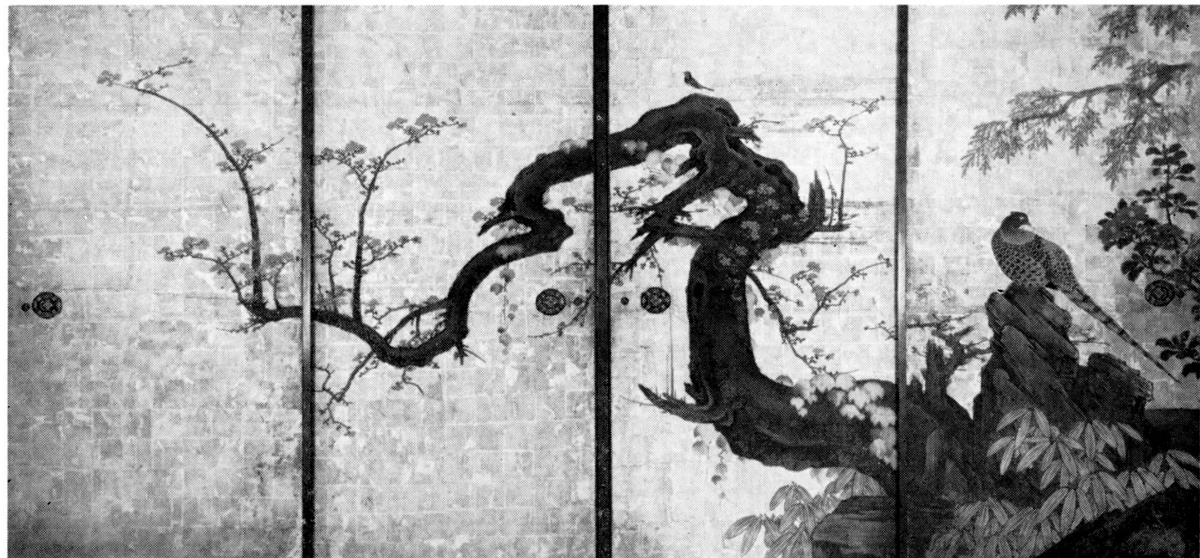

50. *Attributed to Kano Sanraku:* Flowers and Birds. Fusuma, *colors and gold on paper; 185 × 94 cm. 1631.* Hojo, *Tenkyu-in, Myoshin-ji, Kyoto.*

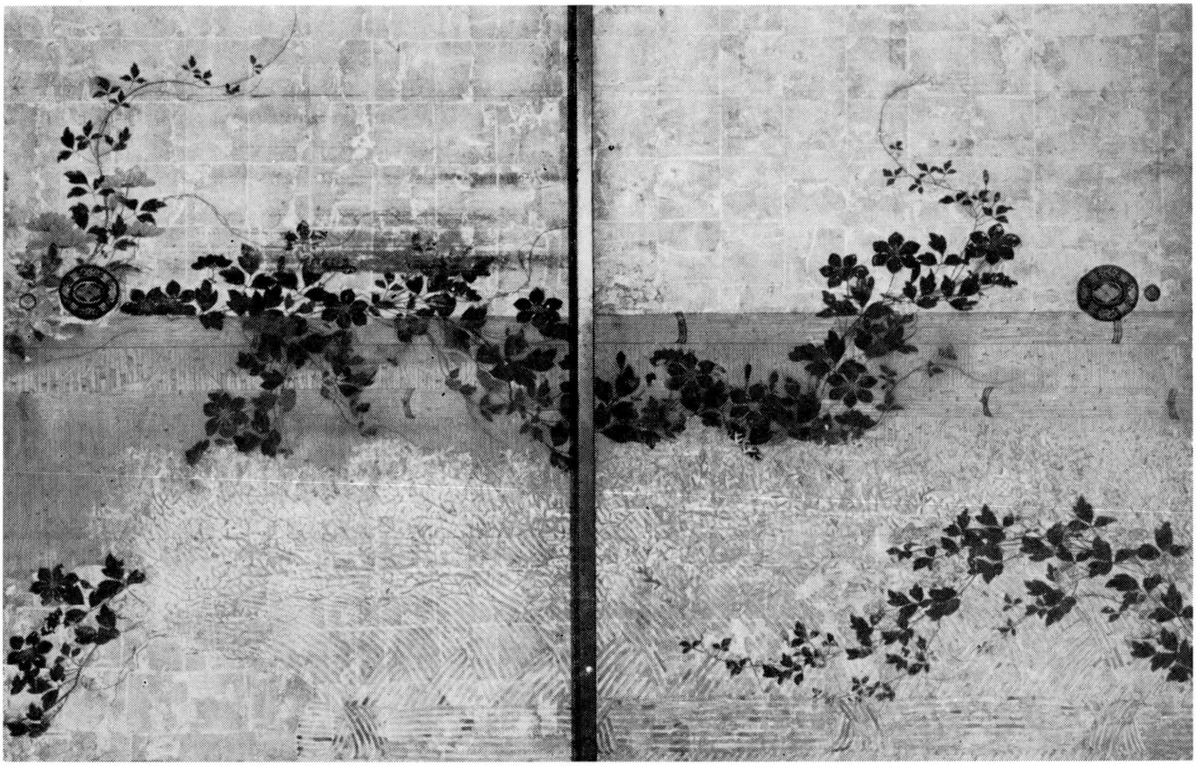

51. *Attributed to Kano Sanraku: detail from* Morning-glories and Clematis. Fusuma, *colors and gold on paper; 184 × 94 cm. 1631.* Hojo, *Tenkyu-in, Myoshin-ji, Kyoto. (See also Figure 116.)*

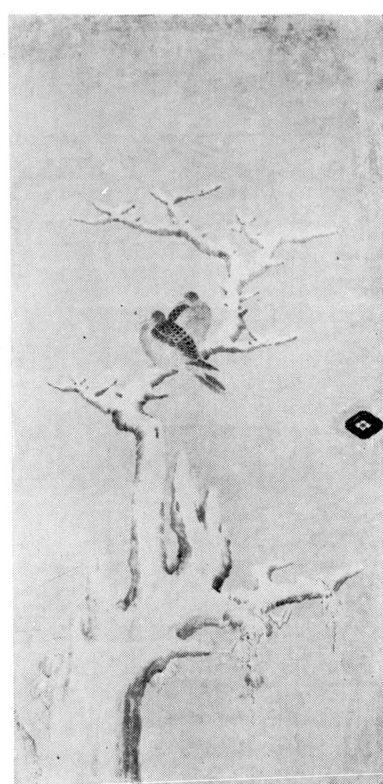

52. *Kano Sansetsu:* Two Doves in an Old Tree. Fusuma, *ink on paper; 157.5 × 77.5 cm. Early seventeenth century.* Shoin, *Daitsu-ji, Shiga Prefecture. (See also Figure 115.)*

It may seem strange that colors and gold on paper, suggesting a sensuous beauty, were used in painting at a time when the simple charm of *kanga* ink painting was predominant. However, when one remembers that the brilliant Kinkaku-ji, or Golden Pavilion, in Kyoto was built in the early part of this period, it is easy to understand that while objects of refined simplicity were highly appreciated, there was also a desire for contrasting gay and bright objects. According to the fifteenth-century *Zenrin Kokuho-ki,* a record of Japanese relations with China and Korea, folding screens covered with gold leaf were among the gifts that the shogun Ashikaga Yoshimitsu, who ruled Japan in the late fourteenth century, sent to the ruling dynasty in China. Because the screens themselves were highly decorative, it is probable that some gold-leaf screens of that time were further adorned with decorative paintings in the *yamato-e* style.

In view of the general increase in the use of gold along with other beautiful colors in *yamato-e* picture scrolls produced during the Muromachi period, the appearance of folding screens and *shoheki-ga* in colors and gold on paper is not surprising. For example, the *Boki Ekotoba* (Fig. 107), a pictorial biography of the priest Kakunyo, comes to mind. This work is composed of ten scrolls. All except the first and the seventh were painted in 1351. Replacements for scrolls one and seven were painted by Fujiwara Hisanobu in 1482. Among the representa-

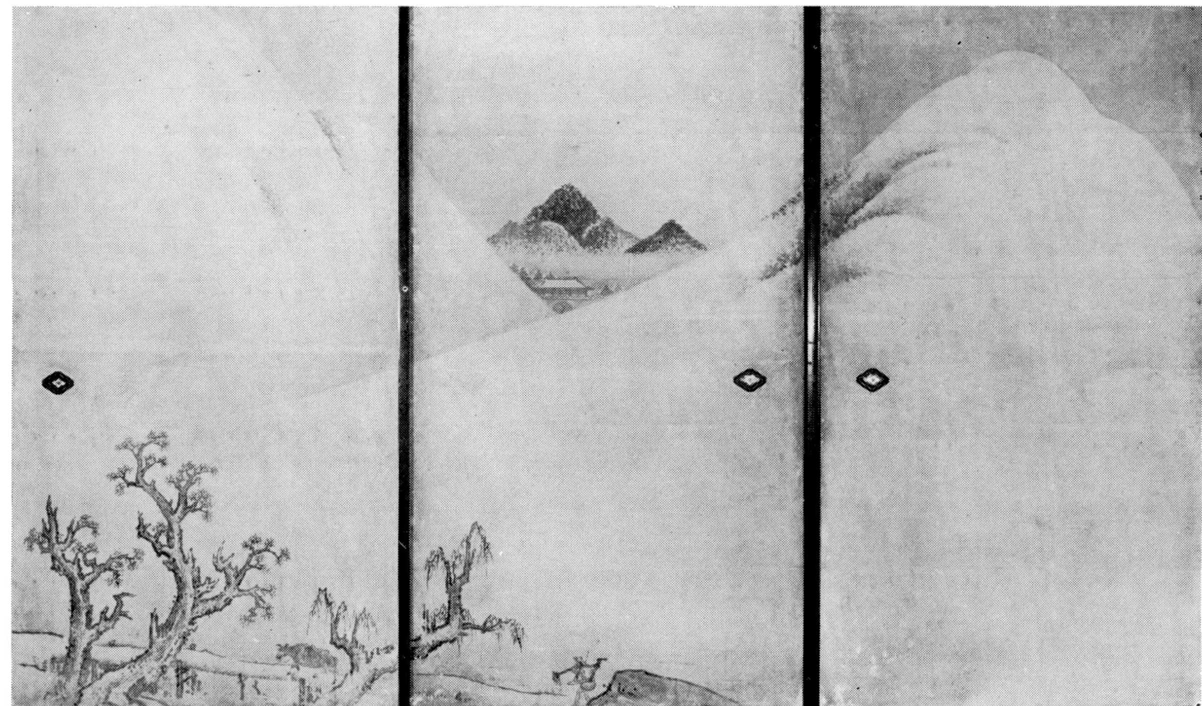

53. *Kano Sansetsu:* Snowy Landscape. Fusuma, *ink on paper; 172 × 92 cm. Early seventeenth century.* Shoin, *Daitsu-ji, Shiga Prefecture.*

tions of gold-leaf *fusuma* and wall paintings in the replacement for scroll one are *yamato-e* pictures of pines, bamboo, and cranes in colors and gold on paper. Also shown in the scroll is a gold-leaf folding screen with pictures painted on fan-shaped pieces of paper pasted on the screen. These examples make it clear that *yamato-e shoheki-ga* painted in the *kimpeki* style had appeared as early as the latter half of the fifteenth century.

Pictures of gold-leaf folding screens decorated with *yamato-e* paintings are frequently seen in scrolls painted after this time. Examples are the *Kitano Tenjin Engi,* a pictorial biography of the great statesman and man of letters Sugawara Michizane (d. 903) that also tells the story of the origin of the

Kitano Tenjin Shrine in Kyoto, painted by Tosa Mitsunobu in the early sixteenth century; the *Shinnyodo Engi,* a set of picture scrolls depicting the origin of the Shinnyodo temple in Kyoto, painted by Kamonnosuke Hisanobu in 1524; and the *Kuwanomi-dera Engi,* a picture scroll showing the origin of the Kuwanomi-dera temple, painted by Tosa Mitsumochi in 1532. It is interesting to note that the scrolls depicting the origin of the Shinnyodo contain pictures of both *shoheki-ga* in colors and gold on paper and *kanga*-style *shoheki-ga* in ink.

Thus there is considerable evidence to support the contention that the *kimpeki* style of painting in colors and gold on paper had already been adopted in *yamato-e* screen and *shoheki-ga* paintings of the

54. Kano Sansetsu: Landscape. Fusuma, *ink on paper; 165 × 85 cm. Early seven-teenth century.* Shoin, *Jinno-ji, Yawata-cho, Kyoto Prefecture.*

Muromachi period, though all the *shoheki-ga* themselves have been lost along with the buildings housing them. However, a few screen paintings have survived, and these are valuable source materials for the study of the *kimpeki*-style paintings of that period. The *Sun and Moon* screens (Fig. 120) belonging to the Kongo-ji in Osaka Prefecture are examples. Some argue that these screens belong to the Edo period, but it seems more reasonable to accept them as late Muromachi works.

CHAPTER THREE

Shoheki-ga and Castles

AT NO TIME in their long history did *shoheki-ga* flourish as vigorously as during the brief but brilliant Momoyama period. The opening of the period literally ushered in the golden age of *shoheki-ga*.

The fine arts of the Momoyama period were no longer religious in inspiration. It is true that this was a time of reconstruction, when the shrines and temples devastated by the civil wars of the preceding hundred years were being revived and rebuilt. New images were carved and religious pictures painted for Buddhist temples. However, religion no longer formed the true basis of the fine arts. The Buddhist images carved at this time lack the nobility of those of the past, more closely resembling cheap religious art. Historically, the most valuable and vigorous carvings of this period were not inspired by Buddhism but were decorative carvings for buildings. Similarly, Buddhist paintings are not of high enough quality to be included among the best works of the time. The greatest masterpieces of the period are decorative *shoheki-ga* and screen paintings.

AZUCHI CASTLE Castle architecture set the stage for the florescence of *shoheki-ga*. As an integral part of the castles where the heroes of the day lived, *shoheki-ga* partook of the glory of the lords of the new age.

It goes without saying that castles were built before the mid-sixteenth century. The rise of the warrior class from the end of the twelfth century to the middle of the sixteenth century accelerated the pace and scope of castle building. There was a remarkable development in the art of building fortifications between the mid-fourteenth and mid-sixteenth centuries as the struggles among the warrior clans continued.

The completion of Azuchi Castle in 1576 marked the beginning of a new era of castle architecture in Japan. The castle was built in Azuchi (present Shiga Prefecture) by Oda Nobunaga (1534–82), the most powerful warrior and feudal lord of his time. The majestic and commanding air of this castle, built around a seven-storied donjon, signaled a departure from earlier castles. While boasting a grand and solid structure executed on a large scale, the donjon and surrounding buildings were elegantly decorated to display the immense power of their master. To this end the very best in architecture, carving, painting, and crafts was concentrated in Azuchi Castle. *Shoheki-ga* played an important role among the paintings used to decorate the castle. An interesting account of the *shoheki-ga* of Azuchi Castle is given in the *Shincho Koki*, a biography of Nobunaga by Ota Gyuichi, completed in 1587. An entry from 1576 under the heading "Details of the Donjon on Azuchi Hill," parts of which are paraphrased in the following paragraphs, gives a detailed account of the sumptuously decorated donjon.

The donjon consisted of seven stories including

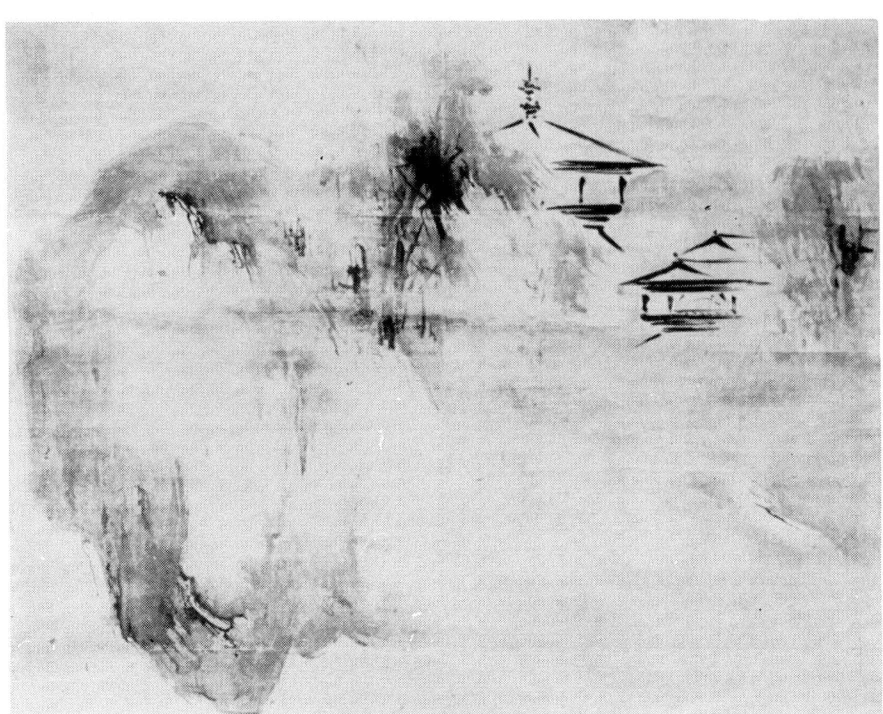

55. *Kaiho Yusho: detail from* Landscape. *Hanging scroll, ink on paper; 199 × 186 cm. 1599. Kennin-ji, Kyoto.*

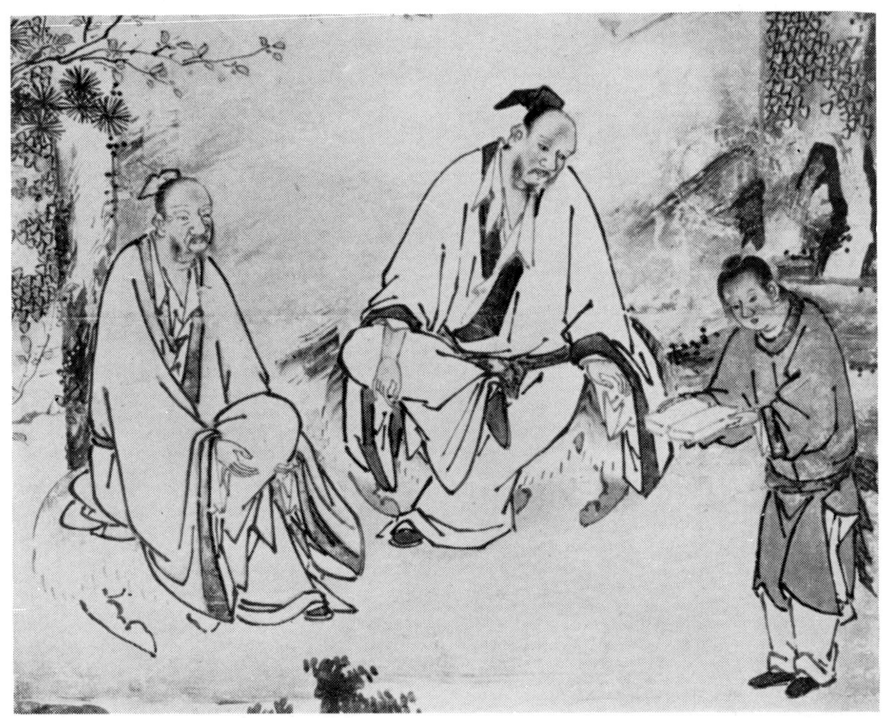

56. *Kaiho Yusho: detail from* Landscape and Figures, *illustrating the four gentlemanly accomplishments. Hanging scroll, ink and light colors on paper; 185 × 190 cm. 1599. Kennin-ji, Kyoto.*

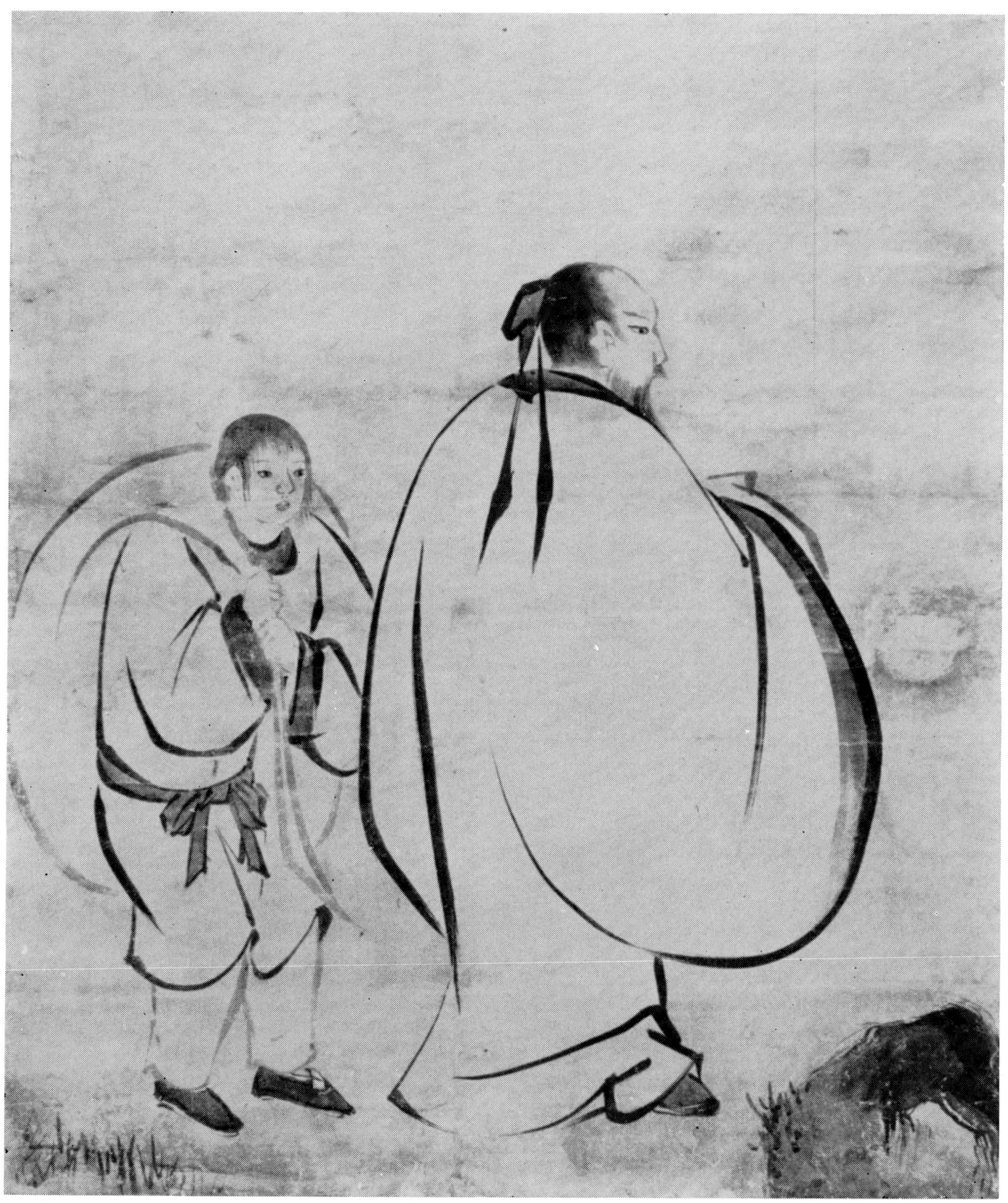

57. *Kaiho Yusho:* The Seven Sages of the Bamboo Grove. *Hanging scroll, ink on paper; 185 × 160 cm. 1599. Kennin-ji, Kyoto.*

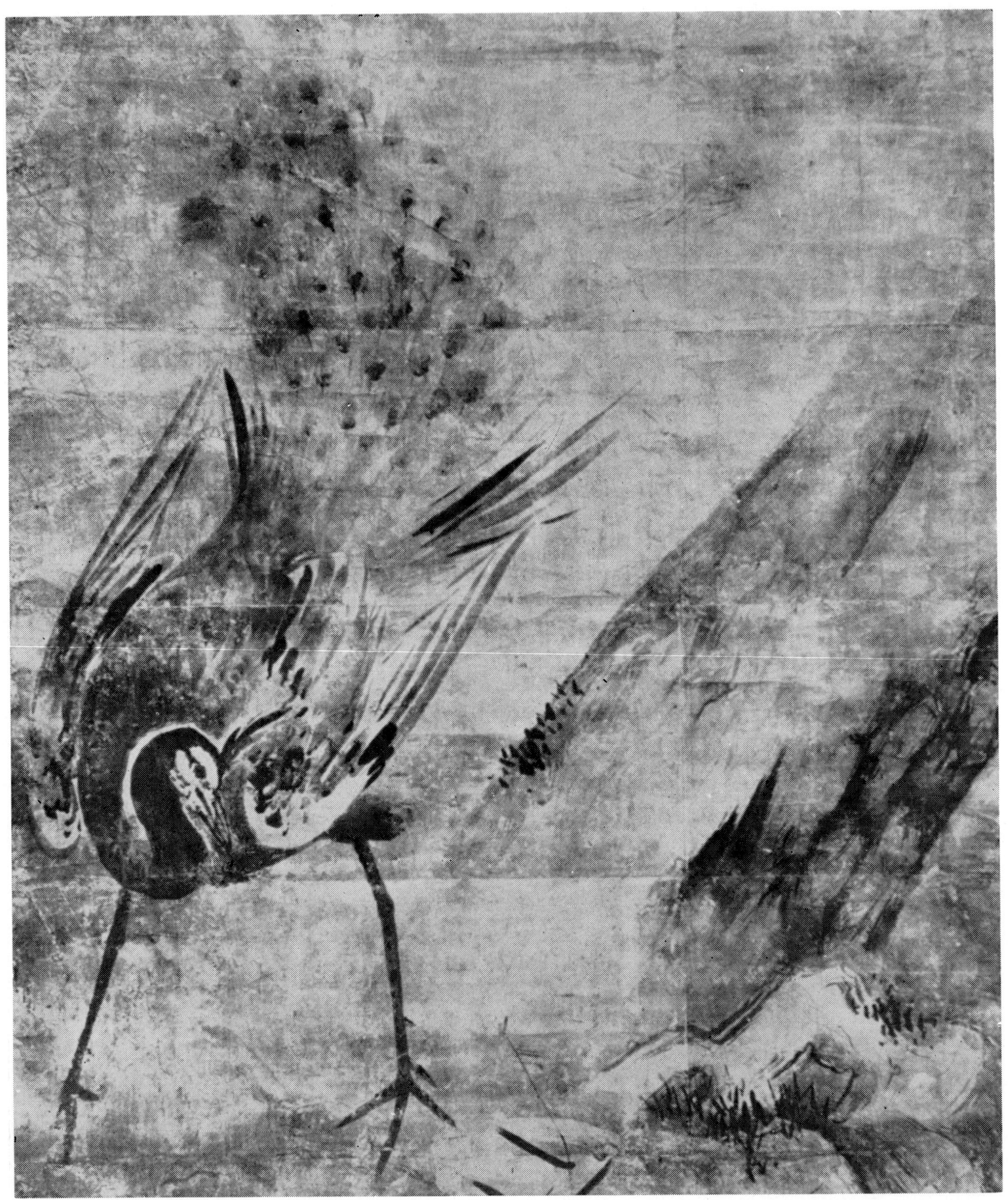

58. *Kaiho Yusho: detail from* Flowers and Birds. *Hanging scroll, ink on paper; 188 × 225 cm. 1599. Kennin-ji, Kyoto.*

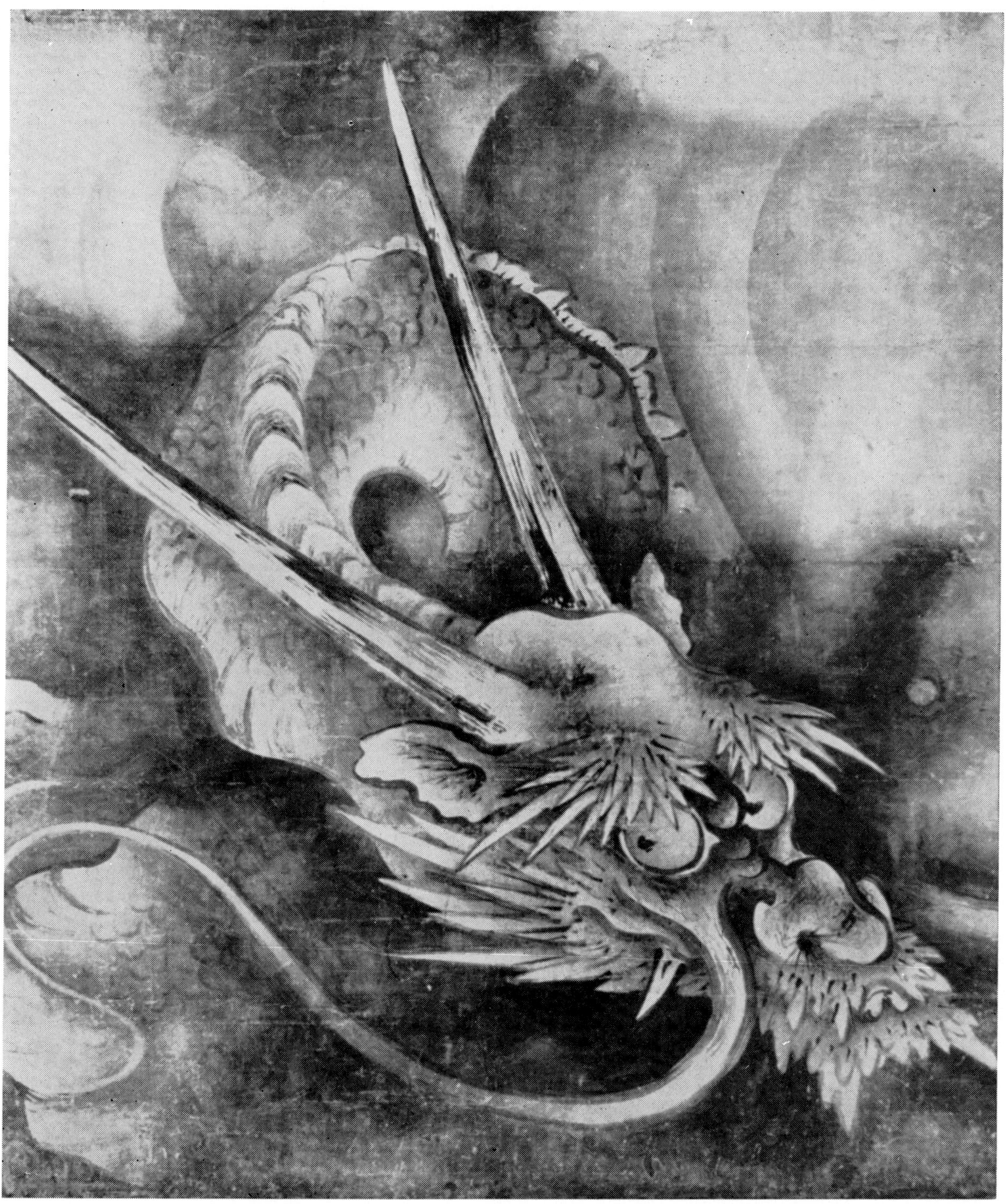

59. *Kaiho Yusho:* Dragon in Clouds. *Hanging scroll, ink on paper; 197 × 186 cm. 1599. Kennin-ji, Kyoto.*

the storage area on the ground floor. The second story was approximately 119 feet long north to south, 101 feet long east to west, and 95 feet high, and had 204 pillars. Kano Eitoku was commissioned to paint *Plum Tree* in ink in the 12-tatami room on the west side. All the rooms with paintings were golden from top to bottom. Paintings in the various rooms on this floor included the landscape *Evening Bell from a Distant Temple,* doves, geese, a pheasant showing affection for its young, and Chinese Confucian scholars.

On the third story, the 12-tatami Kacho-no-ma contained paintings of flowers and birds (*kacho*), as did a 4-tatami room. To the south was the Kenjin-no-ma, or Room of Sages, with a painting of a hermit producing a horse from a gourd. On the east side was the Jako-no-ma, or Civet Room. Other rooms contained pictures of hermits, horses at pasture, and the female Immortal Hsi Wang Mu. There were no paintings on the west side.

On the fourth story were the Iwa-no-ma, with paintings of rocks (*iwa*) and trees; a room with a painting of a dragon and a tiger fighting; the Takè-no-ma with paintings of bamboo (*take*); the Matsu-no-ma with pictures of a variety of pine trees (*matsu*); the Ho-o-no-ma showing a phoenix (*ho-o*) and paulownia; a room with a painting of Hsu Yu and Ch'ao Fu; a room with paintings of *temari* bushes; and the Otaka-no-ma with paintings of hawks (*taka*).

There were no paintings on the fifth story.

On the sixth story the outer pillars were painted vermilion and the interior pillars gold. There were paintings of the Ten Great Disciples of the Buddha, the Buddha preaching, hungry ghosts (*gaki*), and demons (*oni*). Imaginary dolphinlike

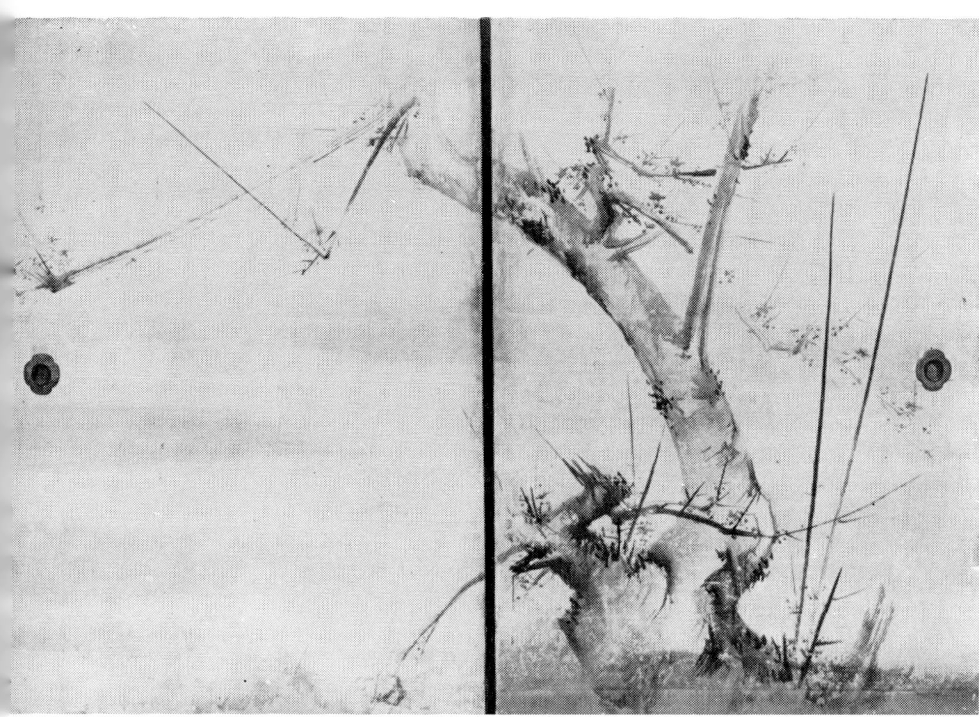

60. *Kaiho Yusho:* Plum Tree. Fusuma, *ink on paper; 173 × 117 cm. Early seventeenth century.* Shoin, *Zenkyo-an, Kennin-ji, Kyoto.*

fish (*shachihoko*) and flying dragons were painted on the paneling around the balcony, and the balustrades around the balcony were decorated with carvings.

The seventh and top story was square, 3 bays (*ken*) to a side, and both the interior and exterior were gilded. Rising and descending dragons were painted on the interior pillars at the four corners. The ceiling bore a painting of a celestial being (*tennin*). Other interior paintings depicted the Three Sovereigns and Five Emperors, legendary rulers of ancient China; the Ten Major Disciples of Confucius; the Four Sages of Mount Shang; and the Seven Sages of the Bamboo Grove.

This description of the Azuchi Castle donjon enables us to imagine the magnificence of the structure and indicates the important role of *sho-heki-ga* in decoration. It is particularly noteworthy that many of these *shoheki-ga* were painted on backgrounds of gold leaf. It is assumed that most of the paintings in these glittering rooms were rendered in the rich colors of the *kimpeki* style, though we know that some were painted in ink, such as *Plum Tree* on the second story. Following is a tentative classification of the widely varied subjects of the donjon's decorative paintings.

Landscape: evening bell from a distant temple
Flowers and birds: flowers and birds, a plum tree, trees and rocks, bamboo, pine trees, a phoenix and paulownia, *temari* bushes, geese, pheasants, doves, hawks
Animals: civet, horses at pasture, a dragon and a tiger fighting, flying dragons, rising and descending dragons, imaginary fish (*shachihoko*)

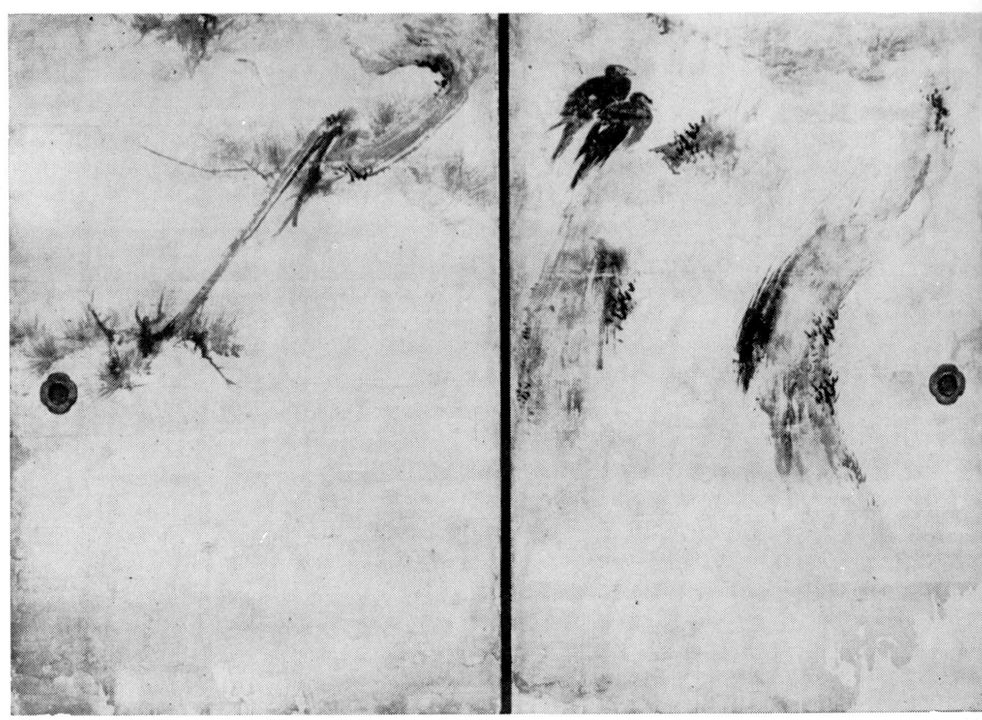

61. *Kaiho Yusho:* Birds Sleeping in Pine Tree. Fusuma, *ink on paper; 173 × 117 cm. Early seventeenth century.* Shoin, *Zenkyo-an, Kennin-ji, Kyoto. (See also Figures 62, 63.)*

Figures: Chinese Confucian scholars, a hermit producing a horse from a gourd, other hermits, the female Immortal Hsi Wang Mu, the Three Sovereigns and Five Emperors, the Ten Major Disciples of Confucius, the Four Sages of Mount Shang, the Seven Sages of the Bamboo Grove *Buddhist subjects:* the Ten Great Disciples of the Buddha, the Buddha preaching, hungry ghosts (*gaki*), demons (*oni*), a celestial being (*tennin*)

Of these paintings, *Evening Bell from a Distant Temple* was the only landscape. It probably represented one of the eight views of the Hsiao and the Hsiang, a favorite subject of *kanga* painters. There must have been a landscape in the background of *Hsu Yu and Ch'ao Fu* on the fourth story, too, for according to the *Shincho Koki* there was a painting of "the homeland of Hsu Yu and Ch'ao Fu." Even so, there is no question that there were very few landscapes among the decorative paintings in the Azuchi Castle donjon. In contrast, the number of paintings of flowers and birds and of figures was remarkably large. It is interesting that an appreciation of flowers and birds characterized the development of Momoyama *shoheki-ga.* All the human figures were Chinese sages, "noble characters," and hermits and Immortals, the usual subjects of the *kanga* tradition of figure painting. Among these paintings were *Four Sages of Mount Shang,* a depiction of four elderly men who lived in seclusion on Mount Shang, in the province of Shensi, to escape the war during the reign of Shih Huang-ti (r. 221–210 B.C.) of the Ch'in dynasty, and *The Seven Sages of the Bamboo Grove,* showing seven recluses who

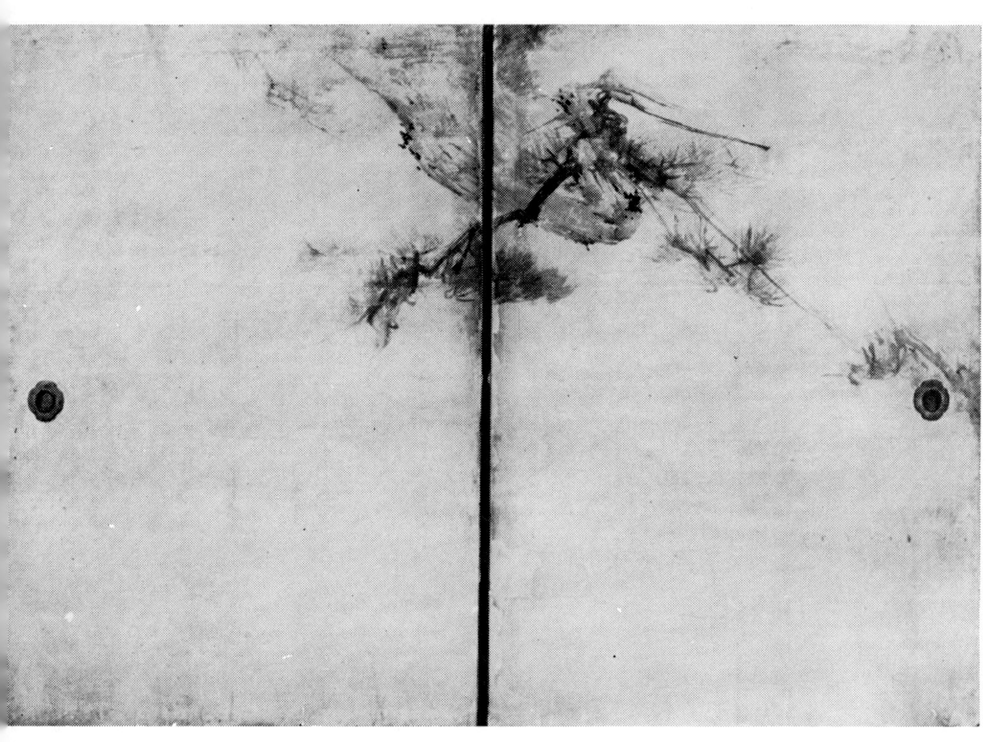

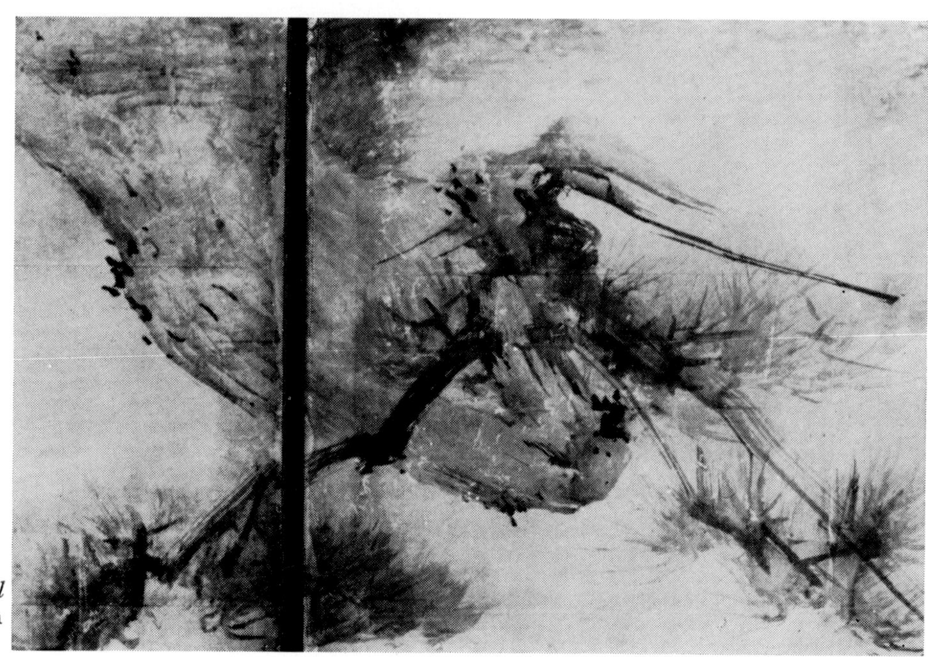

62. *Kaiho Yusho: detail from* Birds Sleeping in Pine Tree.

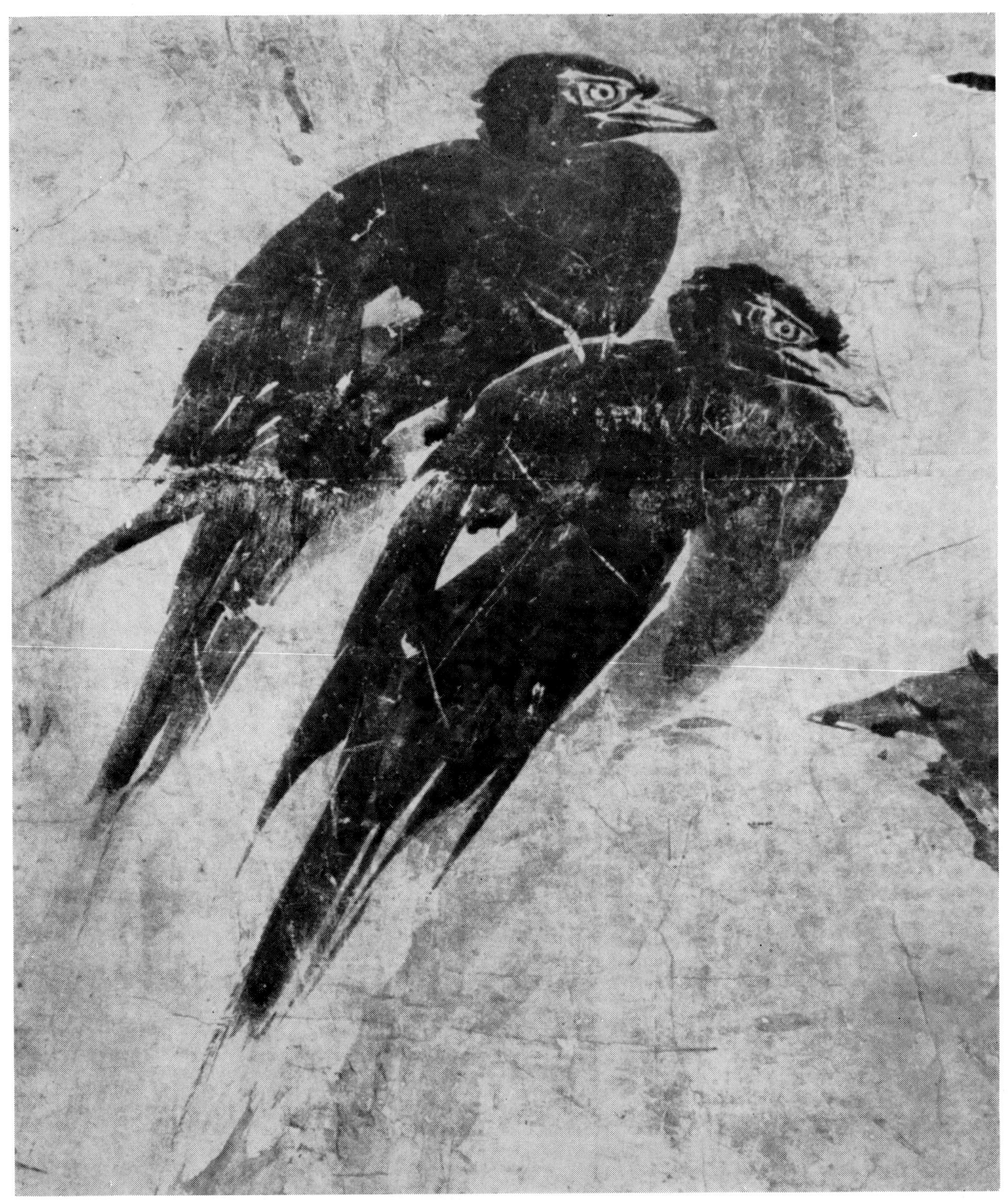

63. Kaiho Yusho: detail from Birds Sleeping in Pine Tree.

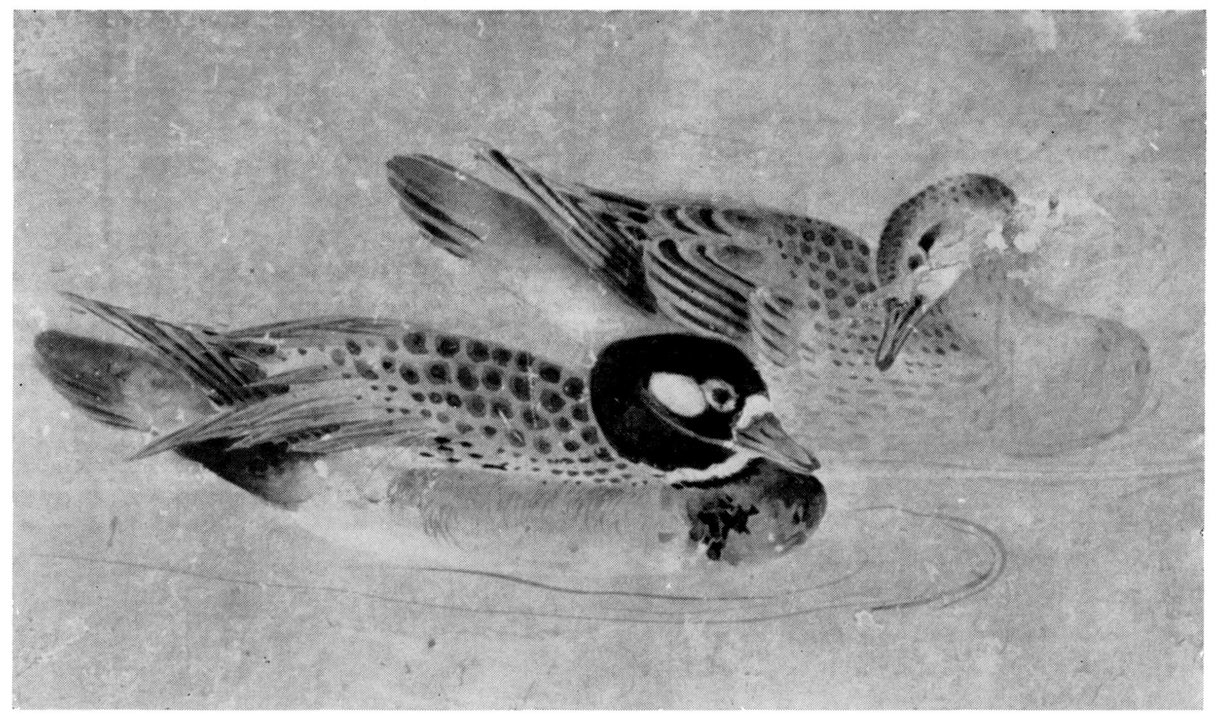

64. *Kaiho Yusho: detail from* Flowers and Birds. Fusuma, *colors on paper; 172.5 × 88 cm. Late sixteenth century.* Shoin, *Reito-in, Kennin-ji, Kyoto. (See also Figure 10.)*

took refuge in a bamboo grove to escape a national crisis during the Ch'in dynasty. There were also paintings of three Taoist hermits, including a woman. The overwhelming influence of the *kanga* tradition is seen in the fact that all the figures painted in the donjon were typical *kanga* subjects.

Many paintings of animals and of Buddhist subjects, including *The Ten Great Disciples of the Buddha,* are also noted. Horses, dragons, and tigers, all considered to be symbolic of valor, were favorite animal subjects in Momoyama painting, and early examples were seen at Azuchi. The reason for Buddhist subjects in decorative paintings in the castle poses an interesting question, as religious subjects are not seen in the later decorative paintings of the period.

KANO EITOKU   Concerning the artists who worked on the Azuchi Castle donjon, the section of the *Shincho Koki* describing the second story states: "Kano Eitoku was commissioned to paint *Plum Tree* in ink in the twelve-tatami room on the west side." Since there is no mention of other artists, it is assumed that Eitoku was entrusted with all the decorative paintings in the donjon, and that he accomplished this task with the help of several artists of the Kano school working under his supervision.

It should not be overlooked that many *shoheki-ga* were also painted in the buildings surrounding the donjon. There are several entries to this effect in the *Shincho Koki*. The entry for January 1, 1578, states that those who came to pay their respects

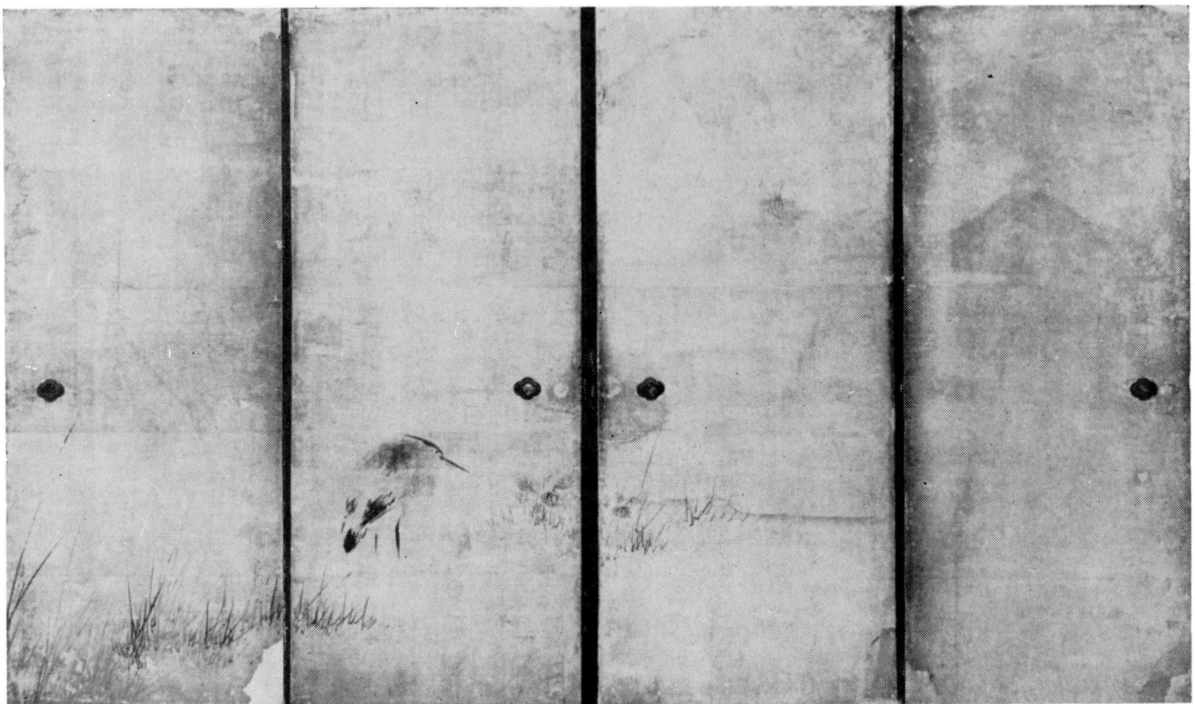

65. *Kaiho Yusho:* Heron and Reeds. Fusuma, *ink on paper; 172 × 69 cm. Late sixteenth century.* Shoin, *Daichu-in, Kennin-ji, Kyoto.*

on New Year's Day were given a tour of the palaces. They were shown all over, "including the lord's chamber in the palace. Scenes from famous places in the 'three countries' were painted by Kano Eitoku in the rich colors of the *dami-e* style of wall painting. Noted products from different parts of the country were gathered here to display the eminence and power of the lord." According to the entry for January 1, 1582, "The rooms were all gold. Kano Eitoku was commissioned to paint pictures in each of these rooms, and a wide variety of pictures was painted there. . . . The roof of the imperial chamber, along with the roof of the hallway leading to it, was thatched with layers of cypress bark. Metal fittings and mountings glittered in the sun. The interior of the palace was all golden. The four sides of the room were covered with gold leaf. Pictures were painted on the gold using thick layers of colors. All the metal fittings were made of gold and had arabesque patterns worked in grains of gold. The room glowed throughout beyond words and imagination. The tatami mats were made with rushes from the province of Bingo, the very best, with silk borders. An area set back approximately twelve feet from the front of the room appeared to be the throne. The floor there was raised, with a screen glittering with gold. The smell of incense floated in the air. It was absolute perfection. There were many rooms to the east. In these rooms various pictures were painted in colors on gold leaf covering the walls." This entry goes on to describe the gorgeous *shoheki-ga* in brilliant *kimpeki* style in the palaces of Azuchi Castle and mentions Kano Eitoku as the artist.

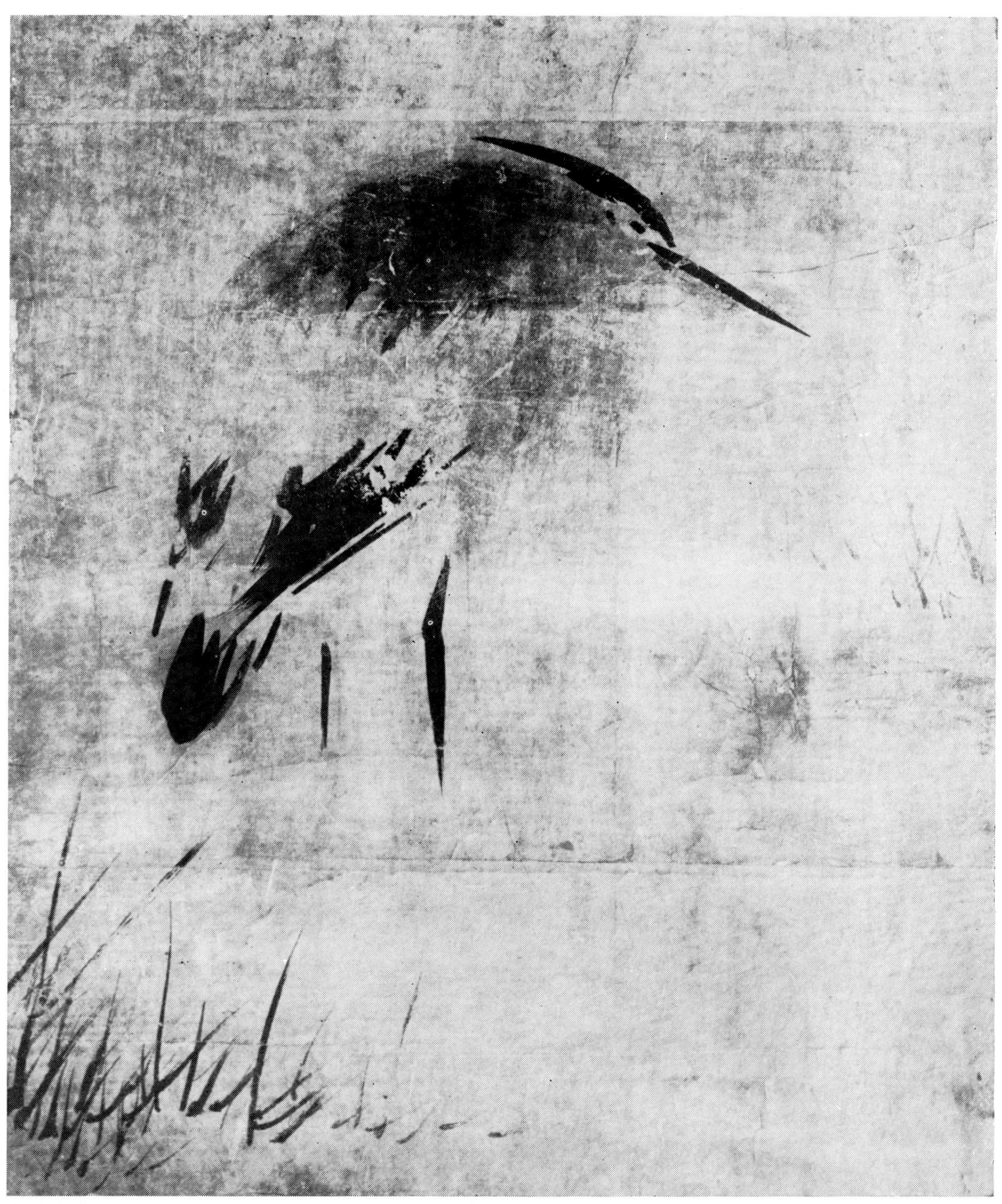

66. *Kaiho Yusho: detail from* Heron and Reeds.

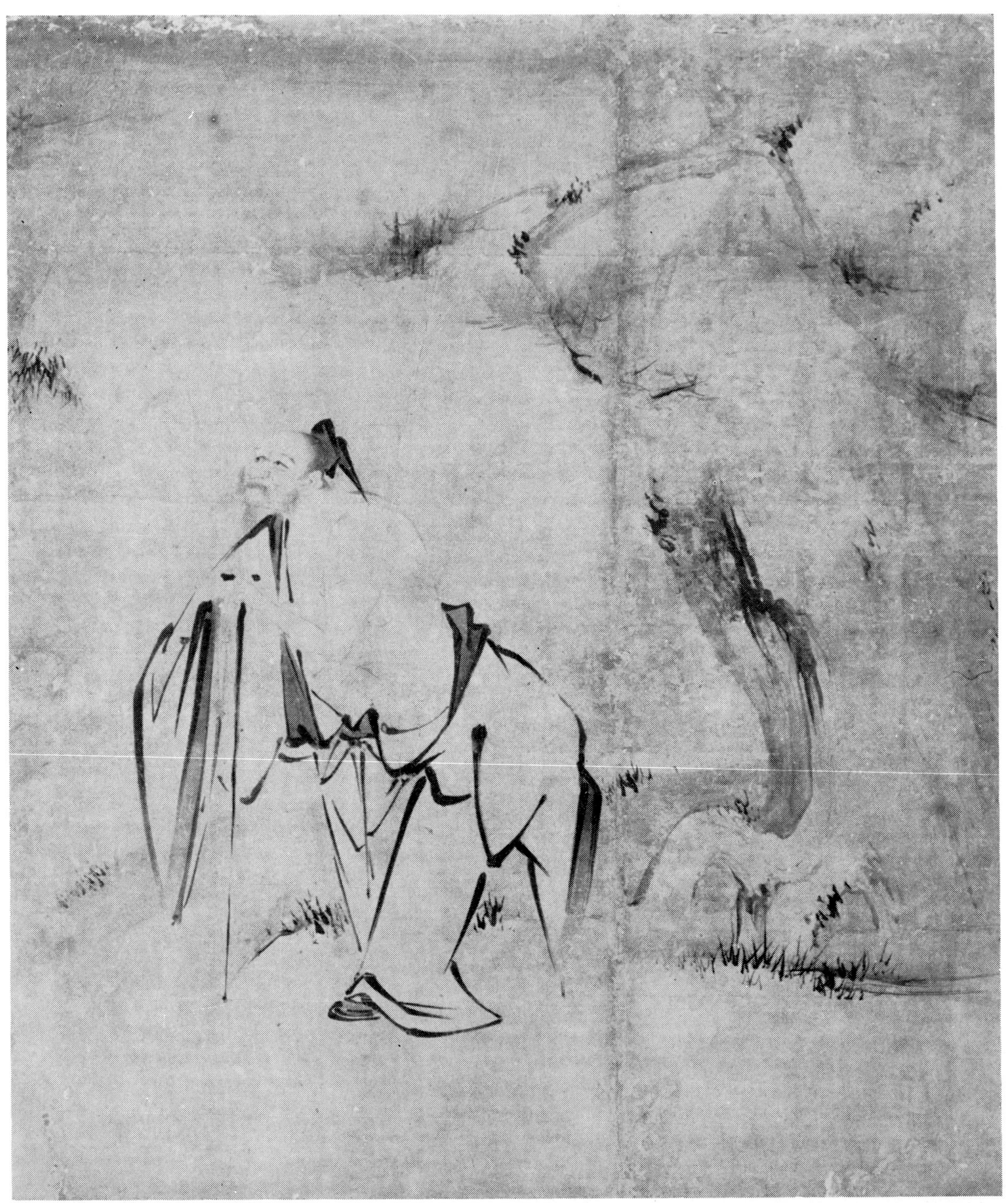

67. *Kaiho Yusho: detail from* Noble Characters *showing Li Po. Ink on paper mounted on a wall; 169 × 181 cm. Late sixteenth* century. Shoin, *Reito-in, Kennin-ji, Kyoto.*

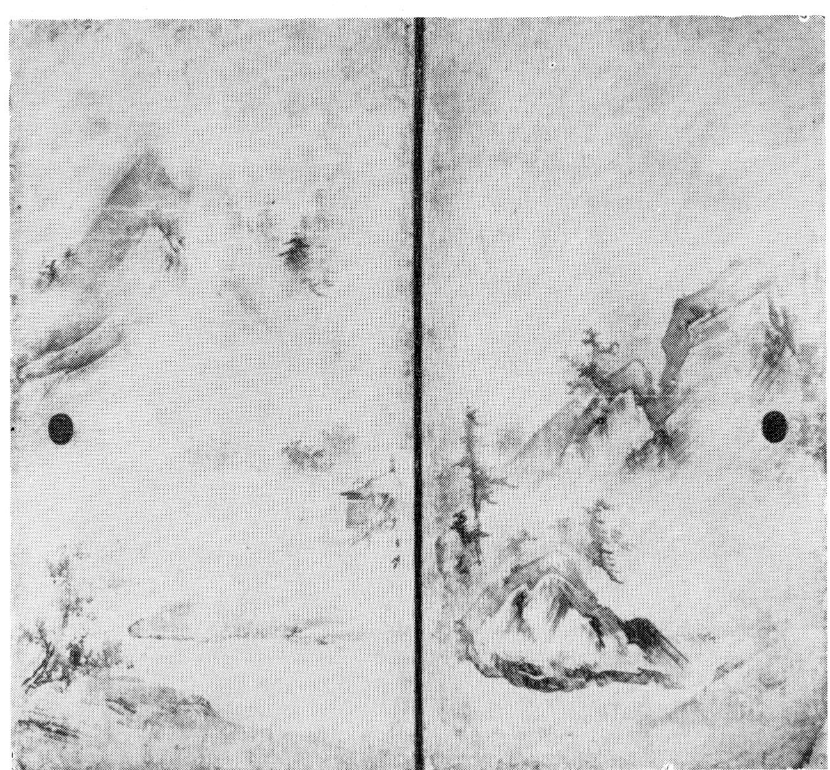

68. Kaiho Yusho: Landscape. Fusuma, *ink and light colors on paper; 173 × 93 cm. Late sixteenth century.* Shoin, *Daichu-in, Kennin-ji, Kyoto.*

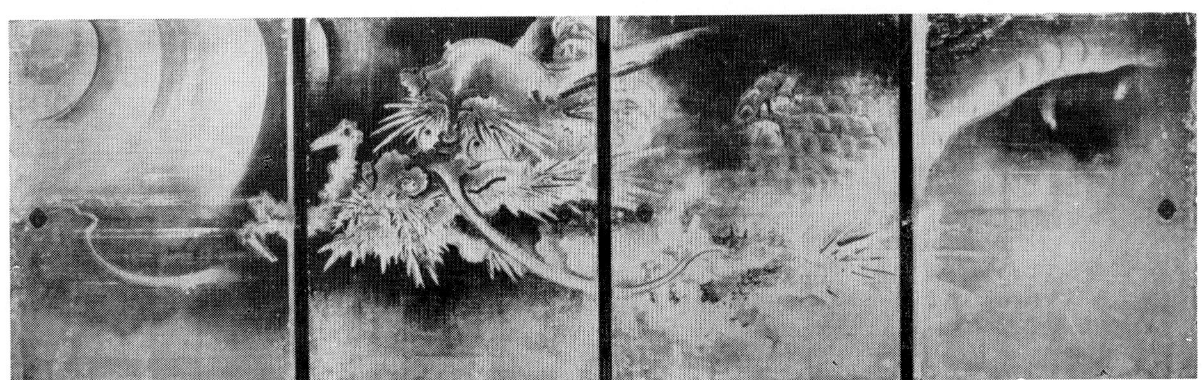

69. Kaiho Yusetsu: Dragon in Clouds. Fusuma, *ink on paper; 188 × 141 cm. 1634. Reception hall, Rinsho-in, Myoshin-ji, Kyoto.*

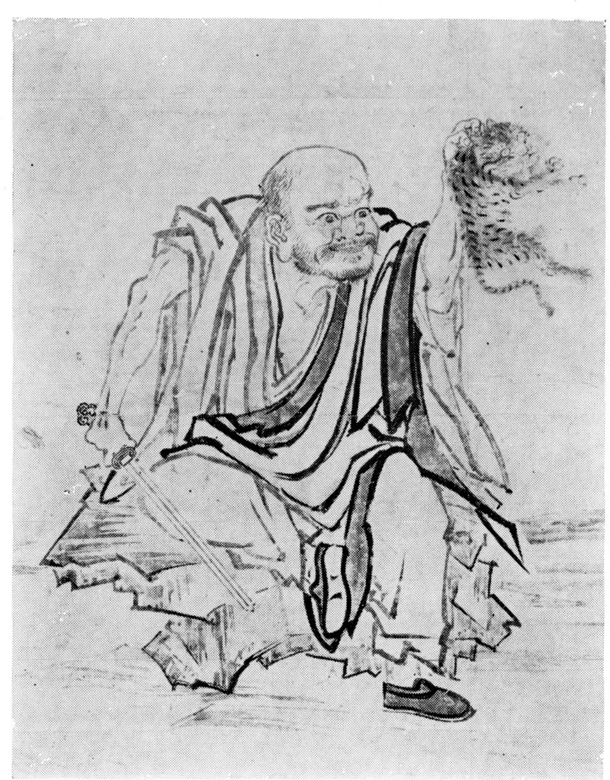

70. *Hasegawa Tohaku: detail from* Zen Patriarchs *showing Nan Ch'uan killing the cat, illustrating a famous Zen anecdote and koan. Fusuma,* ink on paper; *182.5 × 142.5 cm. 1602. Reception hall, Tenju-an, Nanzen-ji, Kyoto.*

THE GOLDEN AGE OF SHOHEKI-GA   With the emergence of Azuchi Castle in the Momoyama period, *shoheki-ga* reached a new and grander stage, advancing toward unprecedented prominence in Japanese fine arts. The magnificence of the *kimpeki* style, seen in Azuchi Castle, set the direction for the subsequent development of *shoheki-ga*. Toyotomi Hideyoshi, who gained control of Japan after the death of Nobunaga in 1582, built a number of castles: Osaka Castle in 1585, Juraku-dai castle-palace in Kyoto in 1587, and Fushimi Castle in Kyoto in 1594. The grand scale and splendor of these castles dazzled the people of that time. *Shoheki-ga*, comprising an important part of the decoration of these castles, flourished phenomenally. The development of *shoheki-ga* in castles eventually stimulated and influenced the decoration of the imperial palaces, the residences of court nobles, shrines, and temples, marking the beginning of the true age of *shoheki-ga* in the history of Japanese fine arts.

CHAPTER FOUR

The Momoyama Painters and Their Milieu

During the unprecedented rise of *shoheki-ga* in the Momoyama period, all the influential artists were excellent *shoheki-ga* painters. The several schools of the *kanga* tradition dominated the scene more than ever before. A branch of the *yamato-e* tradition, the Tosa school, still existed but did not have much influence. Tosa Mitsuyoshi (1539–1613) is about the only noteworthy artist of this school, but no *shoheki-ga* by him have been found.

THE KANO SCHOOL   An important influence during the Momoyama period was the Kano school of the *kanga* tradition. It produced the largest number of distinguished and talented artists of that period. In the late Muromachi period, Kano Motonobu laid the foundations for the prosperity of the Kano school, and his grandson, the master artist Kano Eitoku (1543–90), consolidated a powerful coterie around himself. As the Kano school became officially recognized by the ruling power, it developed into an influential force. Eitoku was commissioned to paint for both Oda Nobunaga and Toyotomi Hideyoshi, executing *shoheki-ga* in Azuchi Castle, Osaka Castle, and Juraku-dai. No other artist matched him in fame.

There were many able artists in the Kano school surrounding Eitoku, however, including his father, Shoei (1519–92), the third son of Kano Motonobu. He outlived his son and also painted important *shoheki-ga*. Eitoku's younger brothers Soshu (1551–1601) and Kyuhaku (1577–1654) were also influential artists who represented the Kano school after Eitoku's death. Although it is assumed that they had distinguished careers, none of their works remain except one painting attributed to Soshu. Eitoku had two noteworthy sons, Mitsunobu (d. 1608) and Takanobu (d. 1618). Both had active painting careers after their father's death. Mitsunobu painted for the Toyotomi clan and Takanobu worked as an artist for the imperial court. Not much attention was paid to Mitsunobu's work until fairly recently, but now he is recognized as a *shoheki-ga* artist of marked individuality who merits attention. Mitsunobu's son Sadanobu (1597–1623) died young, but interest in his work has increased in recent years. Takanobu had three sons: Morinobu, also known as Tan'yu (1602–74), who was an active and representative artist of the early Edo period; Naonobu (1607–50); and Yasunobu (1613–85). Mitsunobu's pupils Kano Koi (d. 1636) and Watanabe Ryokei (d. 1645) also belonged to the Kano school. They began to paint actively in the latter part of the Momoyama period and became influential artists in the early Edo period. *Shoheki-ga* by both survive.

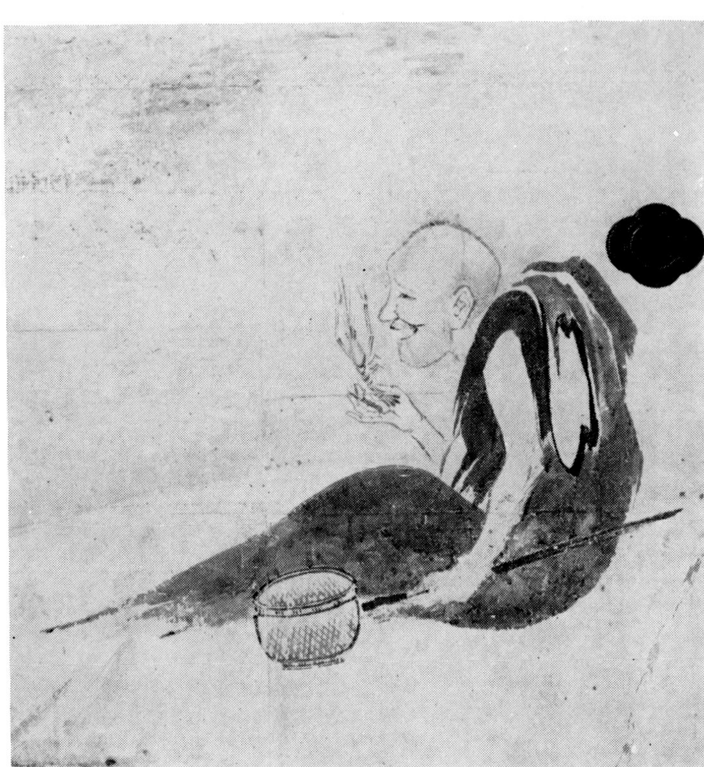

71. *Hasegawa Tohaku: detail from* Hsien Tzu and Chu T'ou *showing Hsien Tzu.* Fusuma, *ink on paper; 179.5 × 93.5 cm. 1601. Reception hall, Shinju-an, Daitoku-ji, Kyoto.*

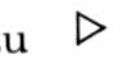

72. *Hasegawa Tohaku: detail from* Hsien Tzu and Chu T'ou *showing Chu T'ou.*

Eitoku's pupil Kano Sanraku (1559–1635) was a Kano-school artist of the Momoyama period who was as renowned as Eitoku. Sanraku's outstanding skill was recognized even during Eitoku's lifetime, and after his teacher's death he won fame as the best artist of the Kano school. His career was brilliant. Naturally he painted many *shoheki-ga,* and superb works of his survive. Like Mitsunobu, Sanraku's successor, Sansetsu (1589–1651), was not considered of much note until recently, but his works have a special quality of their own, and he is now recognized as one of the important *shoheki-ga* artists of the early Edo period.

OTHER SCHOOLS All the above-mentioned artists belonged to the Kano school, but there were other schools within the *kanga* tradition that also produced influential art-ists. One was the Kaiho school. This school was founded by Kaiho Yusho (1533–1615), who had studied under Kano Motonobu. Yusho left many important works, including *shoheki-ga.* He was an artist with a strong, intense style appropriate to a man born into a prestigious warrior family. Yusho's son Yusetsu (1598–1677) was active in the early Edo period. He probably painted many *shoheki-ga,* but few remain today.

The Unkoku school also belonged to the *kanga* tradition. This school was started by Unkoku Togan (1547–1618), who asserted that it was the legitimate successor of Sesshu (1420–1506), one of Japan's best-known artists. Togan served the important Mori clan. Like Yusho, he was originally from the warrior class. Togan's style of paint-ing had a warriorlike intensity, showing the most conservative tendencies among the leading artists

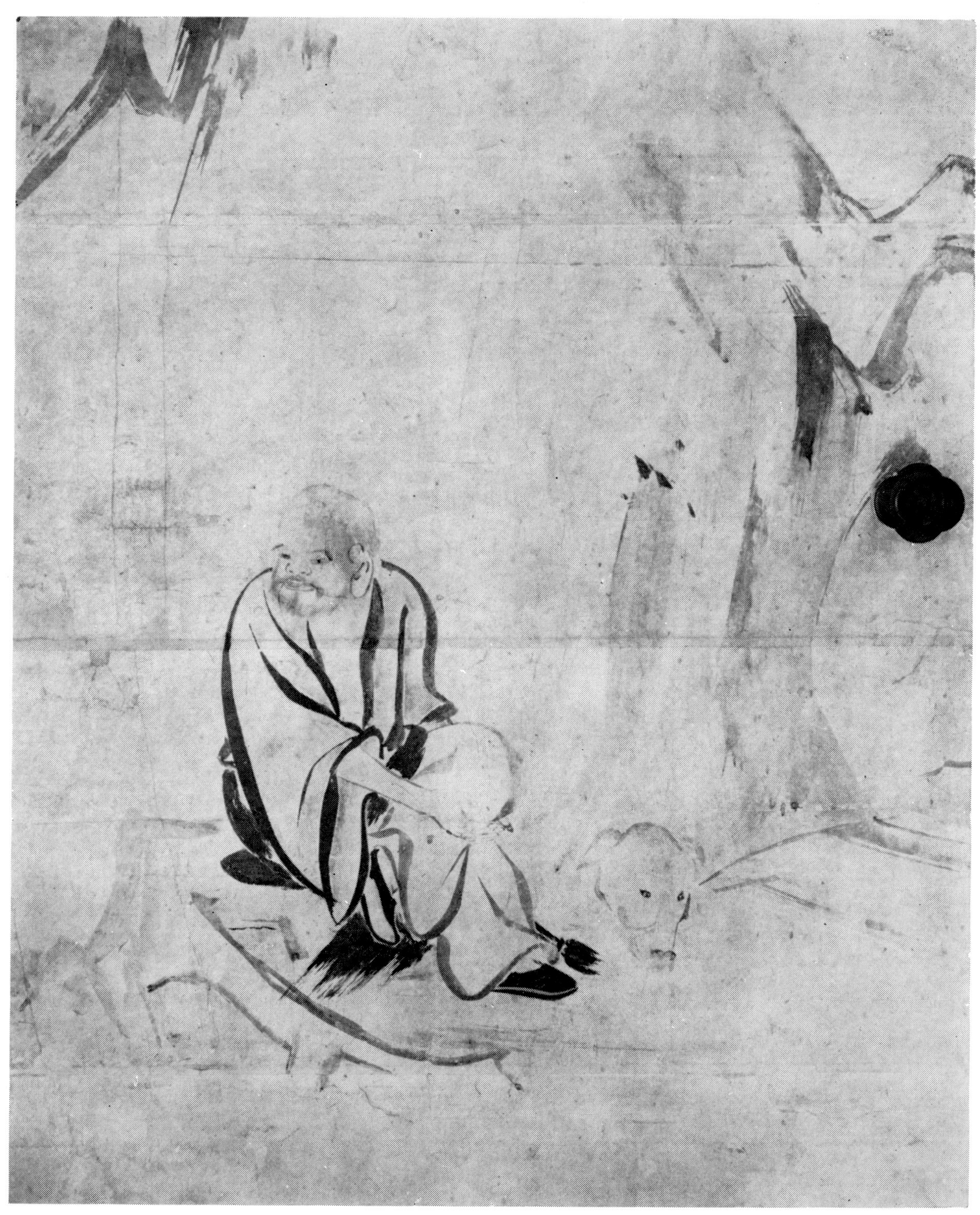

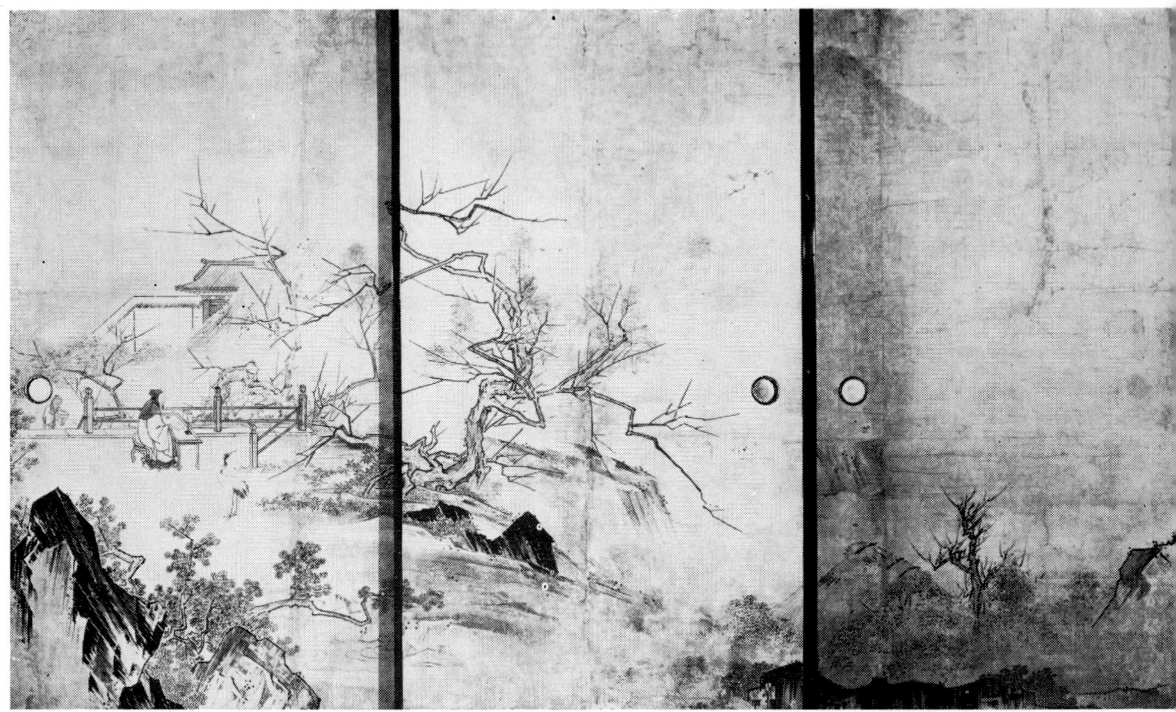

73. *Hasegawa Tohaku:* Four Beloved Flowers. Fusuma, *ink and light colors on paper; two left-hand* fusuma *169 ×
95 cm., four right-hand* fusuma *169 × 93 cm. Early seventeenth century. Uraku-en, Inuyama, Aichi Prefecture. (See also
Figures 74–76.)*

of the Momoyama period. Some *shoheki-ga* painted
in Togan's characteristic style survive. Togan's
second son, Toeki (1591–1644), succeeded Togan
as the head of the family, becoming the most famous artist of the Unkoku school. He too painted
shoheki-ga, but his achievements belong to the early
Edo period. Although there was a rather large
number of artists in this school, their style became
strongly stereotyped. Togan and Toeki are the only
shoheki-ga artists of the school who are considered
worthy of note.

The Hasegawa school of the *kanga* tradition has
left surprisingly fine *shoheki-ga* from the Momoyama
period. The achievements of its founder, Hasegawa
Tohaku (1539–1610), were especially brilliant. He
studied under Toshun, a pupil of Sesshu. Because
of his connection with Toshun, Tohaku professed
to be of the Sesshu school, like Togan. He pro-

pelled himself into the Momoyama painters' circle
as the leader of the Hasegawa school. His contributions in the area of *shoheki-ga* remained unnoticed
for a long time, not coming to light until the Showa
era (1926–present). His brilliant achievements in
this area are now recognized, however. All Tohaku's children—Kyuzo, who died young (1568–
93); Sotaku, who died in 1611; Sakon; and Soya
(1590–1667)—became artists, but only Kyuzo and
Sotaku can be considered to belong to the Momoyama period. In the field of *shoheki-ga,* Kyuzo
should not be overlooked. Tohaku appears to have
had many followers in addition to his sons, though
their names are not widely known. There are a
number of extant *shoheki-ga* recognized as works
of the Hasegawa school.

Another master-artist in the *kanga* style, Soga
Chokuan, was based in Sakai, near Osaka, as was

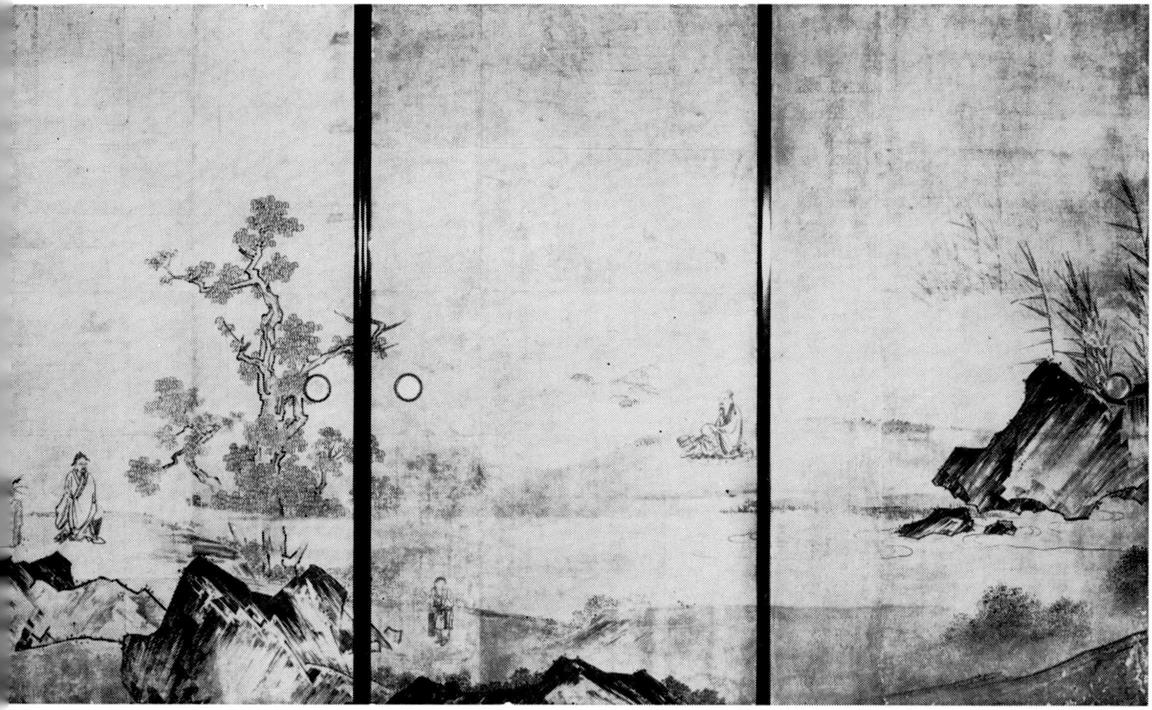

Tosa Mitsuyoshi. Chokuan belonged to the Soga school, which had existed since the Muromachi period. We have many magnificent screen paintings by him. Unfortunately, none of his *shoheki-ga* survive, though as one of the master artists of the Momoyama period, he must have painted *shoheki-ga*. Excellent *shoheki-ga* by his successor, Nichokuan, are extant.

THE PROBLEM OF IDENTIFYING SHOHEKI-GA ARTISTS

Castles provided the major environment for Momoyama *shoheki-ga*. Regrettably, however, most of these *shoheki-ga* have been lost. The only ones remaining are those from Nagoya Castle (Nagoya Castle itself was burned in bombing during World War II), which were painted at the end of the Momoyama period. Fortunately, temples

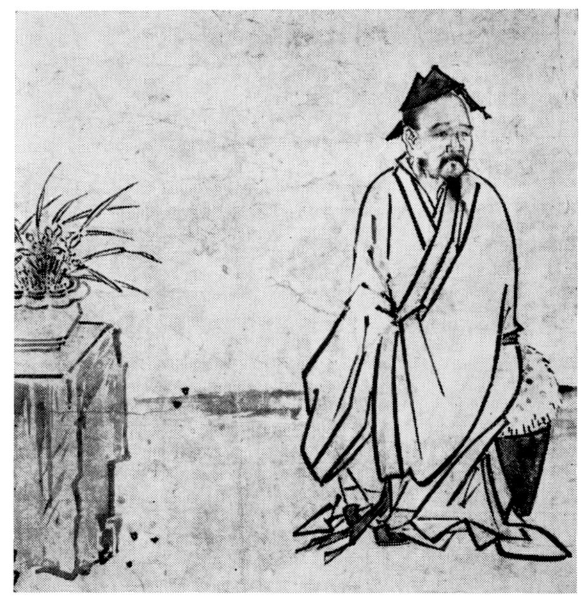

74. *Hasegawa Tohaku: detail from* Four Beloved Flowers *showing Huang Shan-ku and orchids.*

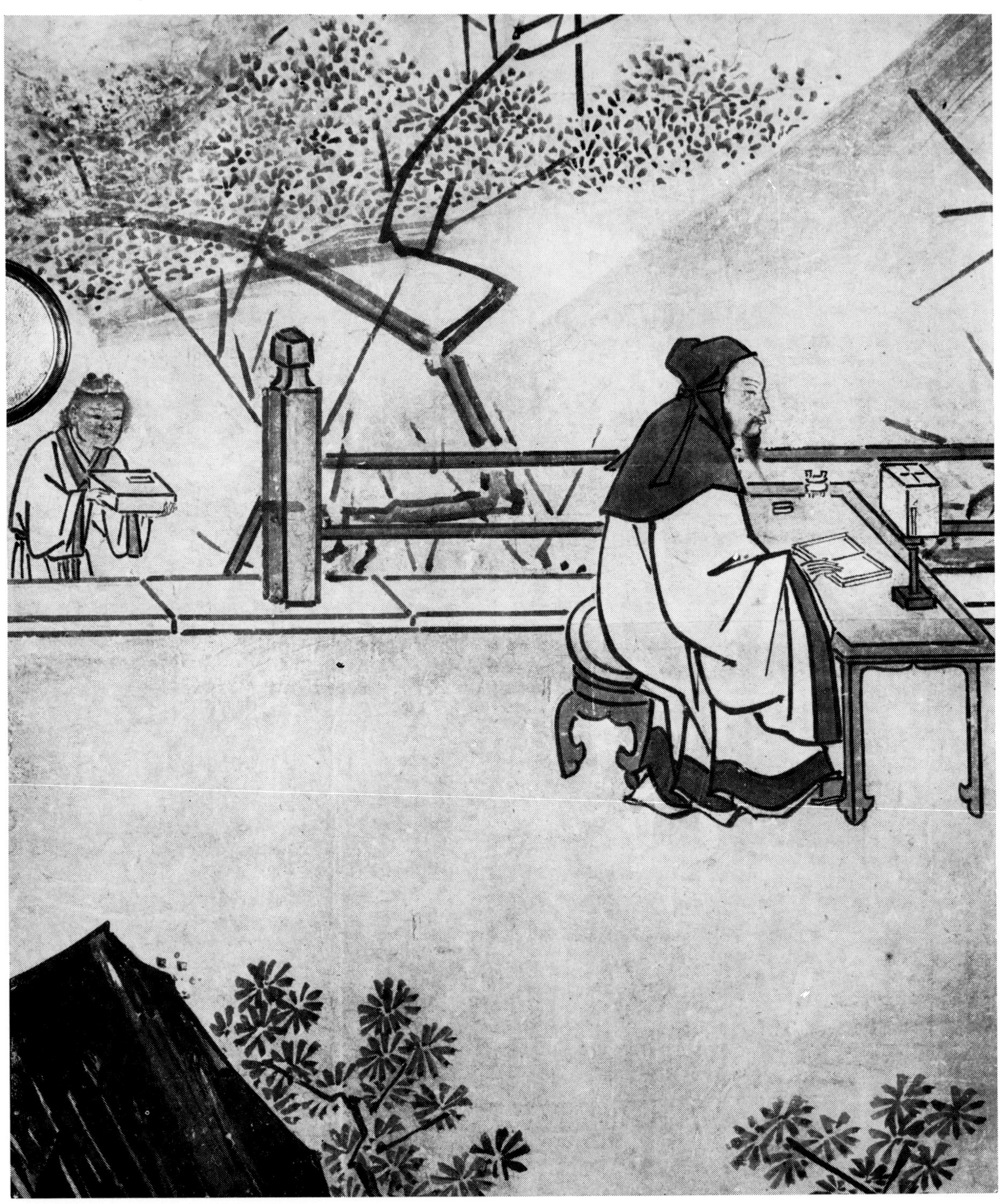

75. *Hasegawa Tohaku: detail from* Four Beloved Flowers *showing Lin Ho-ching and plum blossoms.*

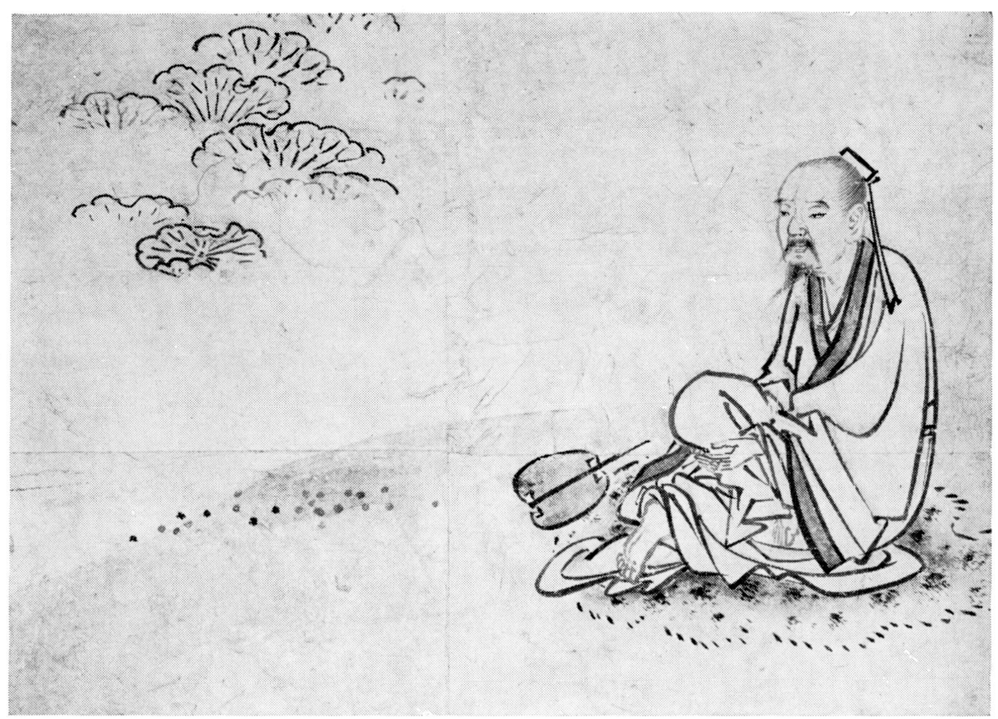

76. Hasegawa Tohaku: detail from Four Beloved Flowers *showing Chou Mao-shu and lotus.*

contain a considerable number of *shoheki-ga* of that period; they are usually found in the *hojo* (the main hall), the reception halls, and the *shoin*. Some also remain in the possession of Shinto shrines. These works are not of exactly the same type as the *shoheki-ga* painted in castles, but it is not difficult to see in them characteristics of the castle *shoheki-ga* of the Momoyama period.

All considered, surviving Momoyama *shoheki-ga* are most abundant in the Buddhist temples in and around Kyoto. Anyone who has visited temples in this area must have noticed the many *shoheki-ga* vividly conveying the vigor and strength of the people of Momoyama times. Most of these works are attributed to specific artists. Guides and the printed leaflets given to visitors explain that this one was painted by Kano Eitoku and that one by Kano Sanraku. Yet careful examination reveals

no artist's signature or seal, nor any inscription or seal of authentication, on these *shoheki-ga*. This in itself is not surprising; it was not customary for an artist to sign or put his seal on wall or *fusuma* paintings. This tradition continued at least as late as the Momoyama period. Artists began occasionally to sign their names on *shoheki-ga* early in the Edo period. Tan'yu's seal and signature on *shoheki-ga*, alongside notations and seals of authentication, are not rare. Even in the early Edo period, however, the tradition of leaving one's work unsigned remained deeply entrenched.

Nevertheless, most *shoheki-ga* of the Momoyama period are attributed to specific artists. Anyone comparing the many *shoheki-ga* that are said to be by Sanraku (these are especially numerous in the temples in and around Kyoto) will be struck by the varied painting styles. If all these paintings

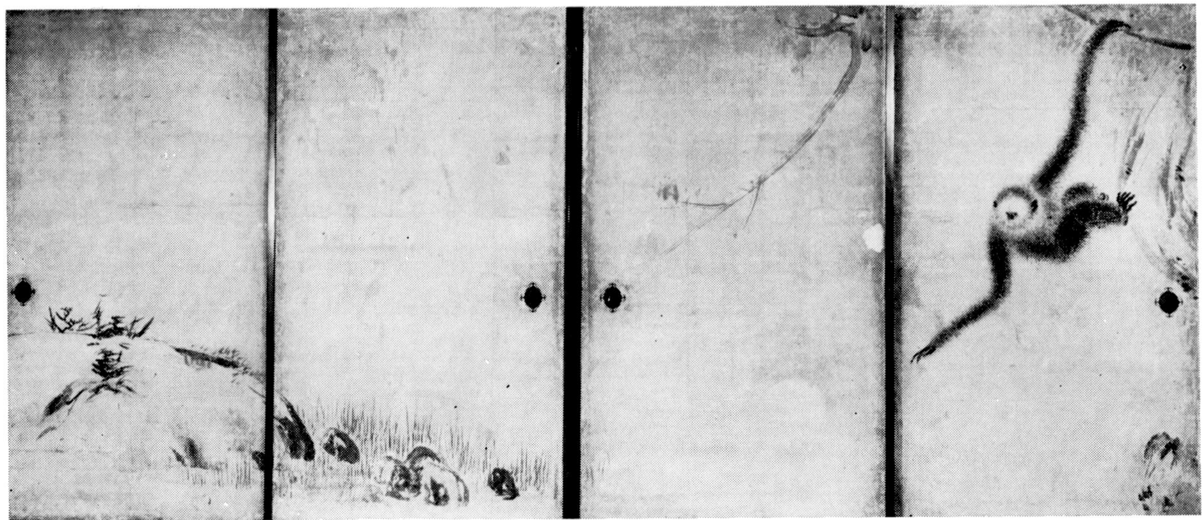

77. *Hasegawa Tohaku:* Monkey Trying to Catch the Reflection of the Moon. Fusuma, *ink on paper; 171 × 89 cm. Late sixteenth century.* Shoin, *Konchi-in, Nanzen-ji, Kyoto.*

were the work of Sanraku, as the temples claim, he was an artist with a remarkably wide variety of styles who painted an incredible amount. Obviously this could not have been the case. Even if some of the works attributed to Sanraku are actually his, a large number must have been done by other painters.

Examination of each of the *shoheki-ga* attributed to Sanraku for positive and dependable documentation to support the attribution shows that most have no documented proof. It was only by word of mouth that a painting came to be attributed to Sanraku. While it cannot be said that none of the works attributed to Sanraku were actually done by him, other methods of verification must be used in order to distinguish between those that are definitely his and those that are not.

AUTHENTICATION BASED ON STYLE AND TECHNIQUE

One method of authentication is based on examination of style and technique. For a painting attributed to Sanraku to be considered actually his, examination must show techniques known to be charac-

teristic of Sanraku. Needless to say, to make this kind of determination, Sanraku's style and technique must be clearly known. It is impossible to make a judgment without certain definite criteria. The characteristics of Sanraku to be considered in making an authentication are learned from works other than *shoheki-ga* having his signature or seal or bearing inscriptions and seals declaring the works to be by Sanraku. These paintings can be screens, hanging scrolls, or anything else. The method of selecting the standard works to be used as criteria poses problems of its own, of course, and is no simple task. Such works are selected only after a careful examination of all their aspects. Naturally, if wrong selections have been made, any evaluation of Sanraku's style and technique based on them will be in error.

Continuing with Sanraku as an example, some of the ways to determine the painter of a *shoheki-ga* without the artist's signature will be discussed here. To learn the true artist of an unsigned *shoheki-ga* of the Momoyama period, it is necessary to find as many reliable and important leads as possible by searching the documents and literature related to

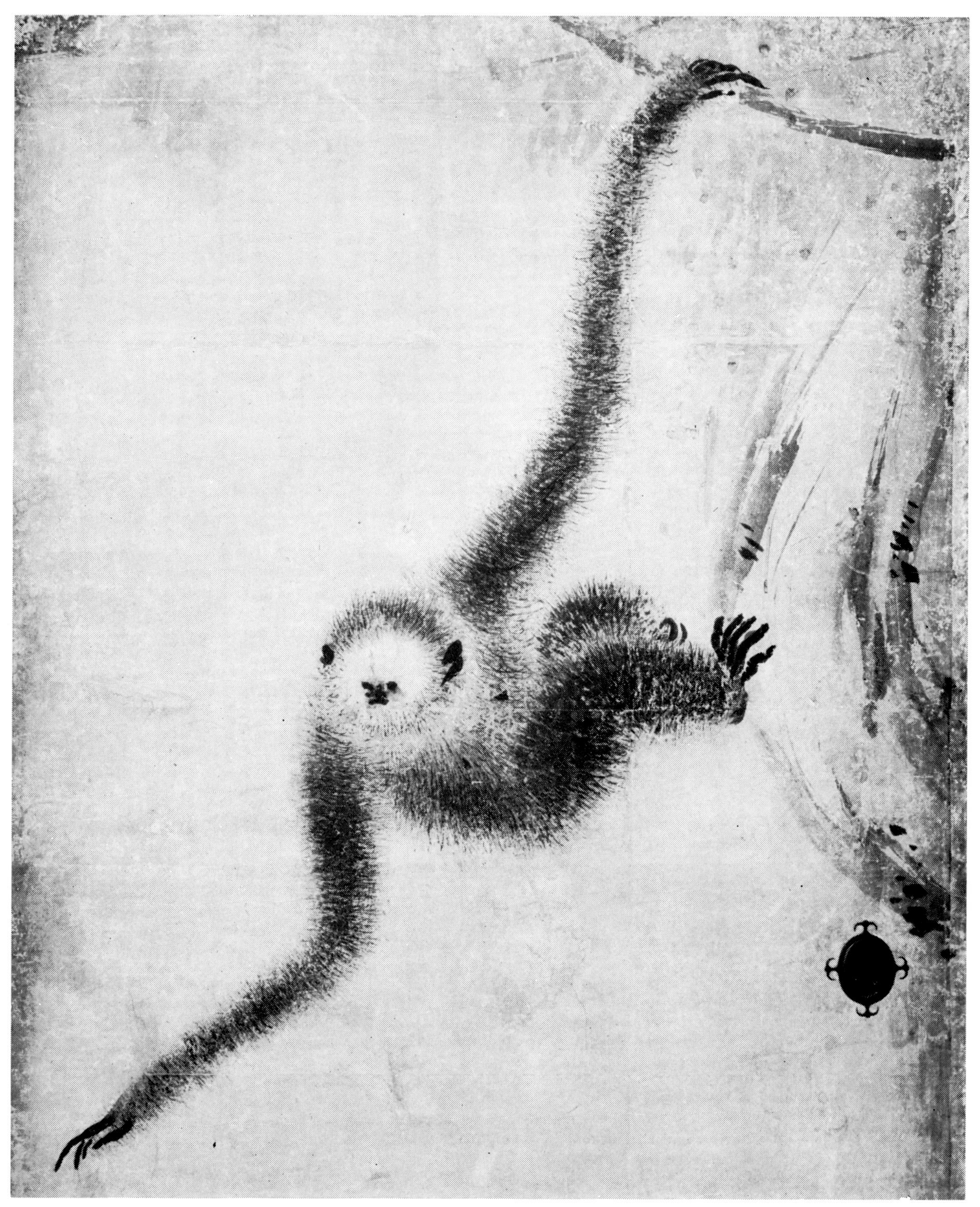

78. *Hasegawa Tohaku: detail from* Monkey Trying to Catch the Reflection of the Moon.

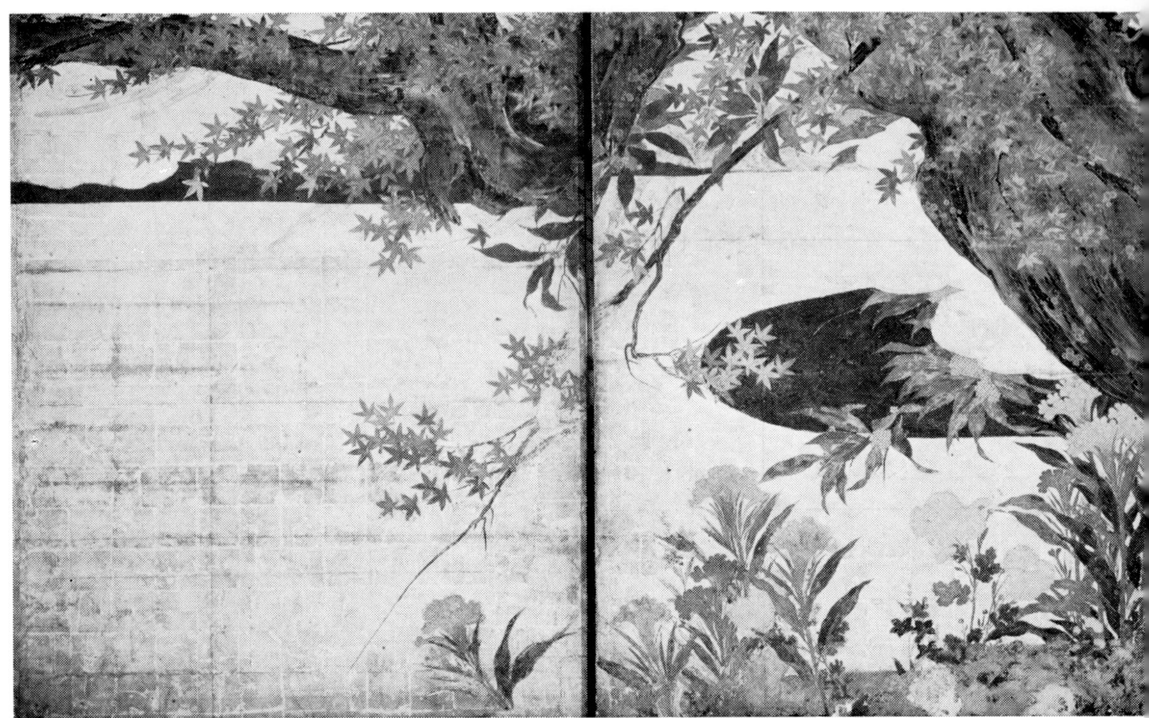

the work, at the same time carefully and diligently studying the characteristics of the work in question, including the painting style and the technique. The artist is finally determined after the characteristics of the painting have been verified against those that are known from the standard works selected as criteria. Obviously it is necessary to have a correct perception of the artist's style and technique, based on reliable paintings selected as criteria and compared not only with those of his famous contemporaries but with those of as many artists of the period as possible. Any discussion of a *shoheki-ga* artist should be based on an evaluation of standard works other than *shoheki-ga*.

OBSERVATION OF DETAILS The study of *shoheki-ga* is not a new area of research. In the Taisho era (1912–26) the art of Eitoku and Sanraku was already being discussed on the basis of their *shoheki-ga*. However, the problems of attribution of *shoheki-ga* were not fully recognized at that time, and scholars tended to swallow the vague stories handed down by the temples. It was not until the following Showa era that critical eyes were cast on apocryphal stories concerning Momoyama *shoheki-ga* and the need for definitive research on the works themselves was recognized.

It goes without saying that in attempting to make an attribution it is important to note the composition of the picture as a whole. The organization of the total composition must show the characteristics of the artist in question. Since the whole is a synthesis of the parts, however, careful attention must also be paid to each detail, such as trees, flowers, rocks, hills and mountains, birds, figures, and buildings. Of course, the characteristics of the lines and brushwork used in drawing

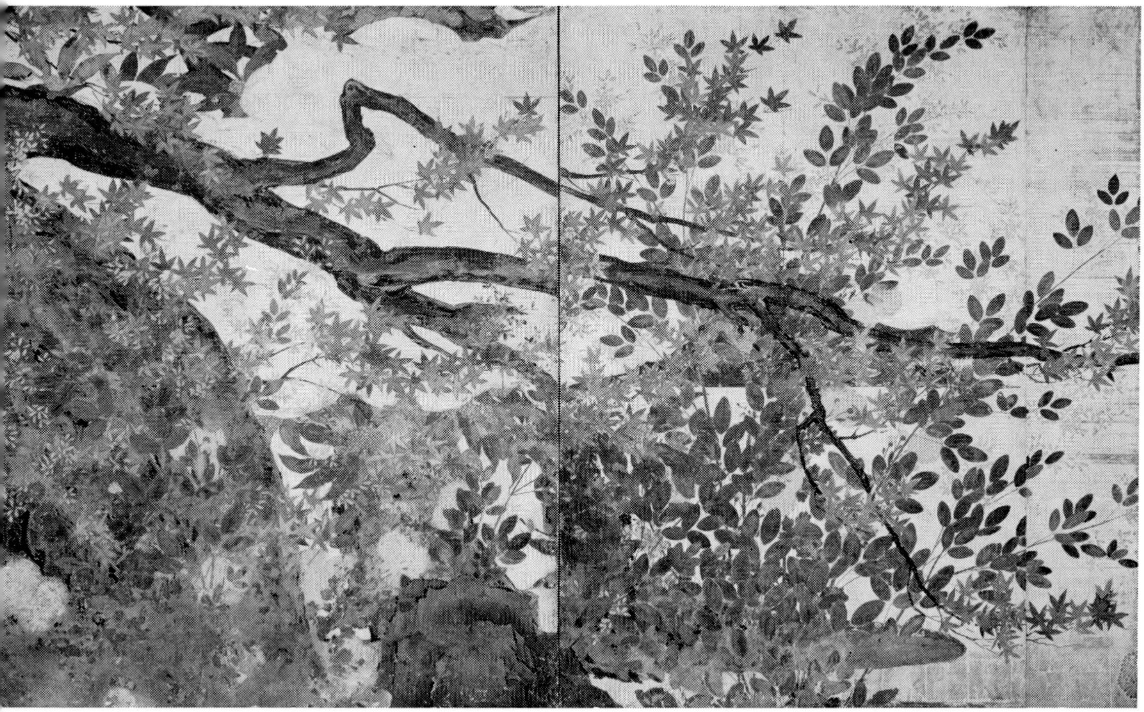

79. *Hasegawa Tohaku:* Maple Tree. *Colors and gold on paper mounted on a wall; 172.5 × 138.5 cm. 1592.* Chishaku-in, Kyoto. (See also Figure 6.)

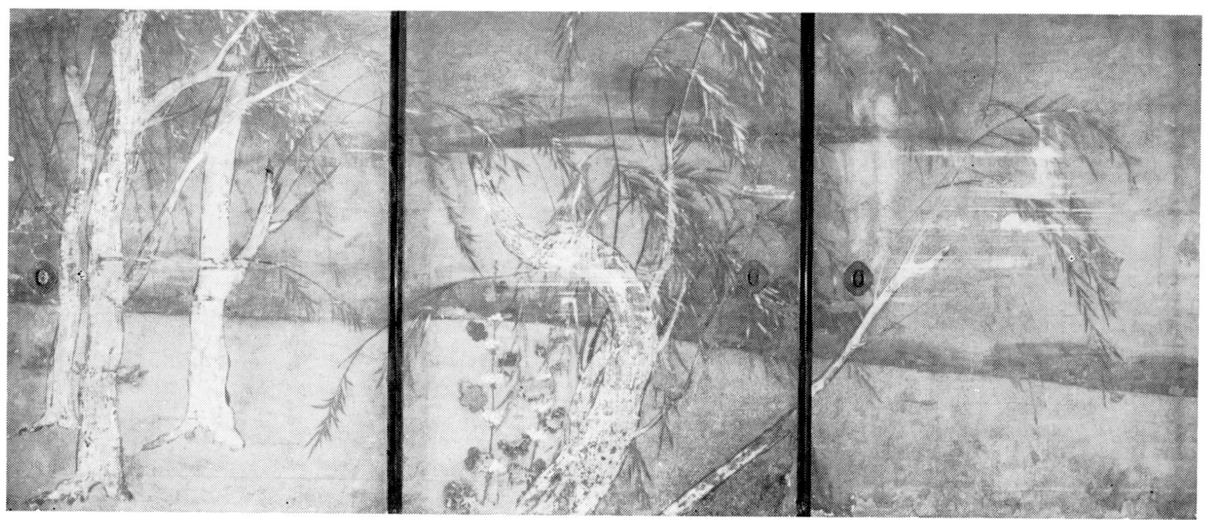

80. *Attributed to Hasegawa Tohaku:* Willow. Fusuma, *colors on paper; 184 × 142.5 cm. Late sixteenth century.* Shoin, Myoren-ji, Kyoto.

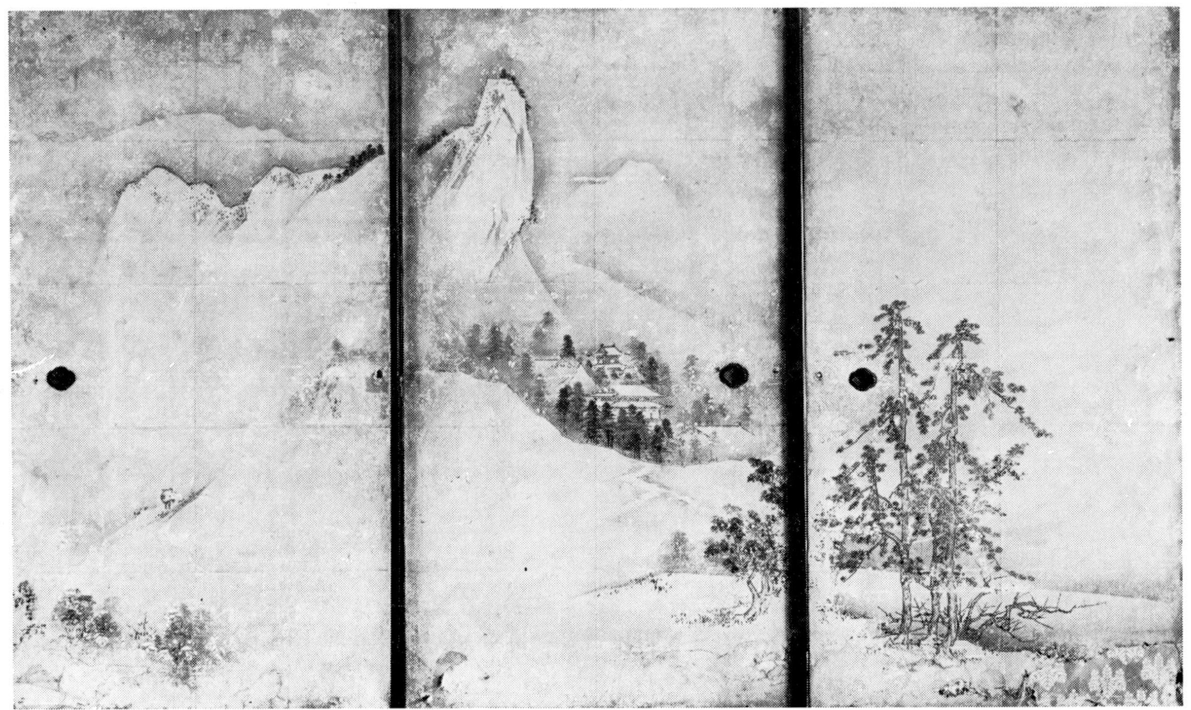

81. *Hasegawa Tohaku:* Landscape. Fusuma, *ink on paper; 177.5 × 94 cm. 1589.* Hojo, *Entoku-in, Kyoto.*

and the use of ink should not be neglected. An important clue in identifying the artists of Momoyama *shoheki-ga* is found in the method used to draw rocks. Among the many objects painted, rocks most clearly exhibit the school an artist belonged to, for rocks are the part of the painting where the individual artist most directly expressed himself. Attentive observation of the way rocks are arranged, the shape and form of each rock, the characteristics of the outlines, the method used to show creases in the rocks, and the brushwork used in shaping these creases frequently gives clues not only to the style and school of the artist but also to the artist himself. For example, as shown in the foldout opposite page 136, Eitoku, Sanraku, and

Mitsunobu of the Kano school and Kaiho Yusho, Hasegawa Tohaku, and Unkoku Togan all had their own characteristic ways of painting rocks.

COLLABORATION AND THE MAIN ARTIST

The importance of observing details as well as the total composition when studying *shoheki-ga* has already been emphasized. Some hold, however, that *shoheki-ga* do not show the individual style of any one artist because they were often the result of collaboration. *Shoheki-ga,* with their huge painting surfaces, especially the elaborately colored works, were not executed single-handedly by the artist who was commissioned to paint them but are

82. *Kano Mitsunobu:* Pine Trees by the Shore. *Colors and gold on paper. Early seventeenth century. Interior of* reioku, ▷ *Kodai-ji, Kyoto.*

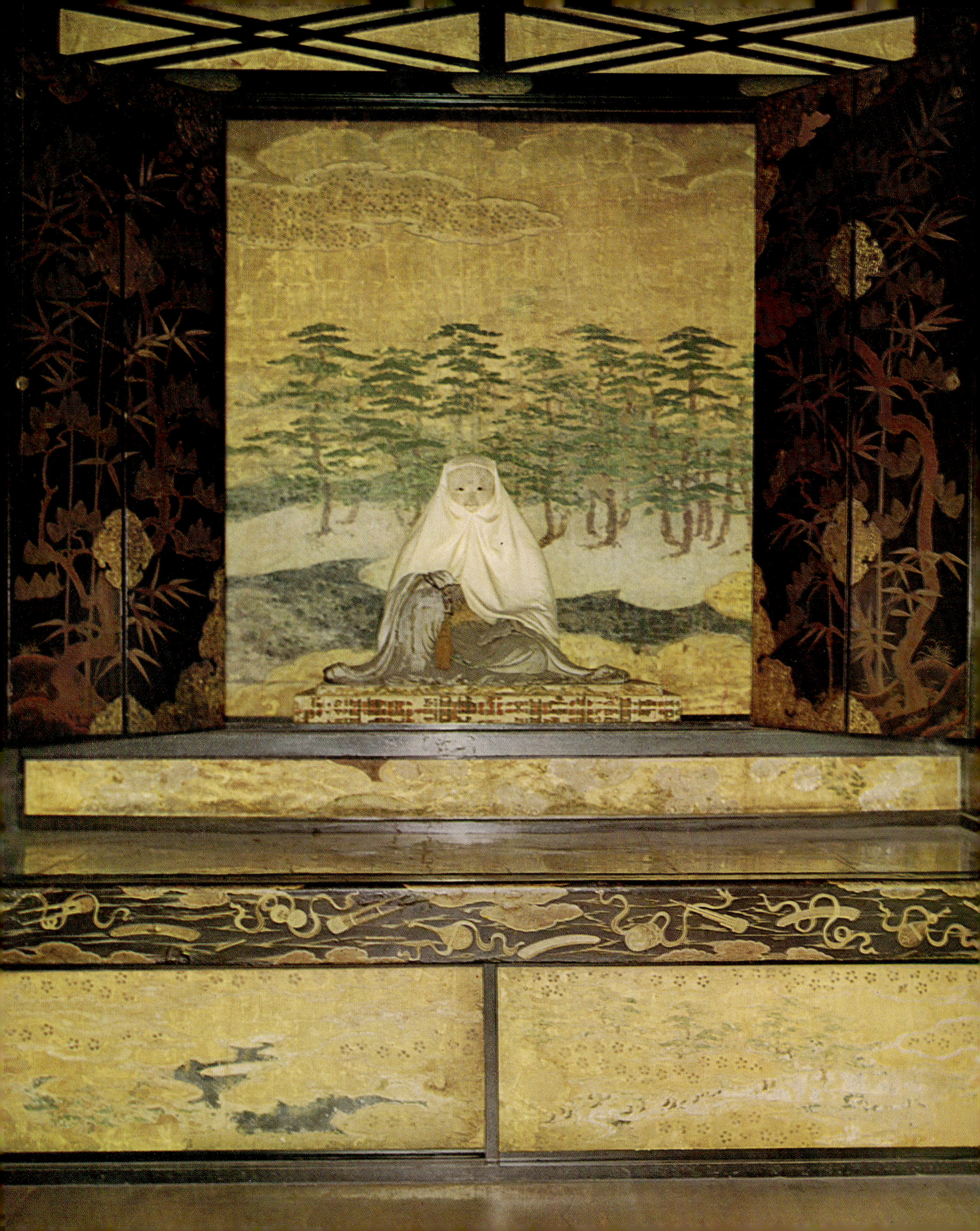

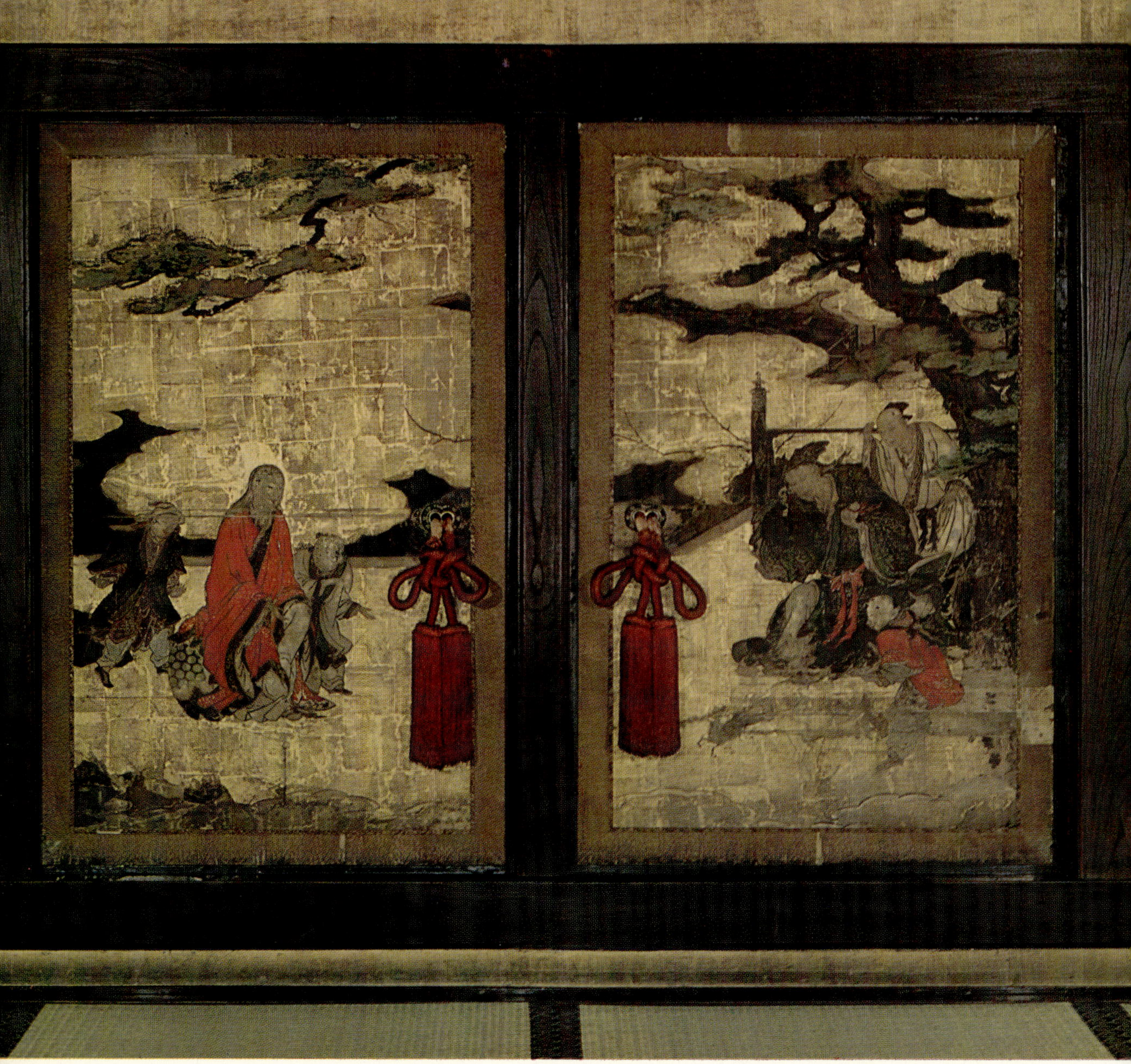

83. *Kano Mitsunobu:* Hermits and Noble Characters. *Colors and gold on paper mounted on* chodai; *121 × 72 cm. Early seventeenth century.* Daishoin, *Myoho-in, Kyoto.*

84. *Kano Mitsunobu:* Flowers *(autumn flowers and pine)*. Fusuma, *colors and gold on paper;* ▷
170.5 × 116 cm. Early seventeenth century. Honden, *Tsukubusuma Shrine, Shiga Prefecture.*

85 *(overleaf). Kano Mitsunobu:* Black Pines and Aronias. ▷
Fusuma, *colors and gold on paper; 167 × 134 cm. Early seventeenth century.* Hojo, *Honen-in, Kyoto.*

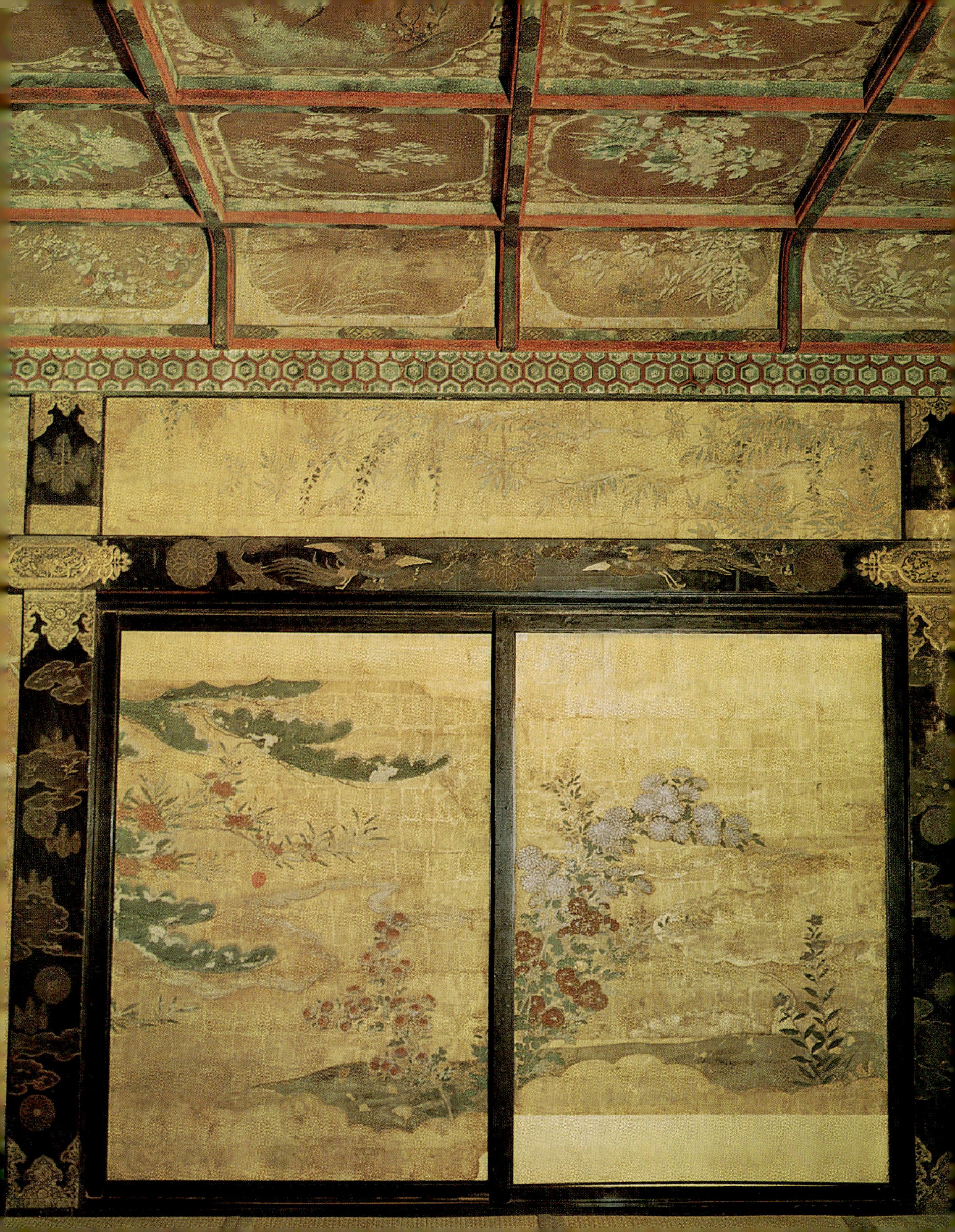

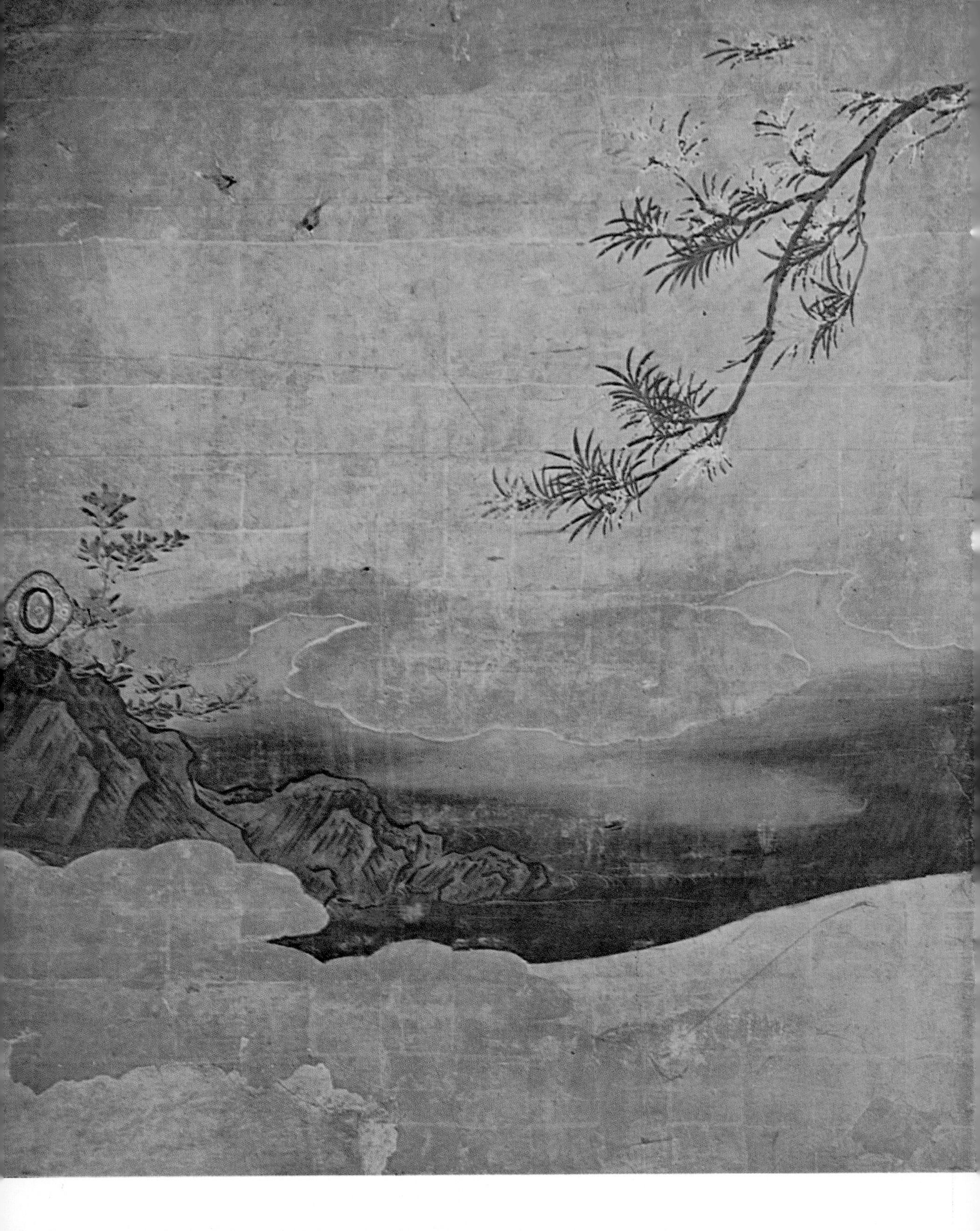

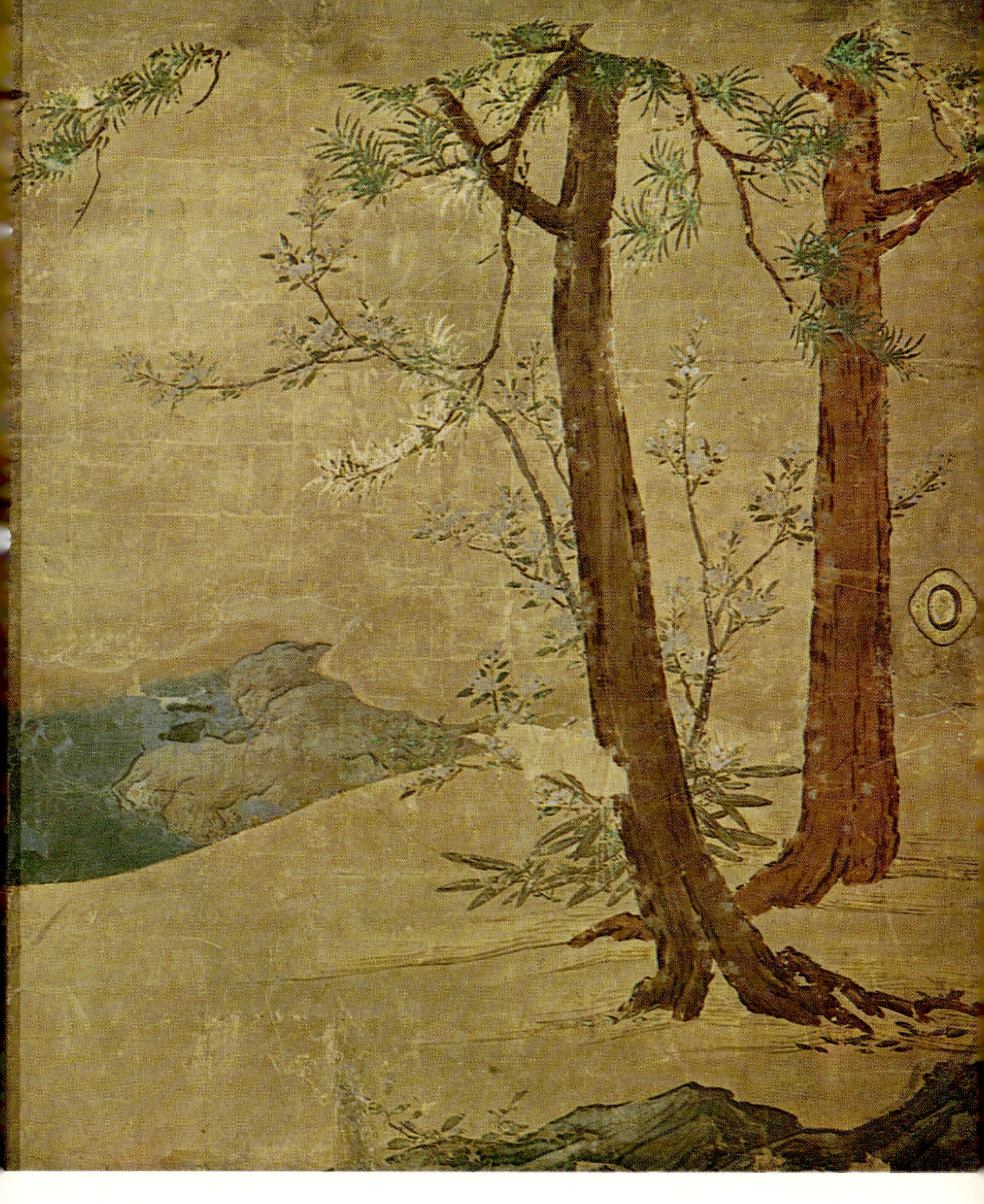

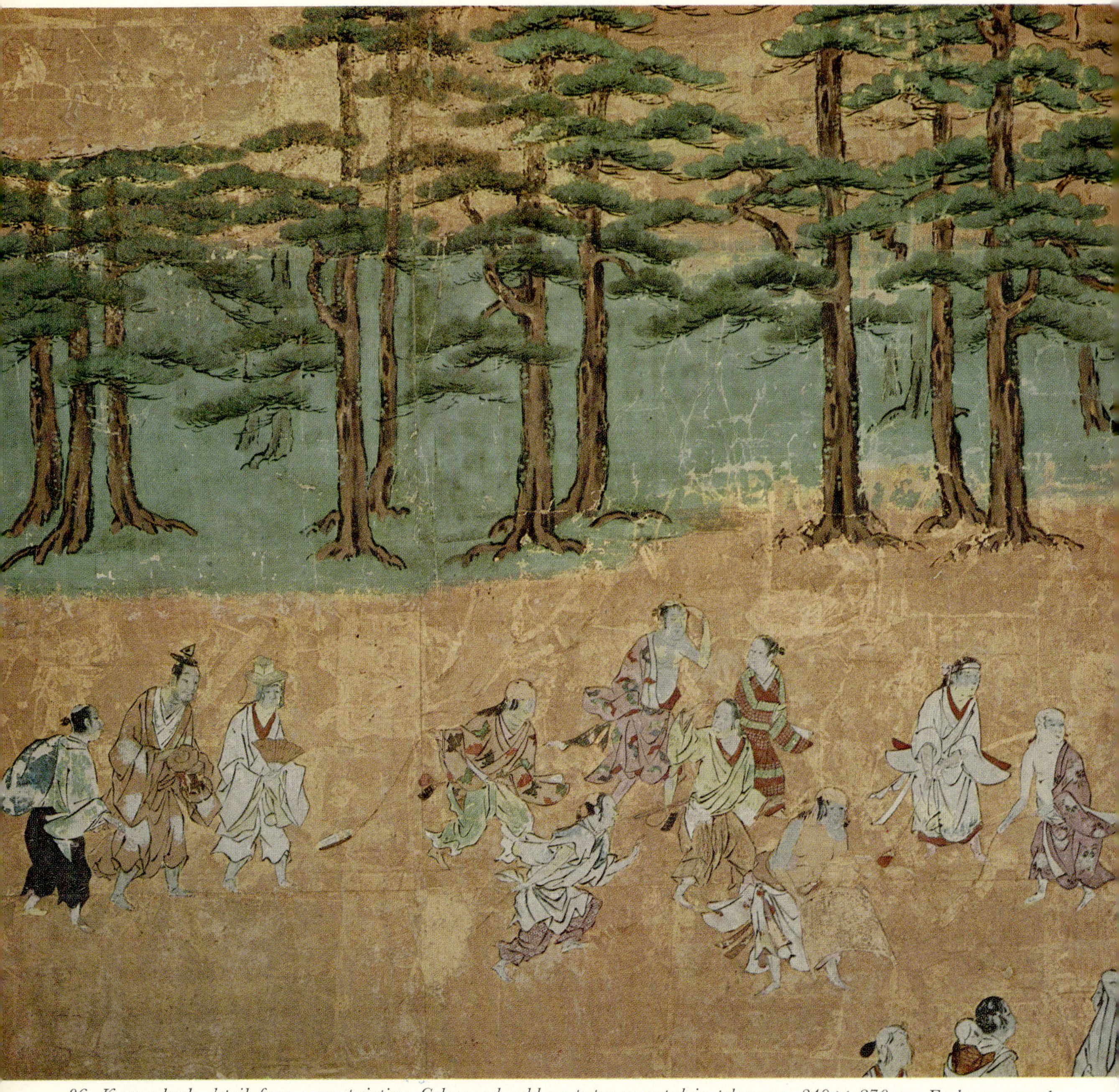

86. *Kano school: detail from genre painting. Colors and gold on paper mounted in tokonoma; 249 × 378 cm. Early seventeenth century. Kyoto National Museum. (See also Figures 26, 27.)*

87. *Kano Takanobu:* Kenjo Shoji *(left, Teng Yu; right, Kuan Chung). Hanging scroll, colors on silk; 207.5 × 113.5 cm. 1612. Ninna-ji, Kyoto.* ▷

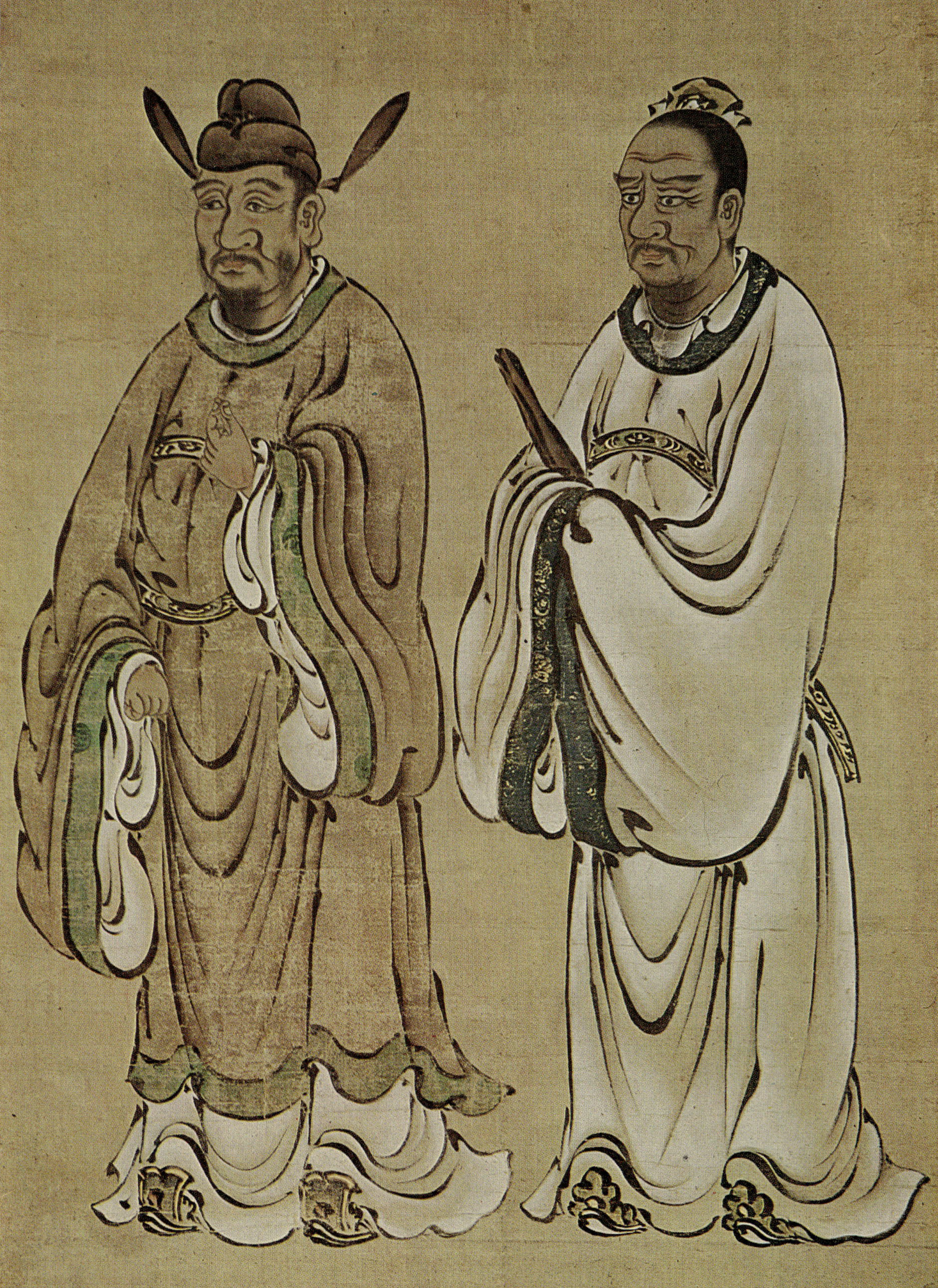

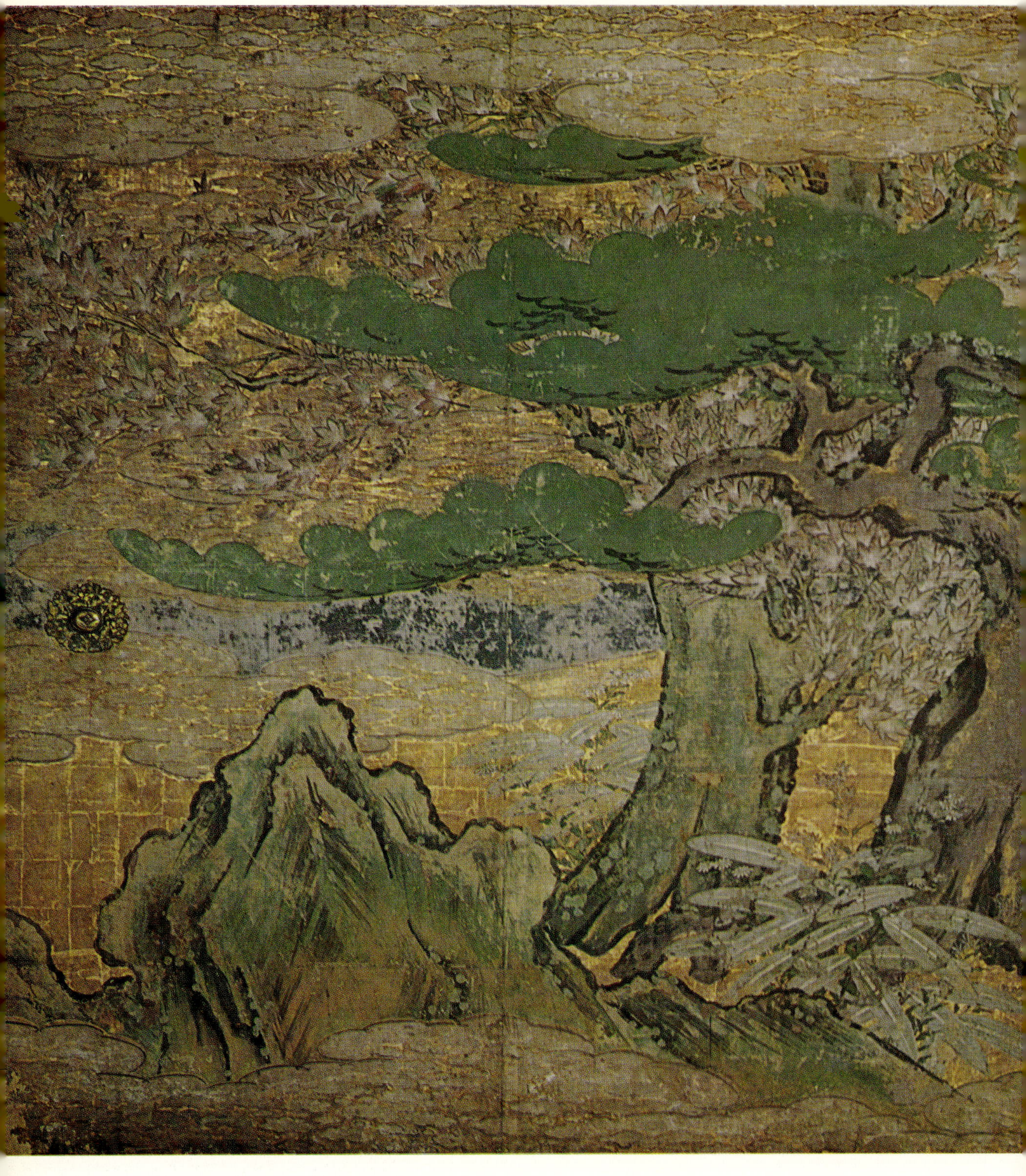

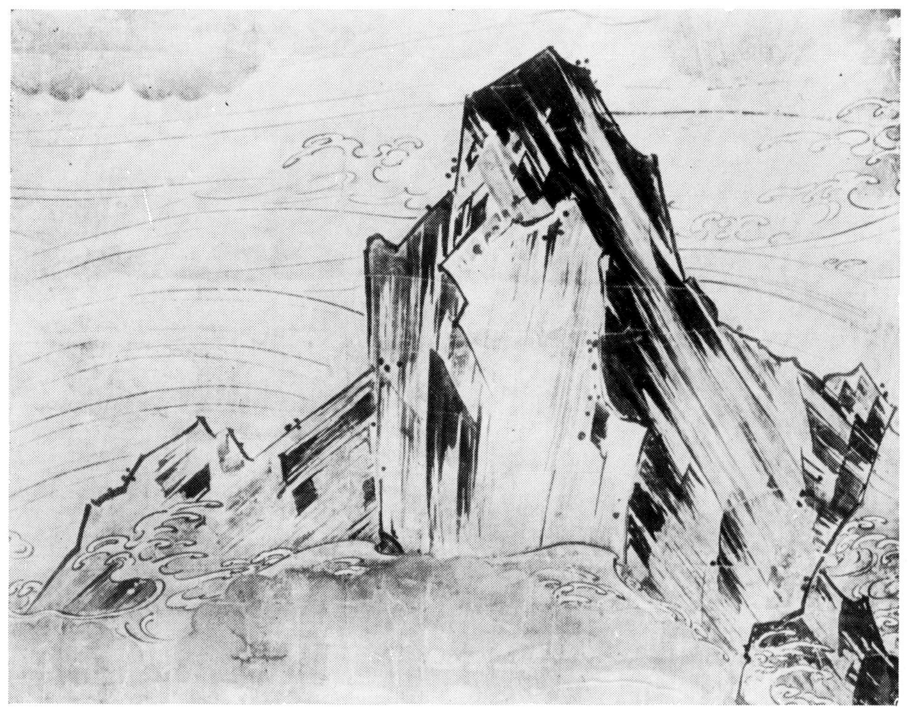

89. *Hasegawa Tohaku: detail from* Rocks and Waves. *Hanging scroll, ink and light colors on paper; 180 × 138.5 cm. Early seventeenth century. Zenrin-ji, Kyoto.*

known to have been painted with the cooperation of several assistants. Naturally, some conclude that it is impossible to learn the artist of a given *shoheki-ga* by studying its style because of the collaborative nature of the work.

However, what must be considered are the method and the meaning of this collaboration. It is believed that when an artist was commissioned to paint a *shoheki-ga* on a large surface, he often used several other artists as his assistants. This is clear from the designations of colors, "white," "vermil-ion," and so on, written in ink and visible on existing *shoheki-ga* where the colors have chipped or peeled off. Following the directions of the main artist, the assistants applied the coloring. In a sense, then, a *shoheki-ga* is a collaborative work. However, what should be noted here is that the assistants who applied colors were assistants in all respects. They worked according to the plan of the main artist as nothing more than extensions of his arm. Some assistants prepared ink and others prepared white paint. One dissolved blue coloring and another prepared green paint. They participated in very small parts of the painting, following orders given by the main artist, who created the scheme of the total picture and executed the underdrawing. In addition, all the important parts of the final outlines drawn in ink after the completion of the coloring must have been the work of the confident brush of the principal artist.

◁ 88. *Kano school:* Flowers and Birds. Fusuma, *colors and gold on paper; 207 × 191.5 cm. 1622. Hondo, Zuigan-ji, Miyagi Prefecture.*

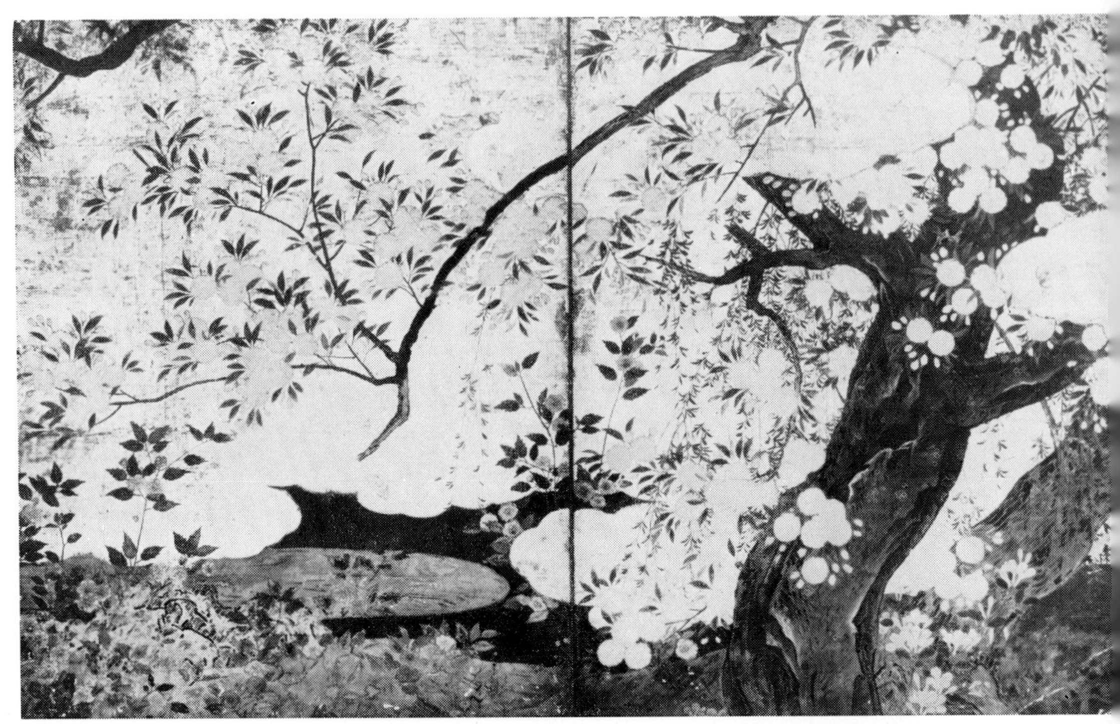

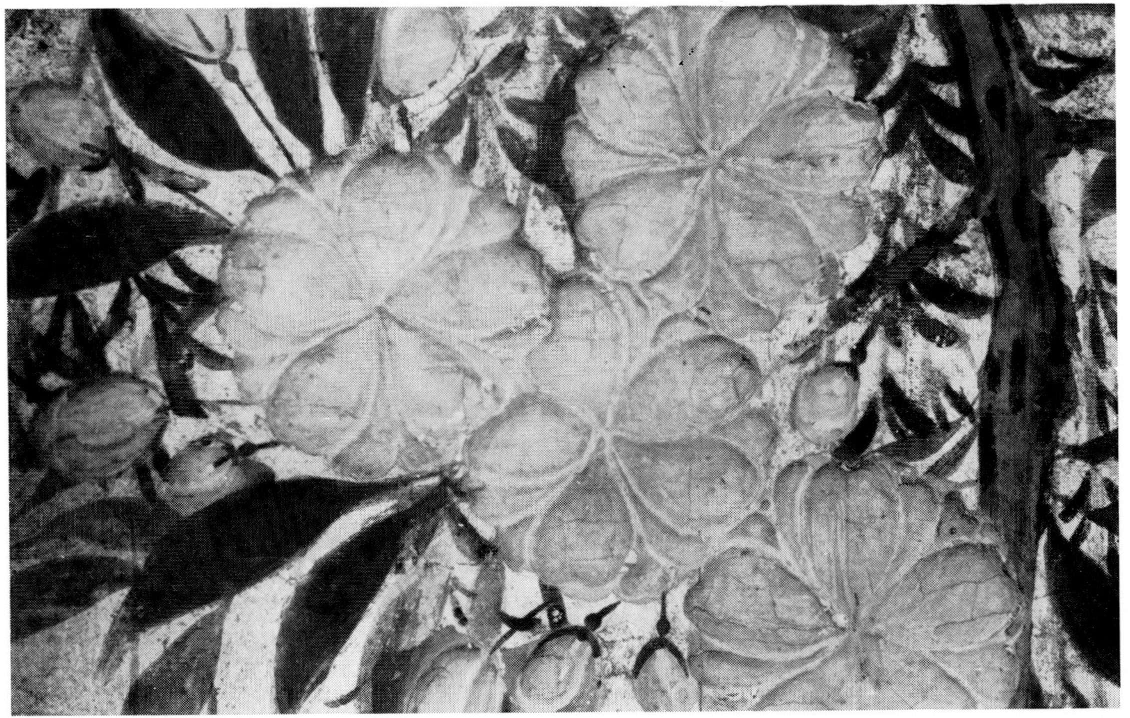

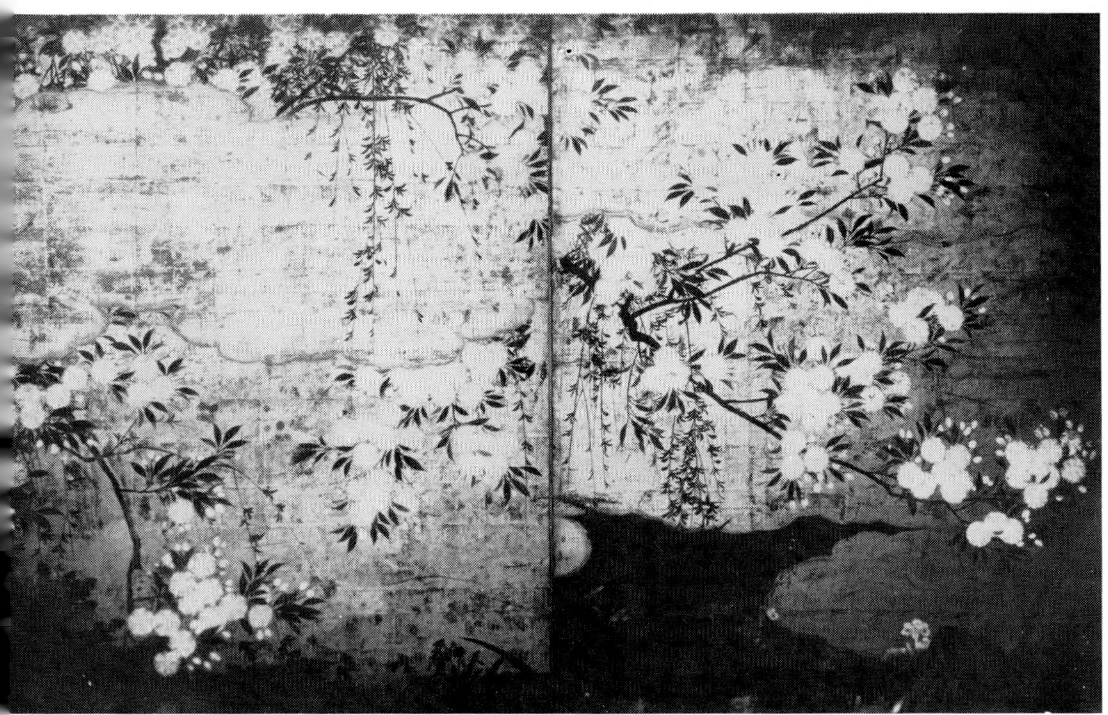

90. *Hasegawa Kyuzo:* Cherry Tree. *Colors and gold on paper mounted on a wall; 172.5 × 139.5 cm. 1592. Chishaku-in, Kyoto. (See also Figure 5.)*

◁ 91. *Hasegawa Kyuzo: detail from* Cherry Tree.

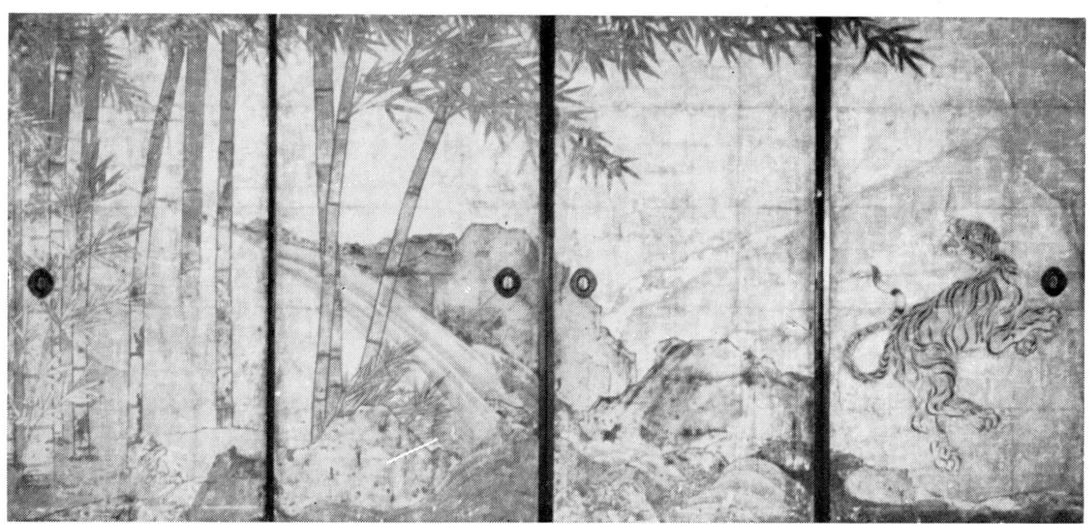

92. *Hasegawa school:* Tiger and Bamboo. Fusuma, *colors and gold on paper; 181.5 × 91 cm. Early seventeenth century. Hojo, Zenrin-ji, Kyoto.*

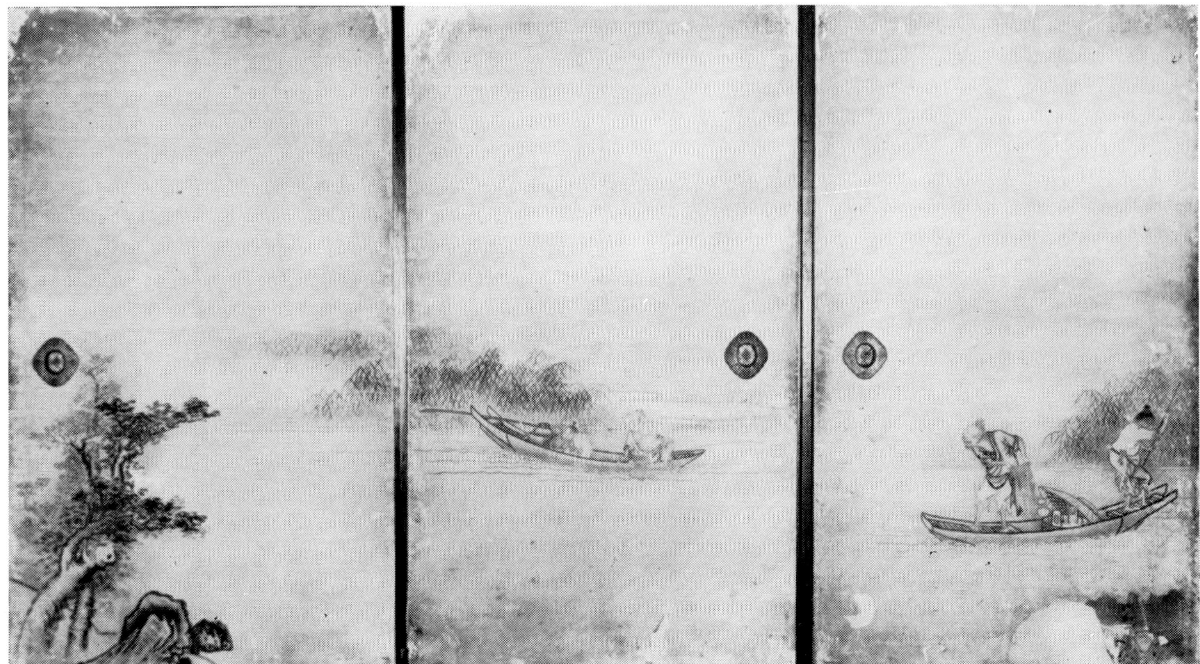

93. *Soga Nichokuan:* Fishing Boats by the Reeds. Fusuma, *ink and light colors on paper; 170 × 109 cm. Early seventeenth century. Naka-no-bo shoin, Taima-dera, Nara Prefecture.*

A work of art created in this manner must be possessed of the style of the main artist. Although the work was a joint creation, the assistants did not participate to express their own styles but only to assist the master in his creative activity. The completed work is not a synthesis of the style of each participant but a work in the style of the main artist. With this interpretation of the collaborative effort, we believe we can determine the principal artist of a *shoheki-ga* by an examination of its style.

CHAPTER FIVE

Characteristics of Momoyama Shoheki-ga

FLOWER-AND-BIRD PAINTING The gorgeous *kimpeki*-style paintings of flowers and birds are representative of Momoyama *shoheki-ga,* showing most clearly its characteristics. In fact, *kimpeki*-style *shoheki-ga* featuring flowers and birds are among the finest of all paintings of the Momoyama period and add luster to the history of Japanese art. Flowers and birds had been favored subjects of the *kanga*-style *shoheki-ga* painters from early times, but none of these early works remain. The *fusuma* paintings in the main hall of the Shinju-an and those in the Yotoku-in, painted in the mid-Muromachi period, are the oldest works that survive. They show the simple and refined style of early ink paintings but lack the sensuous beauty of those done later. Nevertheless, Kano Motonobu painted bright and decorative flowers and birds using colors, as in the *fusuma* paintings in the Daisen-in, Daitoku-ji (Fig. 110). While the influence of the richly colored flower-and-bird paintings of China's Yuan and Ming dynasties is seen in these paintings, the influence of the decorative style of *yamato-e* is also present. Compared to the *kanga* style of flower-and-bird painting before his time, Motonobu's works are unusually rich and have a typically Japanese feeling. Motonobu's grandson Eitoku furthered the Japanization of *kanga*-style flower-and-bird painting and gave birth to the fresh style seen in Momoyama *shoheki-ga*.

BOLD STYLE OF EITOKU In 1566, near the end of the Muromachi period, Eitoku, then twenty-three years old, shared with his father, Shoei, the task of painting *shoheki-ga* in the main hall of the Juko-in, Daitoku-ji. Figures 1, 11–14, 38, and 39 show the son's work, and Figures 2 and 3 that of the father. Paintings of flowers and birds are included. Though painted in ink, those by Eitoku show a remarkably fresh style compared to those of his grandfather, Motonobu, and his father, Shoei. The scale of the composition, the abundance of decorative elements, and the forcefulness of Eitoku's brush strokes surpass those of Motonobu and Shoei. Full of youthful vigor and enthusiasm, his paintings show that the old days were passing; there is a sense of anticipation of a new age.

The completion of Oda Nobunaga's castle in Azuchi in 1576 was an epochal event in the history of Japanese art. Under the stimulus of its construction, architecture, carving, and crafts took on fresh vigor. Painting was no exception. Given the opportunity to display his talents fully, the gifted artist Eitoku, who was charged with decorating the donjon and the surrounding palaces, opened

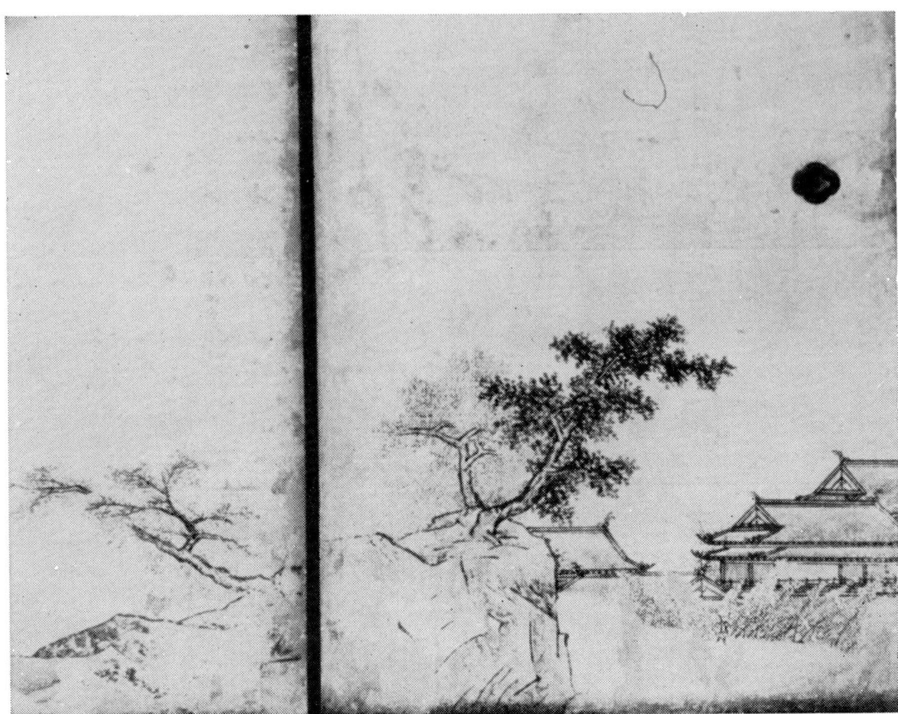

94. *Unkoku Togan: detail from* Landscape. Fusuma, *ink on paper; 181 × 88 cm. 1588. Main hall, Obai-in, Daitoku-ji, Kyoto.*

up unexplored regions for *shoheki-ga* and determined new directions for the many artists who followed him. As mentioned earlier, Eitoku painted in the *kimpeki* style, with rich colors on brilliant golden walls and partitions. Most of these paintings were of flowers and birds, along with Chinese figures, as indicated in the list of the subjects of his paintings given in chapter three. Nobunaga was satisfied with Eitoku's novel and daring expression and style, and Eitoku's contemporaries were overwhelmed by his paintings. Their effect may easily be imagined from the descriptions in the *Shincho Koki* (see pages 69, 74–75).

EITOKU'S UNIFIED COMPOSITION

Eitoku's paintings of flowers and birds in Azuchi Castle must have been executed in a grand and gorgeous decorative style, using the majestic composition and forceful brush-work seen in his flower-and-bird *fusuma* painting in the Juko-in. He had adopted a method employing rich, vibrant colors borrowed from *yama-to-e*. His paintings are thought to have utilized the unified-composition method on a large scale. The method of magnified, close-up composition unifies and systematizes the various subordinate objects arranged around a huge central object. This daring composition method was probably initiated by Eitoku. He had already used it before the construction of Azuchi Castle. The *fusuma* flower-and-bird painting in the Juko-in, executed in 1566, is an example. Here a huge plum tree and a pine tree play the central role in the overall composition. It is assumed that Eitoku applied this method of unified composition on a still grander scale in his *kimpeki*-style *shoheki-ga* in Azuchi Castle; he later used the method extensively when he painted the *shoheki-ga* in Osaka Castle and Juraku-dai. In the

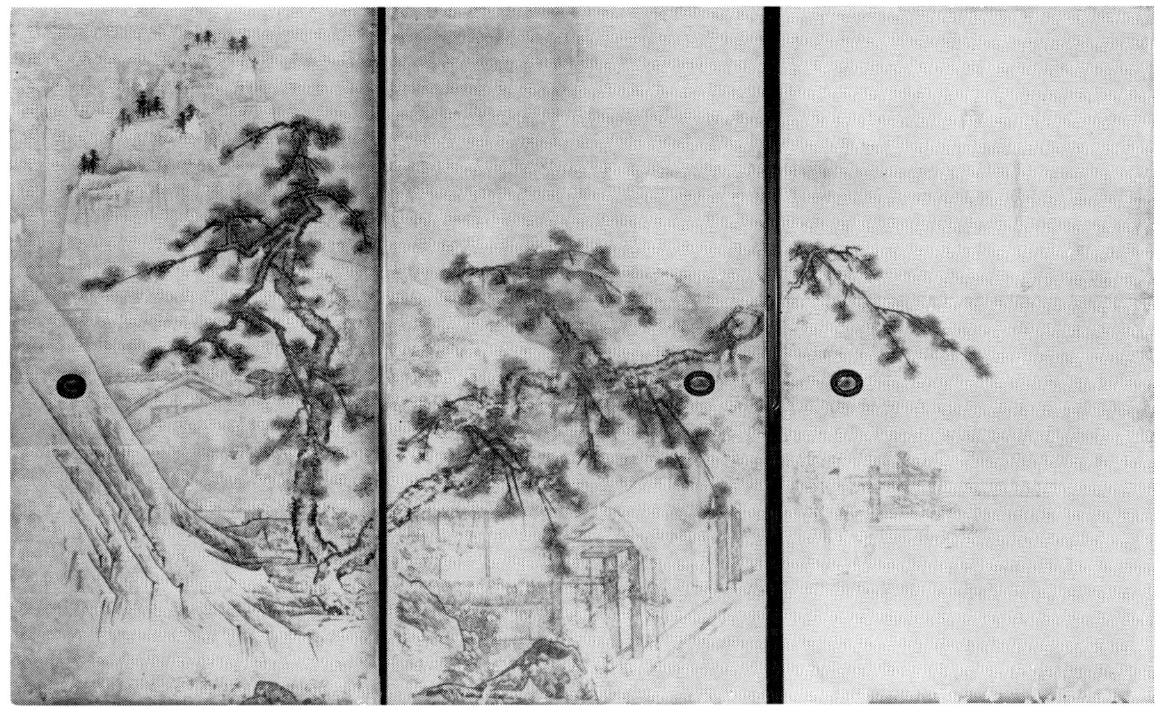

95. *Unkoku Togan:* Landscape and Figures. Fusuma, *ink and light colors on paper; 180 × 92 cm. Late sixteenth century.* Hojo, *Fumon-in, Tofuku-ji, Kyoto.*

section on Eitoku in the *Honcho Gashi,* a history of Japanese painting, Kano Eino wrote in 1693: "He painted splendid and detailed landscapes, figures, flowers, and birds. In the rooms were large-scale paintings [*taiga*] having the forcefulness of flying cranes and dashing serpents. His paintings of figures, rocks, trees, and flowers surpassed those of his father and grandfather. When Toyotomi Hideyoshi built Osaka Castle, Juraku-dai, and other large palaces, he had Eitoku paint pictures on the golden walls. Other feudal lords and high officials also requested Eitoku to paint the golden walls of their palatial residences. Eitoku was too busy with this work to execute detailed paintings [*saiga*] and painted only large-scale works. Some of the pine and plum trees Eitoku painted were ten to twenty feet [about three to seven meters] high, and some of the figures were three to four feet [a meter or more] tall or more. He painted with large, simple,

flowing brush strokes in his own distinctive style, so that it is not a matter of comparing the merits and demerits of Eitoku's paintings with those of Motonobu. For ink paintings Eitoku used a brush with bristles of rice straw. Generally some traces of the style of his grandfather and father are seen in his paintings, but he developed a new style of his own."

The method of unified composition originated by Eitoku was adopted not only by his leading pupil, Kano Sanraku, but also by Kaiho Yusho, Hasegawa Tohaku, Unkoku Togan, and others. Although unified composition was not the only method of painting *shoheki-ga* used in the Momoyama period, it does typify the *shoheki-ga* of that time. The power and magnificence of expression attainable through this method of composition are seen only in the paintings of the Momoyama period. Although artists of the early Edo period also uti-

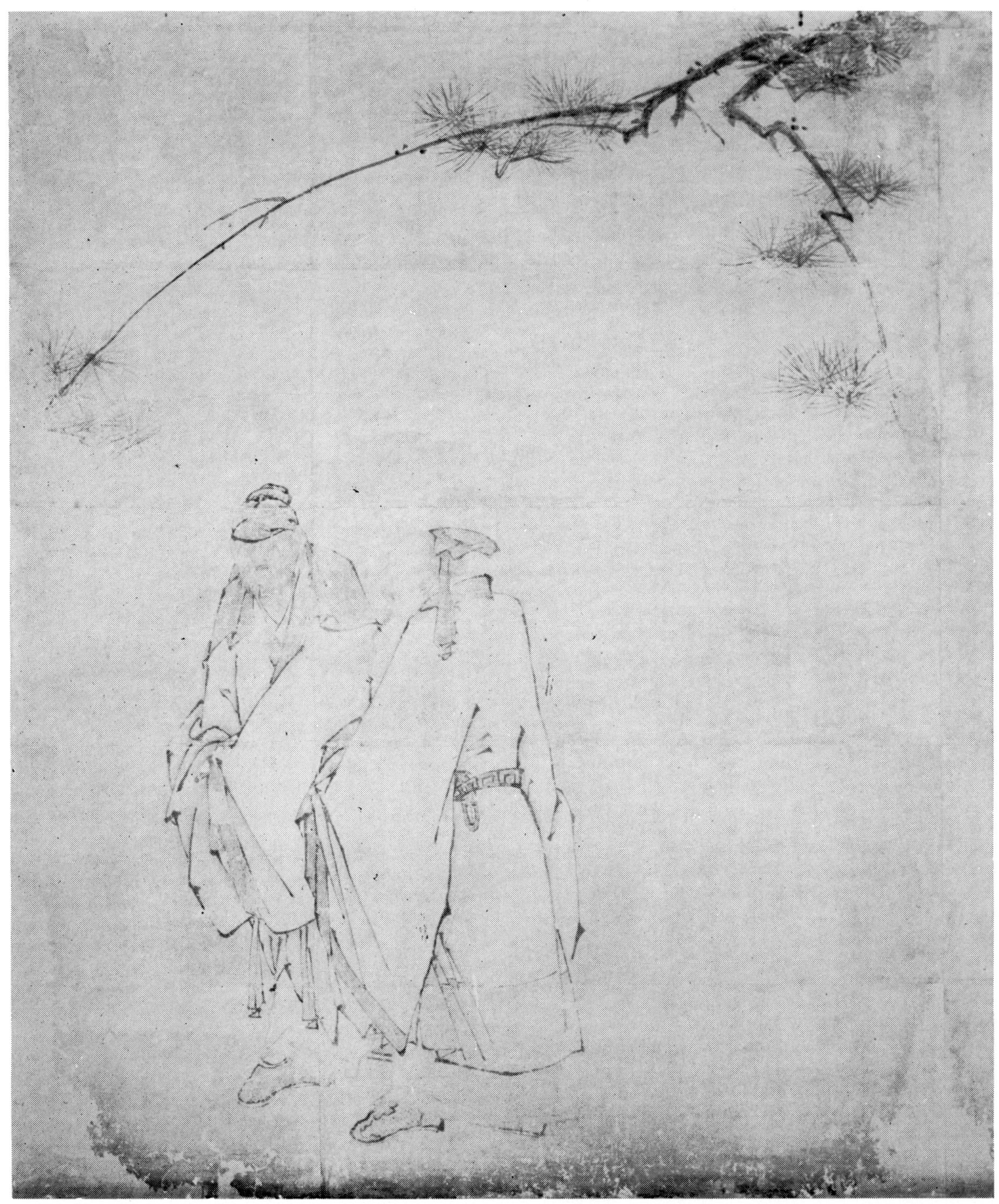

96. *Unkoku Togan: detail from* Noble Characters. *Ink on paper mounted on a wall; 181 × 181 cm. Late sixteenth century.* Hojo, *Fumon-in, Tofuku-ji, Kyoto.*

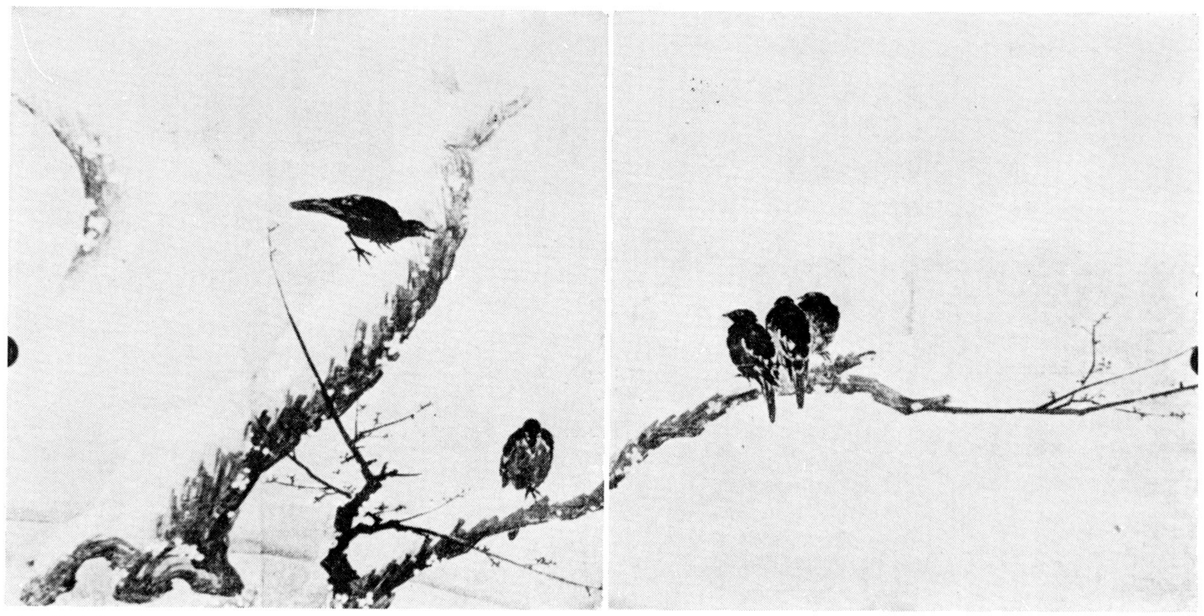

97. *Unkoku Togan:* Plum Tree and Crows. Fusuma, *ink, light colors, and gold on paper; 166.5 × 156.5 cm. Late sixteenth century. Kyoto National Museum.*

lized the unified-composition method in painting *shoheki-ga* on huge surfaces, such as those in the *ohiroma* of Nijo Castle or the reception hall of the Nishi Hongan-ji temple, these later works lack the force and splendor of Momoyama *shoheki-ga.* Only the artists of the Momoyama period proved truly able to handle the unified-composition method.

As mentioned by Eino, Eitoku's painting was not limited to large-scale works, or *taiga,* executed with flowing brush strokes. He also painted detailed pictures, *saiga,* based on elaborate sketches. He painted both in large, sweeping strokes and in detail in the *fusuma* paintings for the main hall of the Juko-in and in the *Rakuchu Rakugai* (Scenes In and Around Kyoto) screens in the Uesugi Collection (Fig. 126). There is no question, however, that it is the grand, flowing style, not the detailed brushwork, that shows Eitoku's true character. He created a style of *shoheki-ga* painting unparalleled in the history of Japanese art.

EXQUISITE STYLE OF SANRAKU

With Eitoku as the leading artist, the *kimpeki* paintings of the early Momoyama period exhibited a positive, vigorous style befitting the constructive phase of a new age. But the *kimpeki* flower-and-bird *shoheki-ga* of the late Momoyama period (1592–1614) differed somewhat from those of the early period. Kano Sanraku and Kano Mitsunobu were representative artists working in this style in the late Momoyama period, though of the two Sanraku retained more of the style of the earlier period. His *kimpeki* flower-and-bird paintings began to show a quieter mood reflecting the end of the excitement of the constructive phase, while retaining force and grandeur. Added elements of realistic detail and delicate artistic effects in the delineation of objects are noted in Sanraku's *kimpeki* works, which exhibit more decorative and sensual characteristics than do early Momoyama paintings.

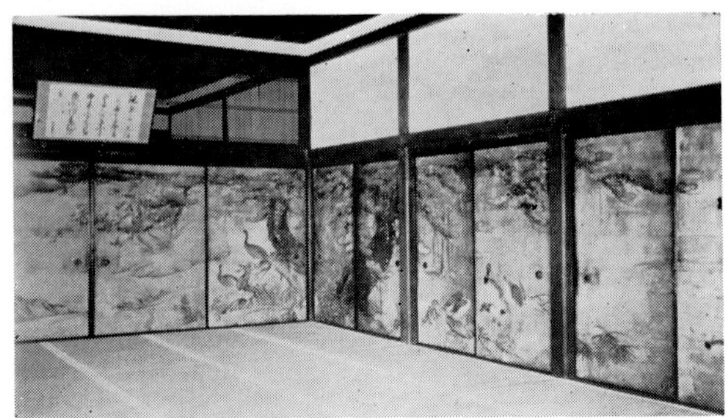

98. *Kano Mitsunobu:* Flowers and Birds. Fusuma, *colors on paper. 1600. Ni-no-ma, Kangaku-in, Onjo-ji, Shiga Pre-fecture.*

99. *(left). Attributed to Kano Tan'yu:* Pine Tree and Hawks. *Colors and gold on paper mounted on a wall. Early seventeenth century. Yari-no-ma,* ohiroma, *Nijo Castle, Kyoto.*

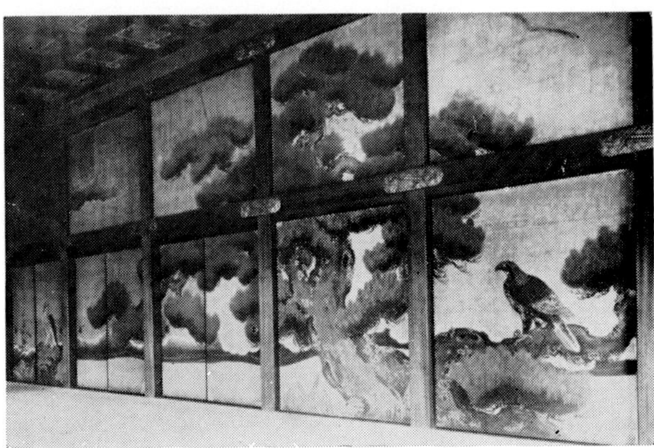

100, 101 *(opposite page). Yoshimura Kokei:* fusuma-*painting sketch (above; colors on paper) and* fusuma *painting (below; colors and gold on paper). 1810. Goedo, Nishi Hongan-ji, Kyoto.* ▷

In the earlier large-scale *shoheki-ga* painted in Eitoku's style the artist did not always draw such objects as flowers and birds realistically because the emphasis was on the majestic and striking composition. Because of the scope of the effort and the huge painting surface, the natural form and delicate mood of individual objects tended to be sacrificed. Eitoku's *Flowers and Birds* in the Juko-in, executed in ink, includes violets and dandelions painted at the base of a huge plum tree. Here the lines and brush strokes are so strong and vigorous that the flowers do not have the gentle feeling associated with wildflowers. Of course, they are superbly painted, vigorous and full of life, but instead of having the shapes of real dandelions and violets, they are strongly subjective and stylized.

Sanraku painted flowers, trees, and birds in more detail than Eitoku, trying to catch the shape and mood of each one. He used smoother and softer lines than Eitoku and tried to incorporate more artistic effects. His large-scale *kimpeki* paintings like *Peonies* (Figs. 7, 44, 45) and *Red Plum Blossoms* (Figs. 46, 47) in the Daikaku-ji in Kyoto show characteristics different from those by Eitoku. His ink *shoheki-ga* in the same temple, *Pine Tree and Hawk* (Fig. 17), shows the same tendency.

QUIET MOOD OF MITSUNOBU Thus, in the latter part of the Momoyama period, changes began to appear in *kimpeki* flower-and-bird paintings. Sanraku followed the traditions carried over from the early Momoyama period, and his paintings, such as *Red Plum Blossoms,* show the majestic force and massive proportions

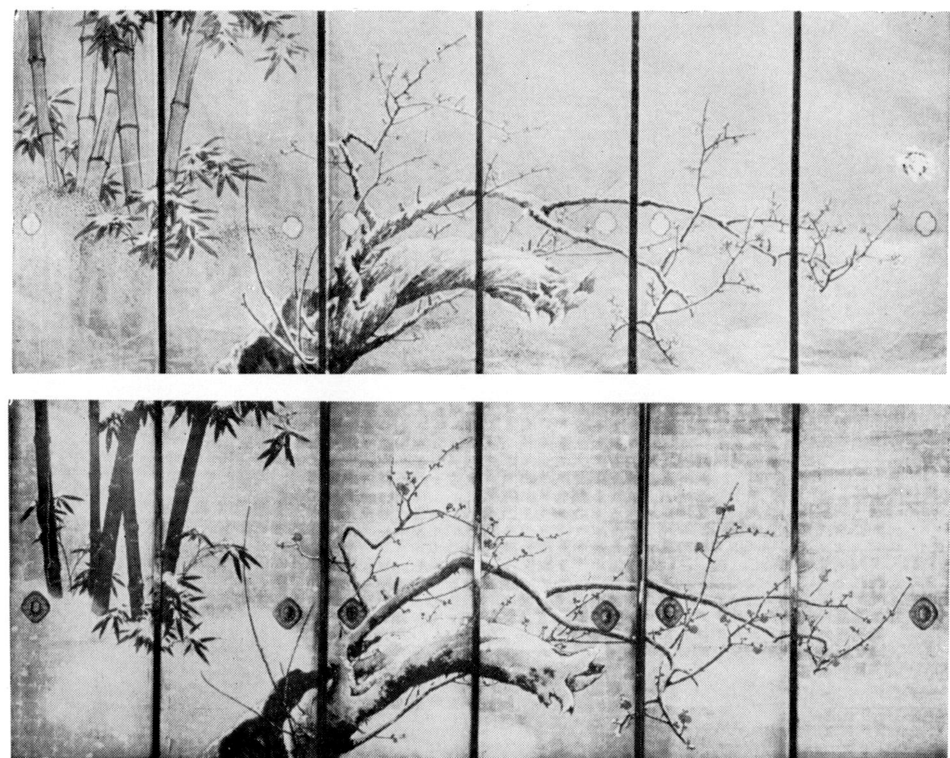

of the unified-composition method, though to a lesser extent than Eitoku's works. Kano Mitsunobu's paintings also include decorative *kimpeki* flowers and birds, but his style differs somewhat from Sanraku's and is very different from Eitoku's.

Sanraku developed the style of the early Momoyama period into one more graphic and romantic, and Mitsunobu carried this tendency still further. Mitsunobu's flower-and-bird paintings lack the overwhelming grandeur and forcefulness of Eitoku's work, but they are filled with a mood of quiet beauty. Gone are the huge trees and massive rocks. Instead, delicate trees are seen growing naturally, and the rock arrangements are not so massive. Bold exaggeration and simplification of objects are no longer seen; the world of flowers and

birds in nature is more gently expressed. The style is no longer overpowering, and the paintings are more inviting and appealing to the viewer. The composition has more depth, realistic three-dimensional space replacing a flat abstract background.

In contrast to the majestic and vigorous style of the early Momoyama period, Mitsunobu's style is characterized by grace and noble elegance, features highly suggestive of the *yamato-e* style. In fact Mitsunobu's knowledge of *yamato-e* was quite profound, as eloquently demonstrated by his paintings of scenes from the *Genji Monogatari*. As mentioned earlier, Eitoku based his *kimpeki* style on a synthesis of the *kanga* and *yamato-e* styles, but he did not achieve a complete harmonization. In particular, he did not fully assimilate the delicate mood traditionally sought in *yamato-e*. It was not until the time

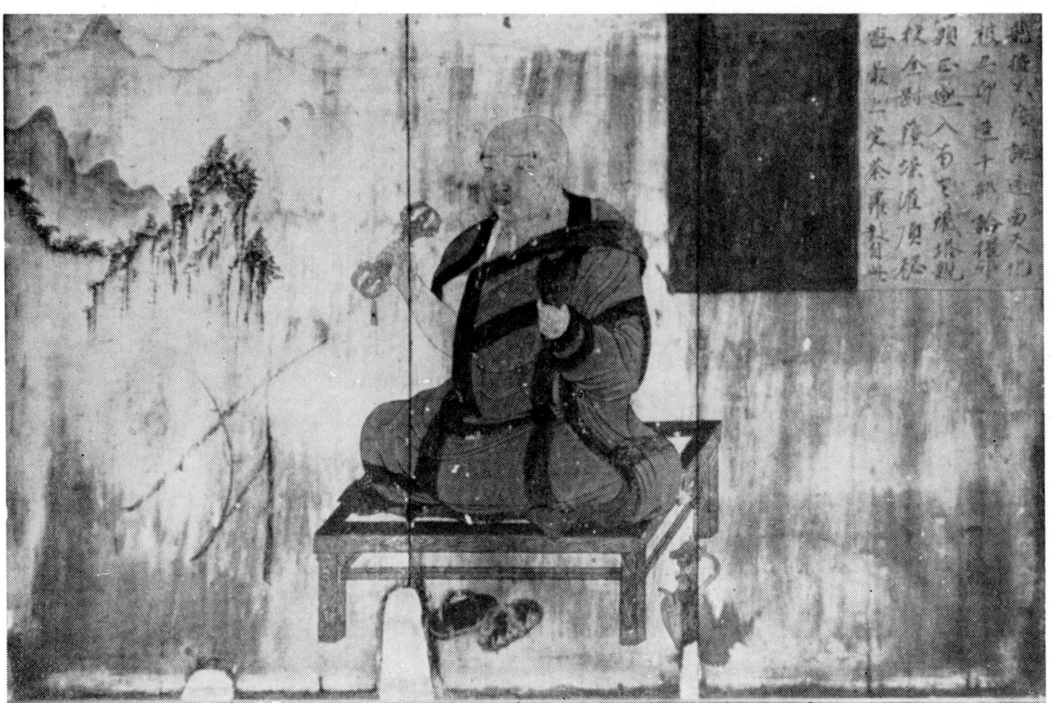

102. *Section of* Portraits of the Eight Patriarchs of the Shingon Sect. *Colors on paper mounted on wood panel. 1407. Five-story Pagoda, Itsukushima Shrine, Hiroshima Prefecture.*

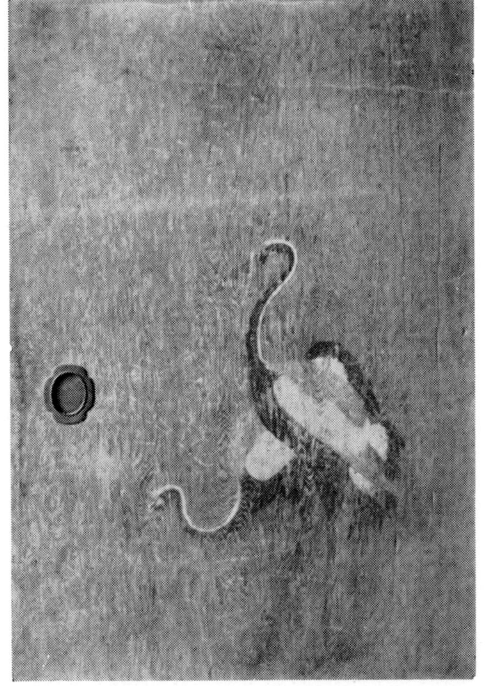

103. Cranes. *Colors on cedar door; 160 × 109.5 cm. 1397. Hondo, Kakurin-ji, Hyogo Prefecture.*

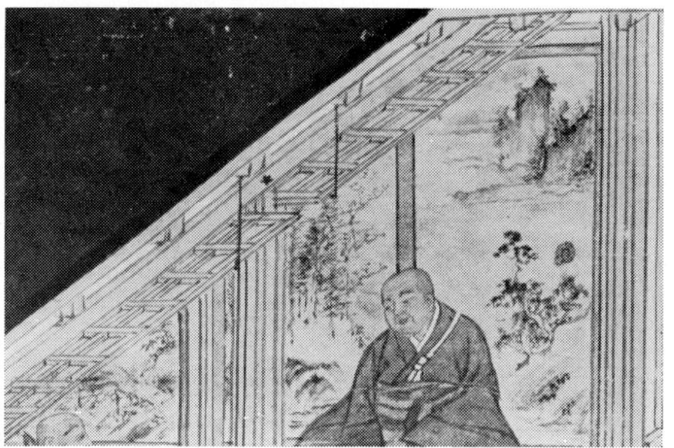

104. Detail from Honen Shonin Eden *(Pictorial Biography of Saint Honen). Colors on paper. Fourteenth century. Chion-in, Kyoto.*

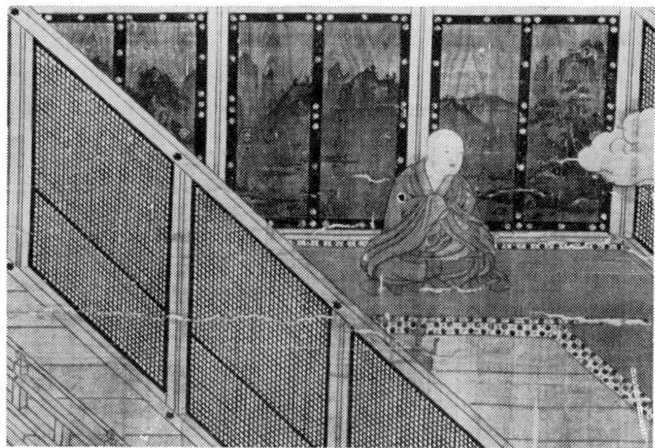

105. Detail from Konda Sobyo Engi *(Origin of the Konda Hachiman-gu Shrine). colors on paper. 1433. Konda Hachiman-gu, Osaka Prefecture.*

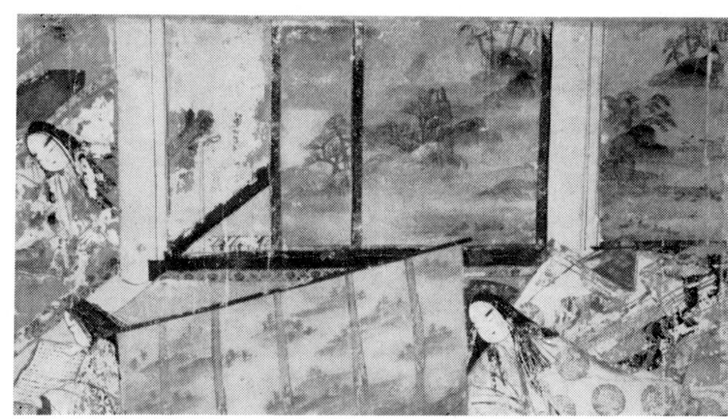

106. Detail from Genji Monogatari Emaki *(Tale of Genji Picture Scroll). Colors on paper. Twelfth century. Tokugawa Reimei-kai, Tokyo.*

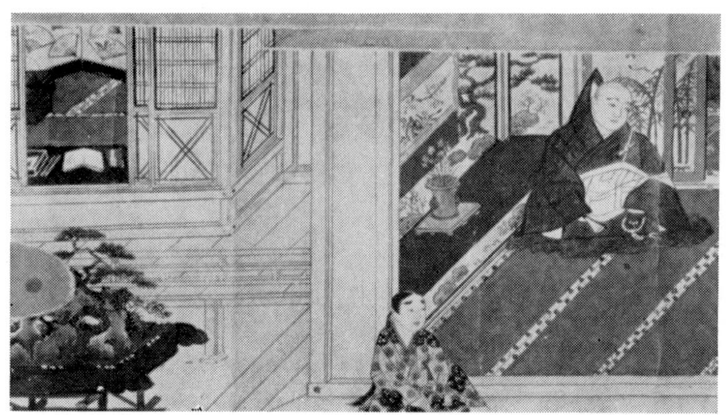

107. Detail from Boki Ekotoba *(Pictorial Biography of Priest Kakunyo). Colors on paper. 1482. Nishi Hongan-ji, Kyoto.*

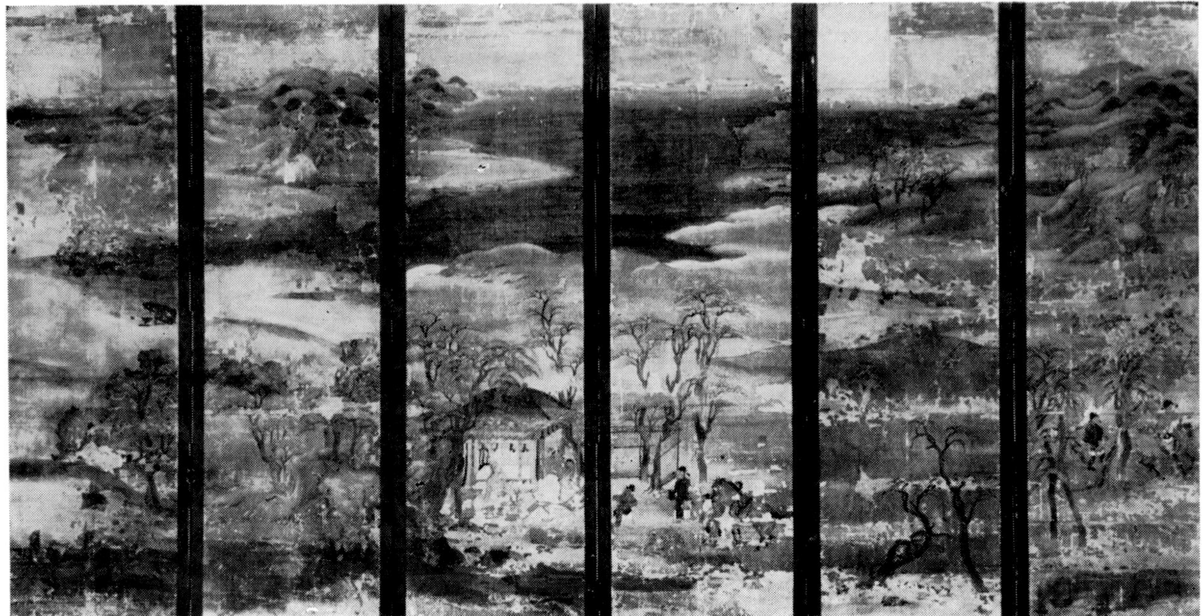

108. *Landscape screen originally belonging to the To-ji, Kyoto. Sixfold screen, colors on silk; each panel 146 × 42.5 cm. Eleventh century. Kyoto National Museum.*

of Sanraku and Mitsunobu in the late Momoyama period that *kanga* and *yamato-e* truly fused and the soft mood of the *yamato-e* style was fully realized in *shoheki-ga*. As seen in his painting *Battle of the Carriages* (Fig. 21), a scene from the *Genji Monogatari,* Sanraku greatly admired *yamato-e* and learned a great deal from it. One of his special talents, skillful delineation of large groups of people, owes much to his study of the classic *yamato-e* picture scrolls. The charming mood of his *kimpeki*-style flower-and-bird paintings is also related to *yamato-e*. The mood of Mitsunobu's painting is slightly different from that of Sanraku's, expressing a pure elegance and a delightfully refreshing ambiance.

The romantic and graphic aspects of the late Momoyama *kimpeki* flower-and-bird *shoheki-ga* of the Kano school are also seen in the paintings of other schools. Examples are the Hasegawa school's *Flowers and Birds* and *Willow* (Fig. 140) from the

scenes of the four seasons in the Sambo-in, Daigo-ji, Kyoto. Naturally the *shoheki-ga* in the Sambo-in show a style clearly different from that of Sanraku or Mitsunobu, but they also show certain features common to all *shoheki-ga* of the period. Though all these works are categorized as examples of the Momoyama style, the *shoheki-ga* of the Sambo-in reveal a world of beauty very different from that depicted by the vigorous and daring style of the early part of the period.

INK PAINTING   So far I have discussed *kimpeki* flower-and-bird paintings as typical of Momoyama *shoheki-ga*. This does not mean, however, that ink flower-and-bird *shoheki-ga* were not painted during this period. On the contrary, some artists produced more works in ink than in colors. Just as the *yamato-e* tradition of *shoheki-ga* painted in rich colors had continued

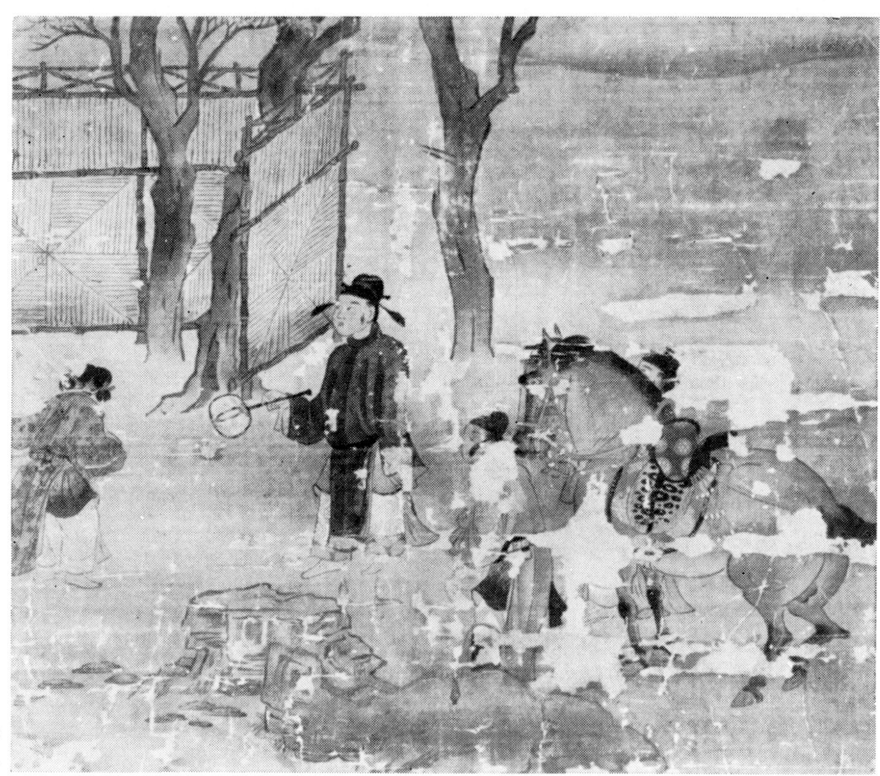

109. *Detail from landscape screen originally belonging to the To-ji.*

during the Muromachi period, when ink *shoheki-ga* predominated, so the painting of *shoheki-ga* in ink continued during the Momoyama period, when brilliant *kimpeki* painting flourished. This persistence was due partly to the influence of the *kanga* tradition. Many ink-painting masterpieces were produced, and many of the first-rate Momoyama artists did excellent work in both colors and ink. Hasegawa Tohaku, Kaiho Yusho, and Unkoku Togan, in particular, painted superb pictures of flowers and birds in ink. Their works demonstrate one characteristic typical of this period, a strong decorative tendency in composition.

FIGURE PAINTING   As we have observed, many of Eitoku's *shoheki-ga* in the Azuchi Castle donjon featured subjects popular in the *kanga* tradition, such as Chinese sages, noble personages, and hermits. This trend continued throughout the Momoyama period, these typical *kanga* subjects remaining the favorite figures seen in *shoheki-ga*. *The Seven Sages of the Bamboo Grove* and *Four Sages of Mount Shang,* two of the paintings in Azuchi Castle, depicted especially favored subjects, and several masterpieces rendering them survive today. These Chinese figures were painted both in *kimpeki* style and in ink. It should be noted, however, that although the subject matter was Chinese, such *shoheki-ga* exhibited a Japanese style similar to that seen in paintings of other subjects. This is true of both *kimpeki* and ink painting. For example, Kaiho Yusho used a distinctive method of rendering figures called *fukuro jimbutsu*. Although the technique was derived from Liang K'ai, a famous Chinese artist of the Southern Sung dynasty (1127–1279), Yusho successfully assimilated it into his own style. A good example of Yusho's figure painting is his *Seven Sages of the Bamboo Grove* (Fig.

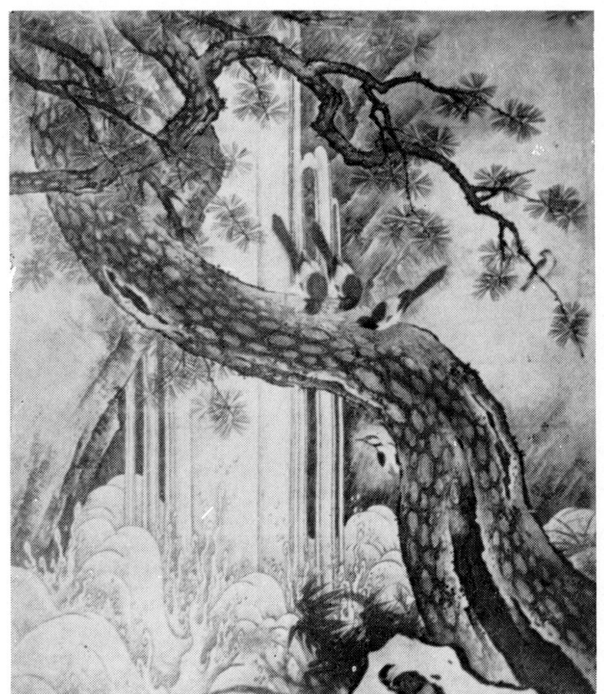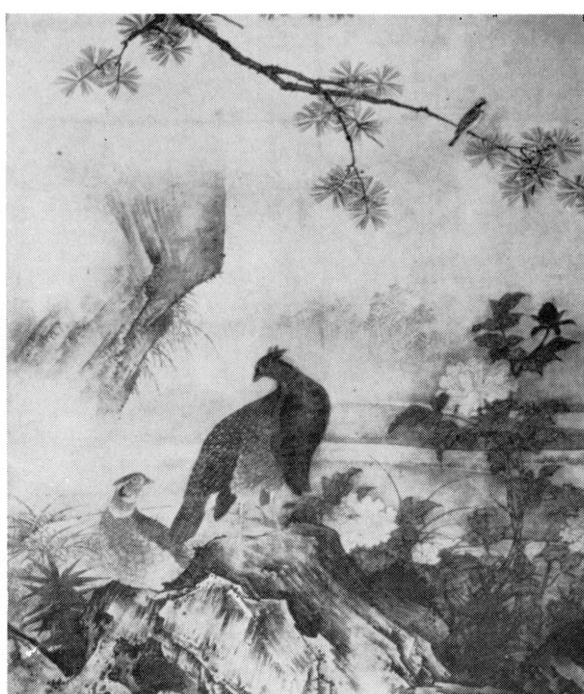

110. Kano Motonobu: details from Flowers and Birds. Fusuma, *colors on paper. 1513. Daisen-in, Daitoku-ji, Kyoto.*

57), painted on *fusuma* in the *hojo* of the Kennin-ji, Kyoto. This kind of grandeur and magnanimity of expression is seen only in Yusho's work.

GENRE PAINTING   Another important development in Momoyama *shoheki-ga* occurred in the field of genre painting, a form of figure painting depicting the lives and customs of the people of the time. All surviving Momoyama genre *shoheki-ga* belong to the latter half of the period. Genre painting already had a long history in the *yamato-e* tradition. Some artists of the *kanga* tradition began to paint genre scenes in the latter half of the Muromachi period, paving the way for the development of the genre painting of the Momoyama and Edo periods. Kano Hideyori and Hasegawa Tohaku are credited with being the pioneers of Momoyama and Edo genre paint-

ing. Most Momoyama genre paintings were executed by *kanga* artists.

These genre paintings depict a cross section of the cheerful and wholesome lives of the people of the time. The scenes vary widely. They include such seasonal pastimes as picnicking under the cherry blossoms in the spring and maple viewing in the fall, festivals at shrines and temples, horse training by warriors, archery practice on horseback, falconry, craftsmen working, and women's Kabuki, which was highly popular with the general public. A type of genre painting with a uniquely exotic mood is seen in the *namban* screens depicting the newly arrived Europeans, who were referred to as *namban,* "southern barbarians." The *Rakuchu Rakugai* paintings of scenes in and around Kyoto also display many of the characteristics of genre painting.

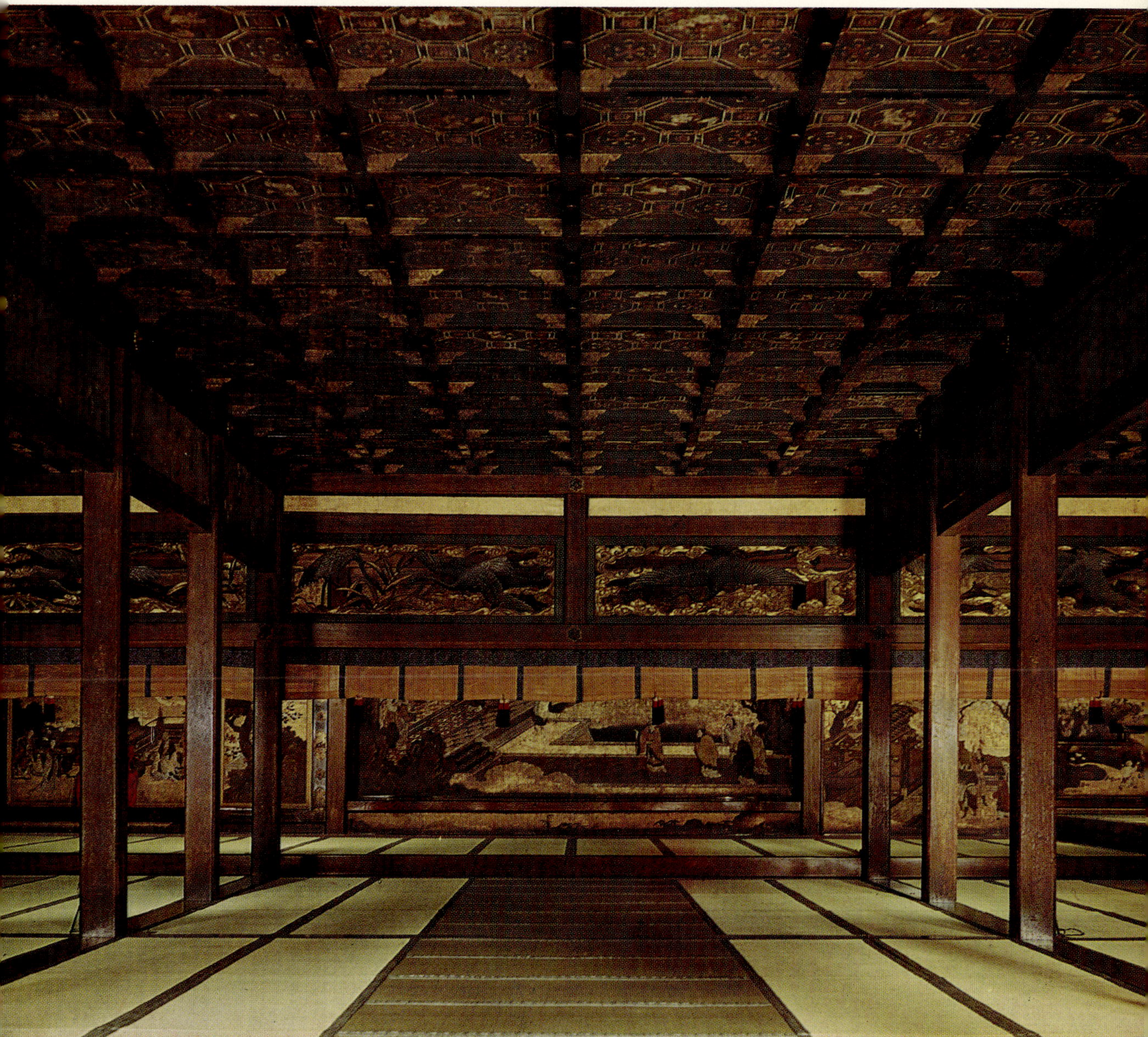

111. Watanabe Ryokei: Figures *and* Flowers and Birds. *Colors and gold on paper. Early seventeenth century. Reception hall, Nishi Hongan-ji, Kyoto.*

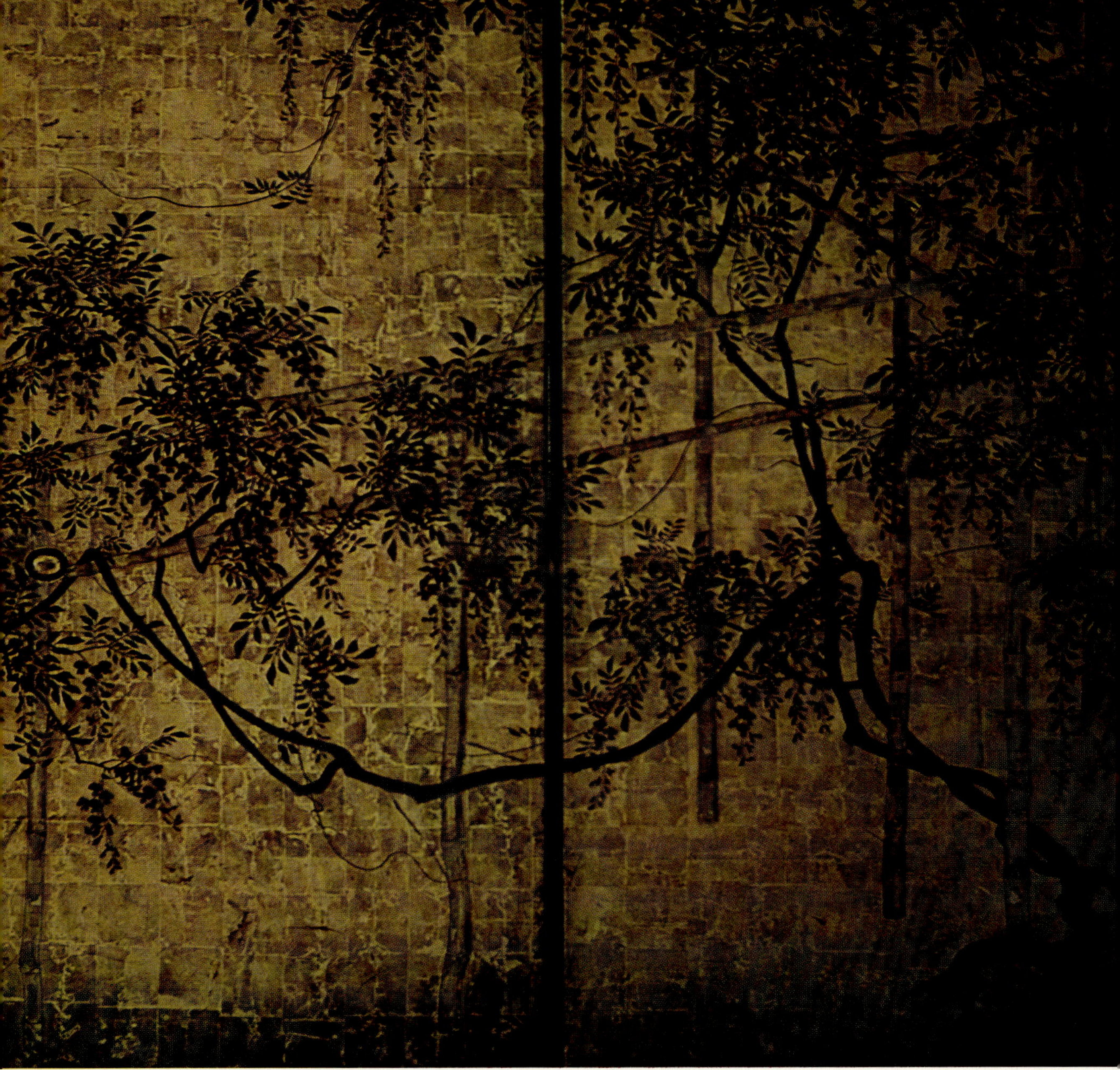

112. *Kano school:* Wisteria. Fusuma, *colors and gold on paper; 178 × 93 cm. Early seventeenth century.* Shoin, *Daian-ji, Osaka Prefecture.*

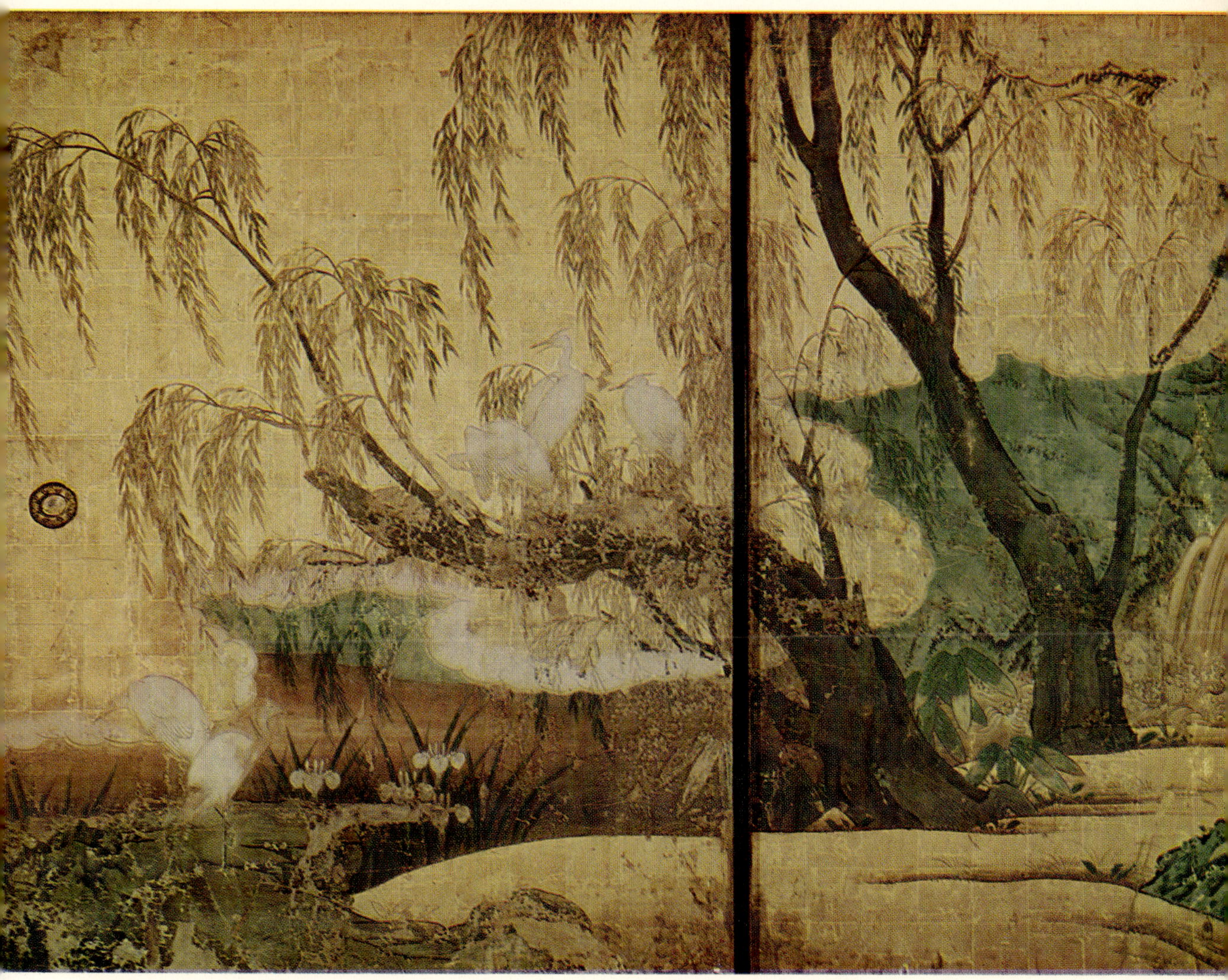

113. *Kano school:* Willows and Herons. Fusuma, *colors and gold on paper; 180 × 140 cm. Early seventeenth century.* Hojo, *Fumon-in, Tofuku-ji, Kyoto.*

114 (overleaf, left). *Attributed to Kano Sanraku: detail from* Flowers and Birds. Fusuma, ▷ *colors and gold on paper; 189 × 142 cm. 1631.* Hojo, *Tenkyu-in, Myoshin-ji, Kyoto.*

115 (overleaf, right). *Kano Sansetsu: detail from* Two Doves in an Old Tree. Fusuma, *ink* ▷ *on paper; 157.5 × 77.5 cm. Early seventeenth century.* Shoin, *Daitsu-ji, Shiga Prefecture. (See also Figure 52.)*

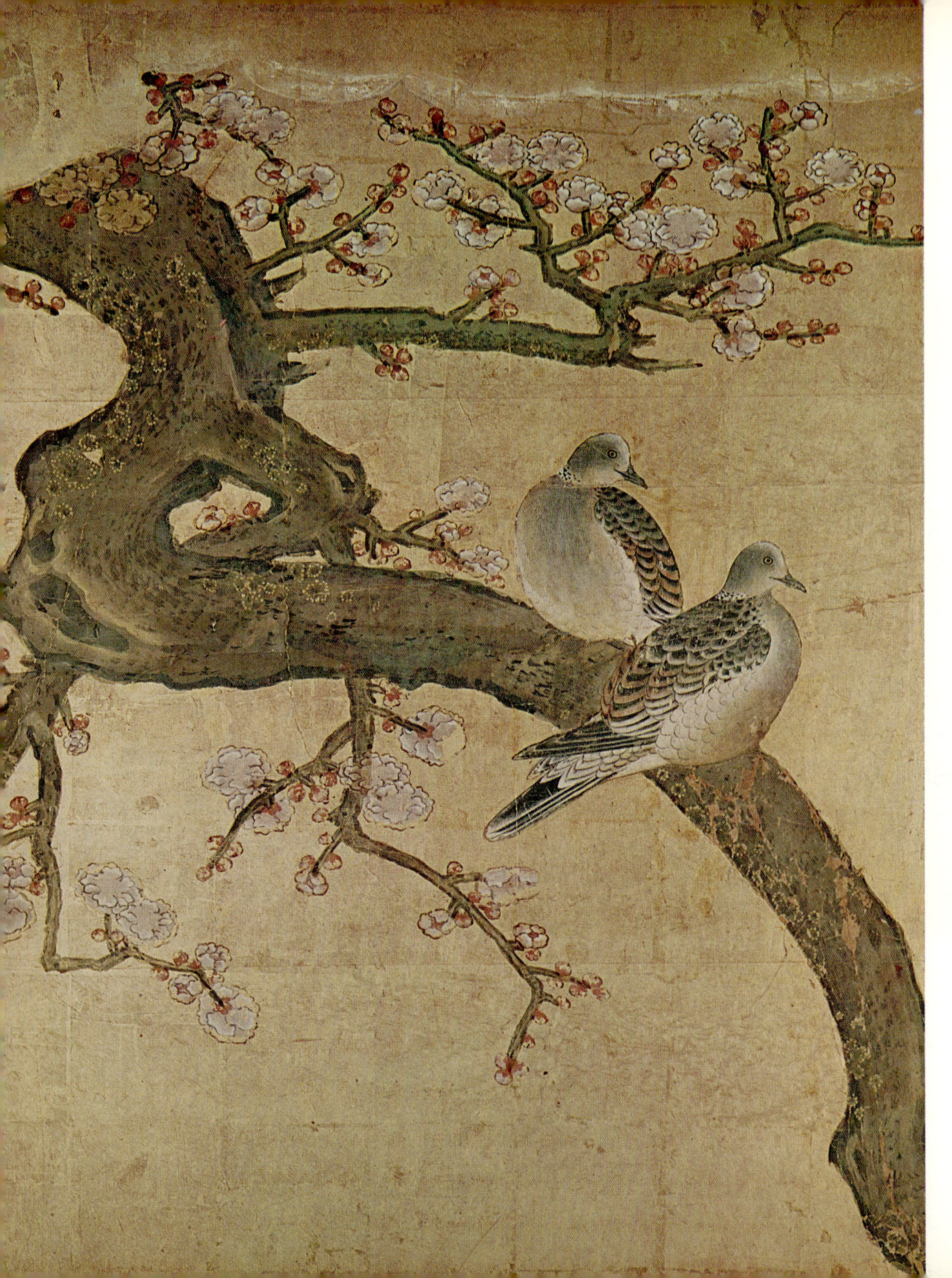

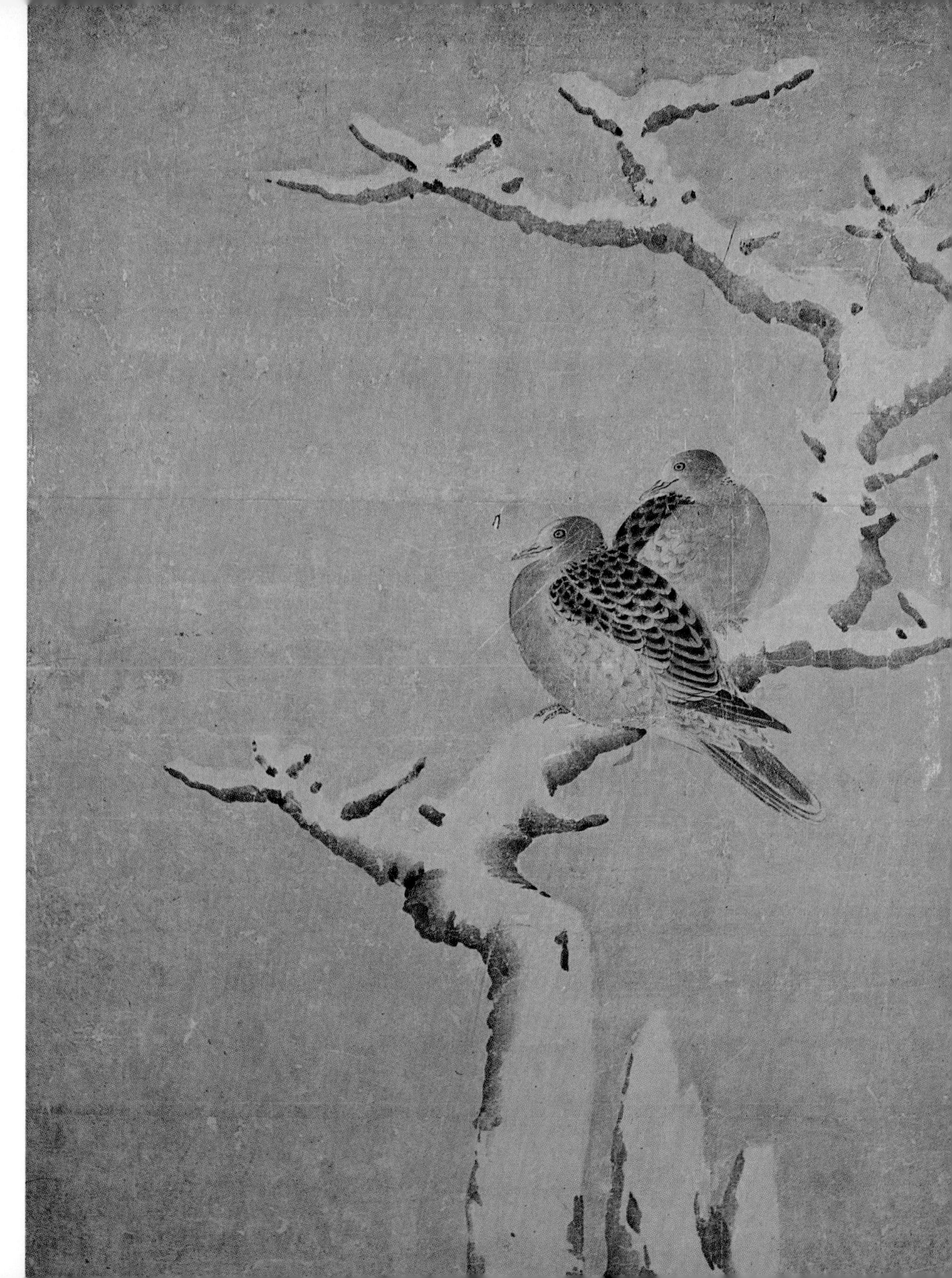

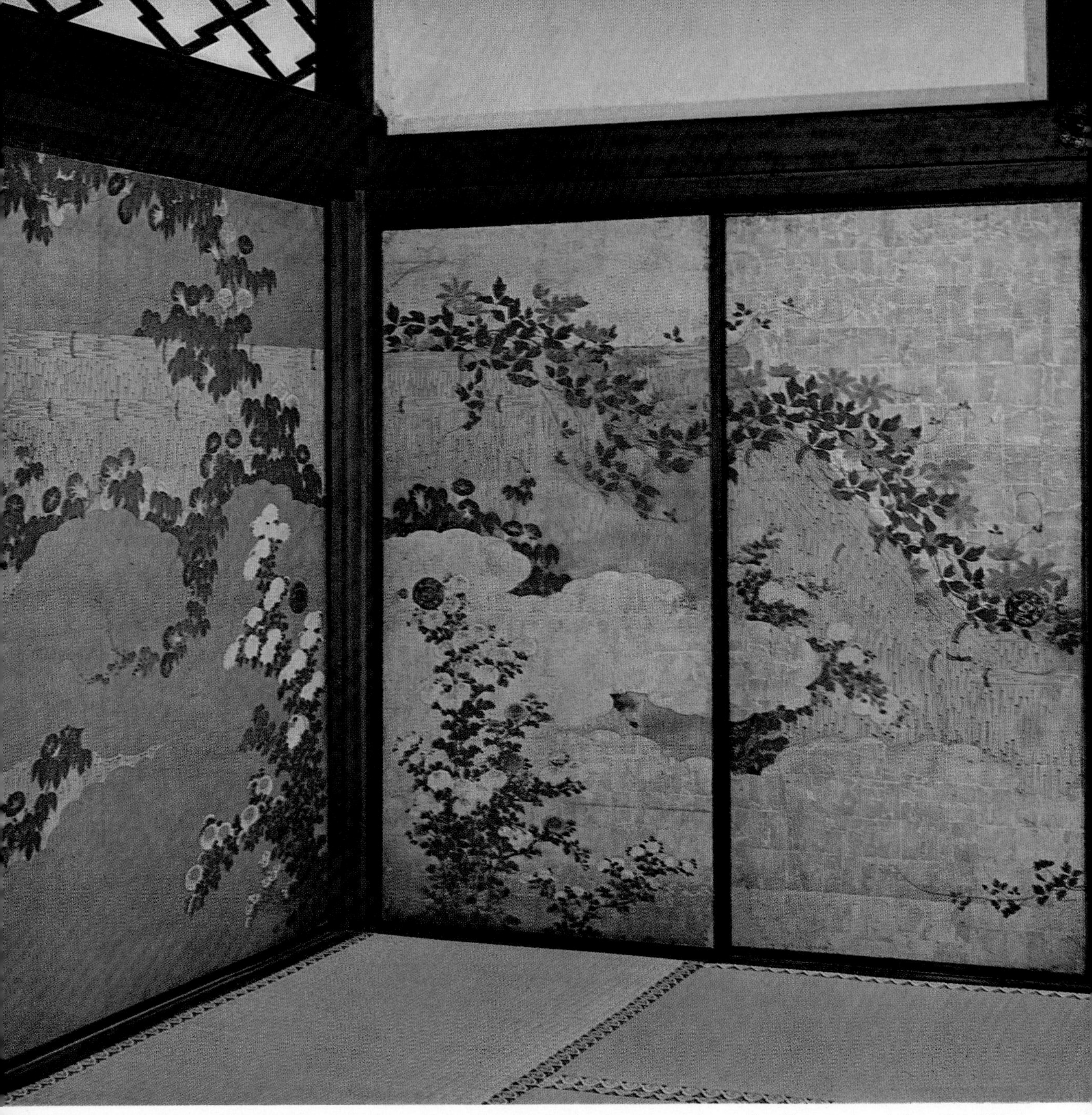

116. *Attributed to Kano Sanraku:* Morning-glories and Clematis. Fusuma, *colors and gold on paper; left section 189 ×
142 cm., right section 184 × 94 cm. 1631. Hojo, Tenkyu-in, Myoshin-ji, Kyoto. (See also Figure 51.)*

117. *Kano Sansetsu:* Flowers and Birds. *Colors on cedar doors; 161 × 85.5 cm. Early seventeenth* ▷
century. Shoin, *Myoki-an, Kyoto Prefecture.*

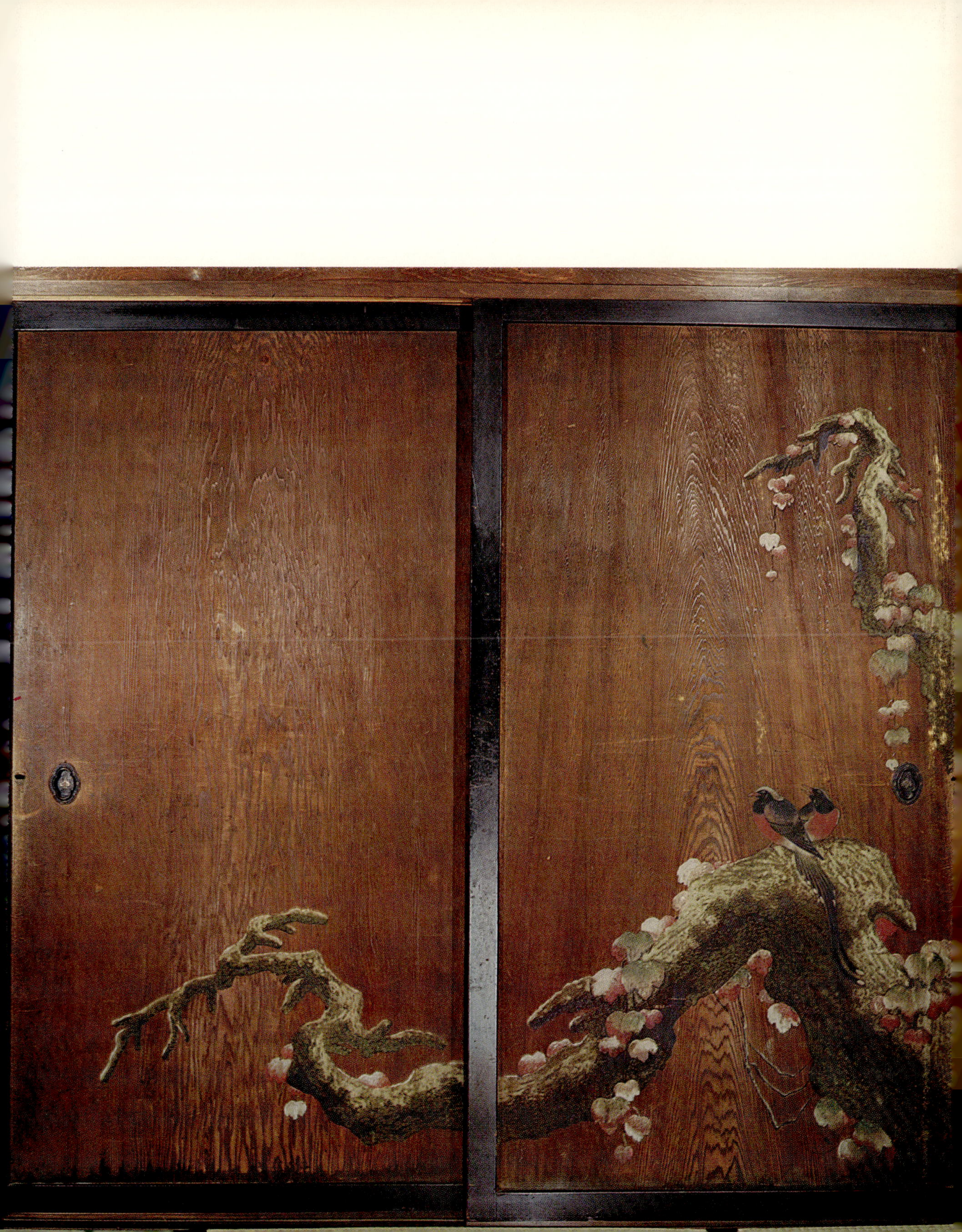

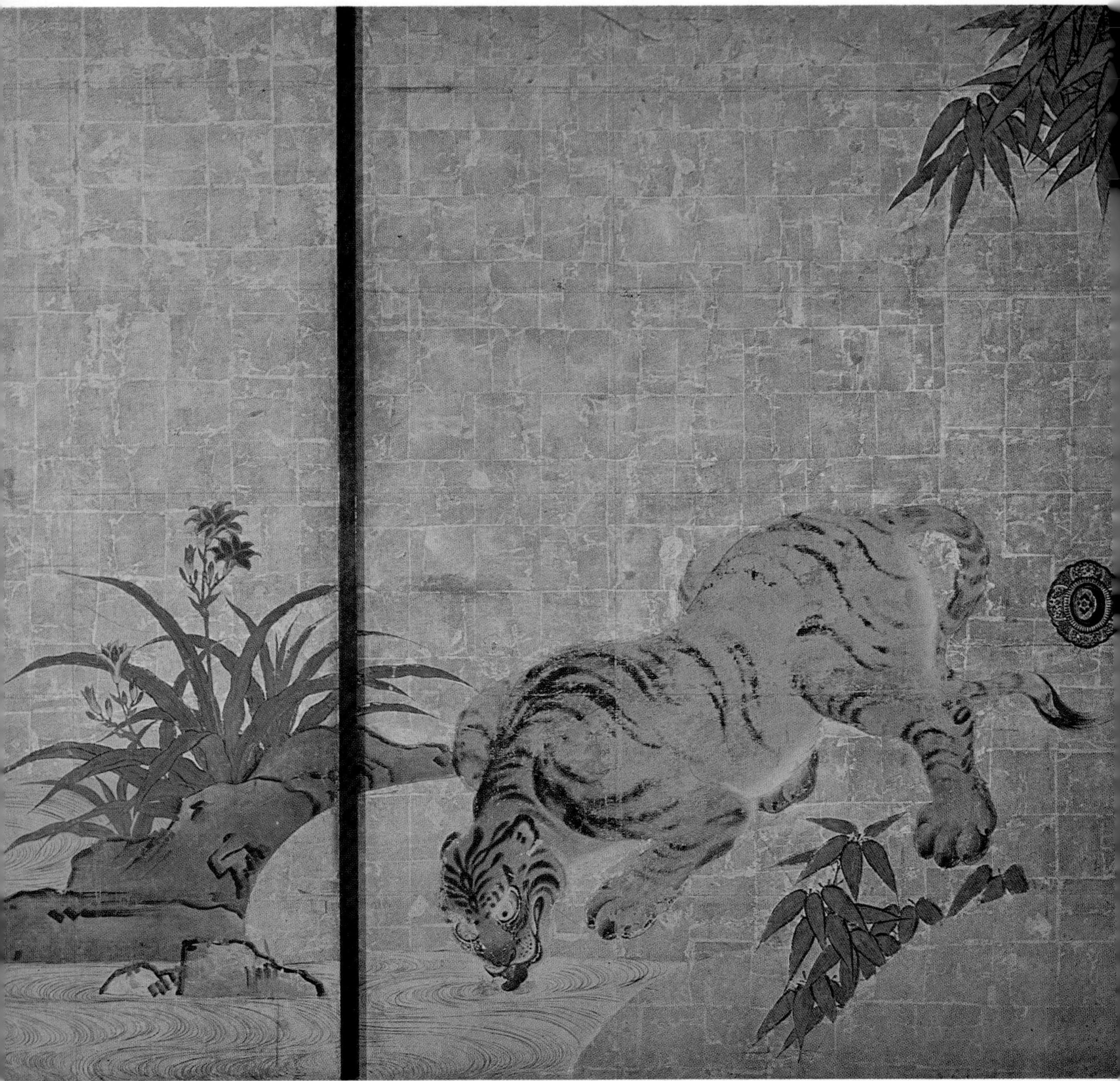

118. Kano Tan'yu: Tiger and Bamboo (Tiger Drinking). Fusuma, *colors and gold on paper; 183 × 139 cm. Early seventeenth century.* Kohojo, *Nanzen-ji, Kyoto.*

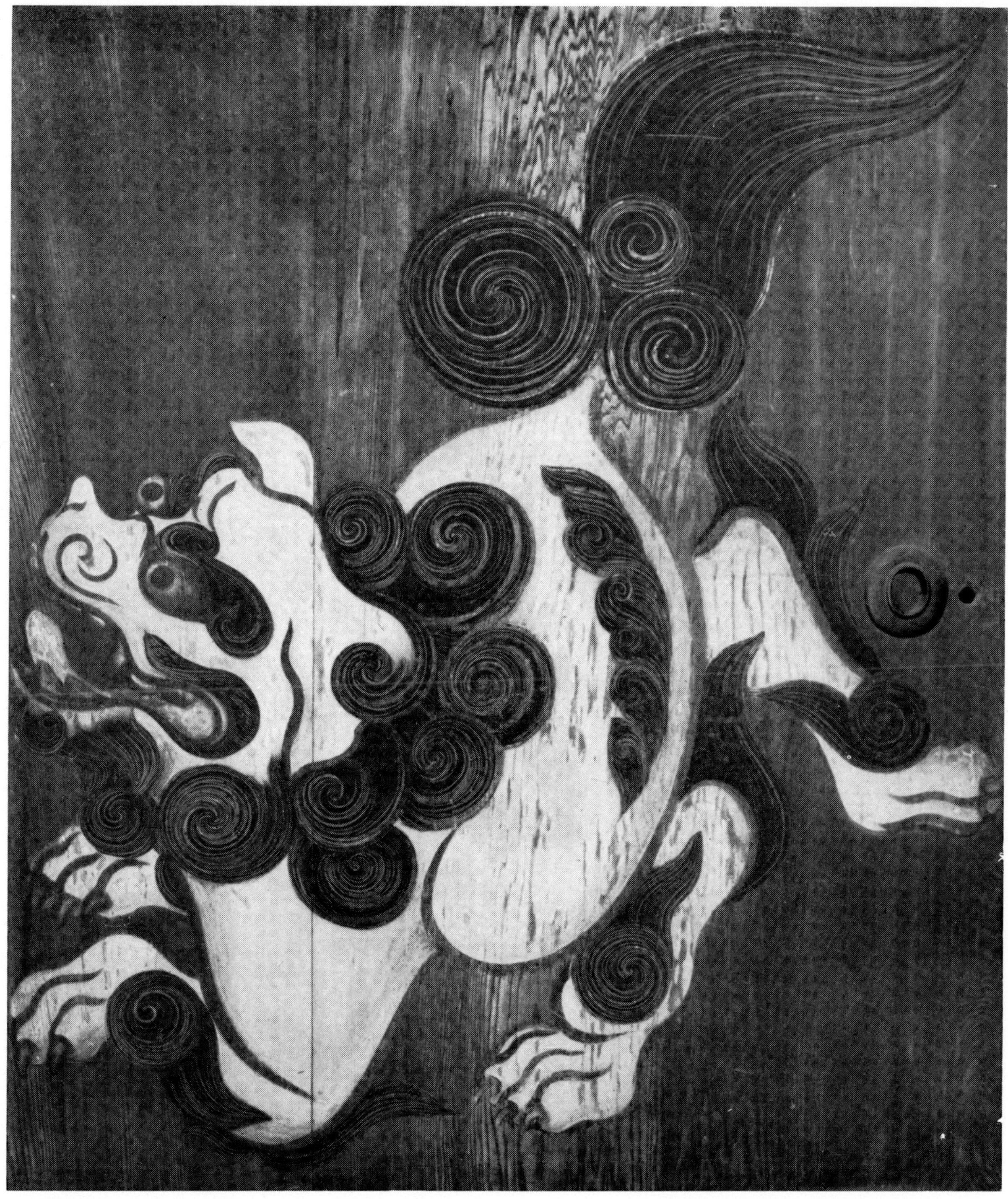

119. *Tawaraya Sotatsu:* Chinese Lion. *Colors on cedar door; 182 × 121 cm. 1621. Reception hall, Yogen-in, Kyoto.*

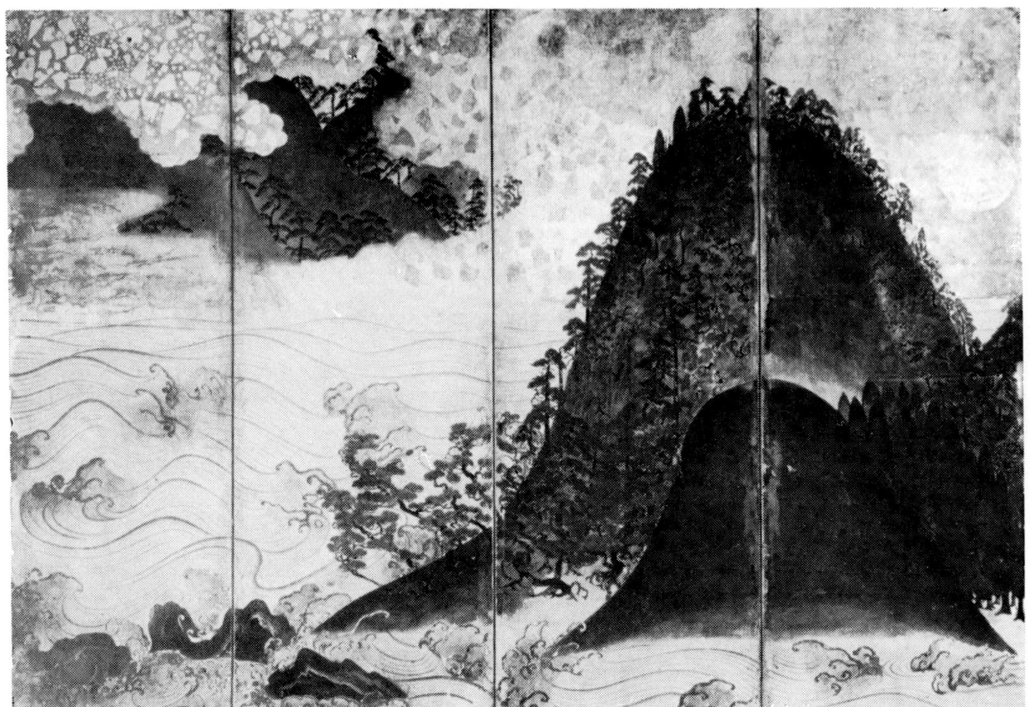

120. *Detail from* Sun and Moon. *One of a pair of sixfold screens, colors and gold on paper; 149 × 317 cm. Late sixteenth century. Kongo-ji, Osaka Prefecture.*

The genre paintings formerly in the Shinden of the Emman-in, Otsu City (Figs. 26, 27, 86), in the reception hall of Nagoya Castle, and in the *shoin* of the Dannohorin-ji, Kyoto, are valuable examples of genre *shoheki-ga* because most genre paintings of the time were done on folding screens. All these *shoheki-ga* were painted in the late Momoyama period by artists of the Kano school. The *fusuma* painting in the Dannohorin-ji depicts the Hie Festival in Sakamoto, Otsu City, while the paintings formerly in the Emman-in and in Nagoya Castle are of famous places. Because the backgrounds derive from *yama-to-e,* the feeling differs from that of *kanga.*

LANDSCAPE PAINTING   Momoyama *shoheki-ga* also included landscapes. Aside from the backgrounds of the paintings of famous places mentioned above, most landscapes were idealized in the manner of the *kanga* tradition and were dominated by Chinese-style scenery and buildings. These works were often painted in ink or ink and light colors. As might be expected, the style was characterized by a Japanese feeling although the subjects were Chinese in origin, and each work by the master artists of that period was strongly distinctive. The works of Tohaku and Yusho are especially fine.

CHAPTER SIX

Works of the Kano School

WE HAVE SEEN THAT artists belonging to the various schools of the *kanga* tradition dominated the painters' world of the Momoyama period. Few influential artists belonged to the Tosa school of the *yamato-e* tradition, so that this school did not wield great power. The Kano school in particular formed the core of the painters' world, commanding the largest number of influential artists who distinguished themselves in painting *shoheki-ga*.

SHOEI   It goes without saying that Eitoku is the leading representative of the Kano school in the Momoyama period and occupies the most important place in the history of the fine arts of his time. However, before discussing Eitoku, the *shoheki-ga* of his father, Shoei (also known as Naonobu; 1519–92), should be mentioned. Shoei had an active career as an artist spanning the years from the end of the Muromachi period through the early part of the Momoyama period. Because his career fell between those of the two master artists Motonobu and Eitoku, he has not received much attention. While he was not as outstanding an artist as his father, Motonobu, he should not be scorned, if for no other reason than that he was responsible for sending the great artist Eitoku into the world. Because trustworthy standard works by Shoei survive, it is relatively easy to form a basis for evaluating his *shoheki-ga*. His most important standard work is the great hanging scroll *The Nirvana of the Buddha* (Fig. 122), painted in 1563

when Shoei was forty-four years old. The next most important standard work is *Flowers and Birds,* a pair of sixfold screens in ink (Fig. 121). It bears the same writing and seal as *The Nirvana of the Buddha,* and the style is the same down to the least detail.

Investigation based on these works has resulted in the discovery of a surprisingly large number of paintings identified as Shoei's work. His *shoheki-ga* in the main hall of the Juko-in are considered masterpieces. The task of painting these *shoheki-ga* was shared between Shoei and Eitoku. Shoei painted the ink *Landscape* (Fig. 3) in the Tonan-no-ma, the ink *Tiger and Leopard* and *Monkeys* (Fig. 2) in the Seihoku-no-ma (the above paintings are now in three different rooms), and the ink *Lotus, Herons, Duckweed, and Fish* on the small *fusuma* in front of the altar in the Butsudan-no-ma, the Buddhist Altar Room. These works were all painted in 1566, the year the Juko-in was founded, when Shoei was forty-seven years old. As might be expected from the style of *shoheki-ga* painted just before the Momoyama period, his work shows a strong decorative tendency. While it lacks the forceful brushwork and striking composition of Eitoku's style, Shoei's style has a definite flavor of its own. *Lotus, Herons, Duckweed, and Fish,* especially, has an inviting feeling.

EITOKU   Shoei's son and heir, Eitoku (1543–90), was the leading artist of the Momoyama period. He was laden with official honors as the greatest artist in the long history of the pros-

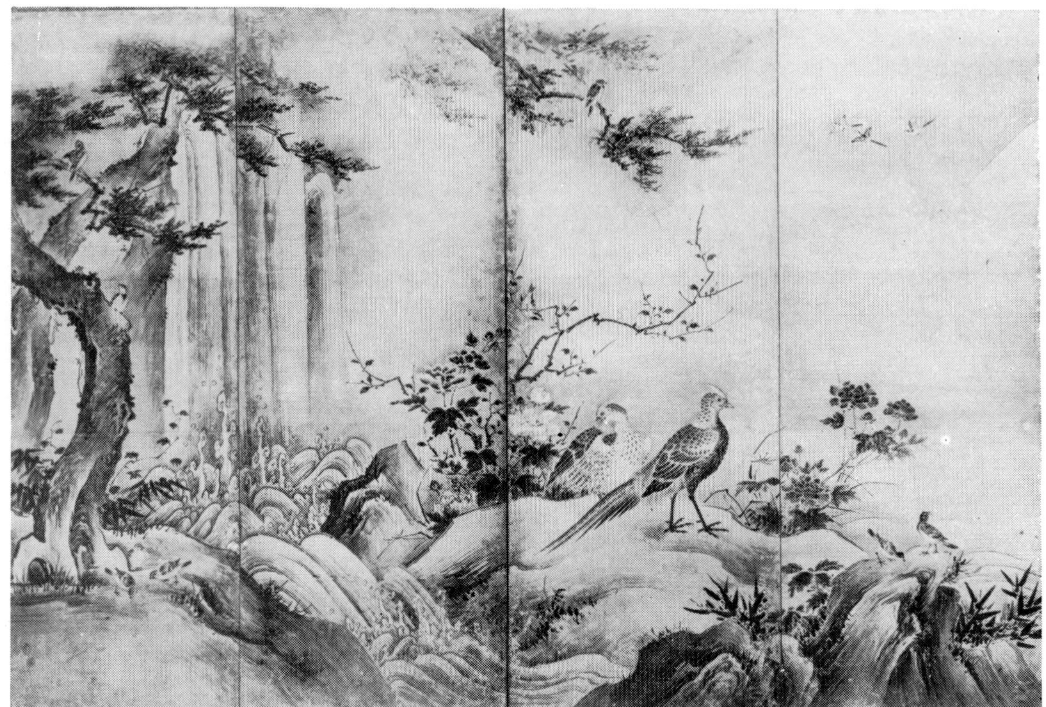

121. *Kano Shoei: detail from* Flowers and Birds. *One of a pair of sixfold screens, ink on paper; 159.5 × 352.5 cm. Late sixteenth century. Nagasaki Collection, Kochi Prefecture.*

perous Kano clan. Fortunately Eitoku, who displayed a talent for painting from an early age, received careful instruction from his grandfather, Motonobu, until he was sixteen years old. Kano Ikkei, the author of the *Tansei Jakuboku-shu,* wrote in his biography of Eitoku that his paintings were forceful, that the movement of his brush strokes was "beyond description," and that even in his youth he surpassed his father. According to the *Tokitsugu Kyo Ki,* a diary by Yamashina Tokitsugu, Eitoku directed one or two other artists of the Kano school in executing paintings in the mansion of the Konoe, an important court family, in 1567 and 1568, when he was twenty-four and twenty-five years old. This confirms the fact that he was already a successful artist by then. Later he enjoyed the favor of Nobunaga. When he executed the decorative paintings in Nobunaga's Azuchi Castle, his fame soared and he became the most popular

artist of the day. He was also patronized by Toyotomi Hideyoshi, who ruled Japan after Nobunaga's assassination in 1582. As Kano Eino wrote, the nobles and feudal lords of the time vied with one another to get Eitoku to paint *shoheki-ga* in their mansions.

Unfortunately, most of Eitoku's *shoheki-ga,* including his works in Azuchi Castle and those in the castles and mansions of nobles and feudal lords, have been destroyed. It is most regrettable that despite his fame so few of his works remain today. In his case, standard works are also rare. The Uesugi Collection's *Rakuchu Rakugai* (Fig. 126), a pair of folding screens said to have been presented to the feudal lord Uesugi Kenshin by Nobunaga in 1574, and the *Chinese Lions* folding screen (Fig. 127), certified by Kano Tan'yu to have been painted by Eitoku, are considered standard works. The former is a detailed painting showing considerable *yama-*

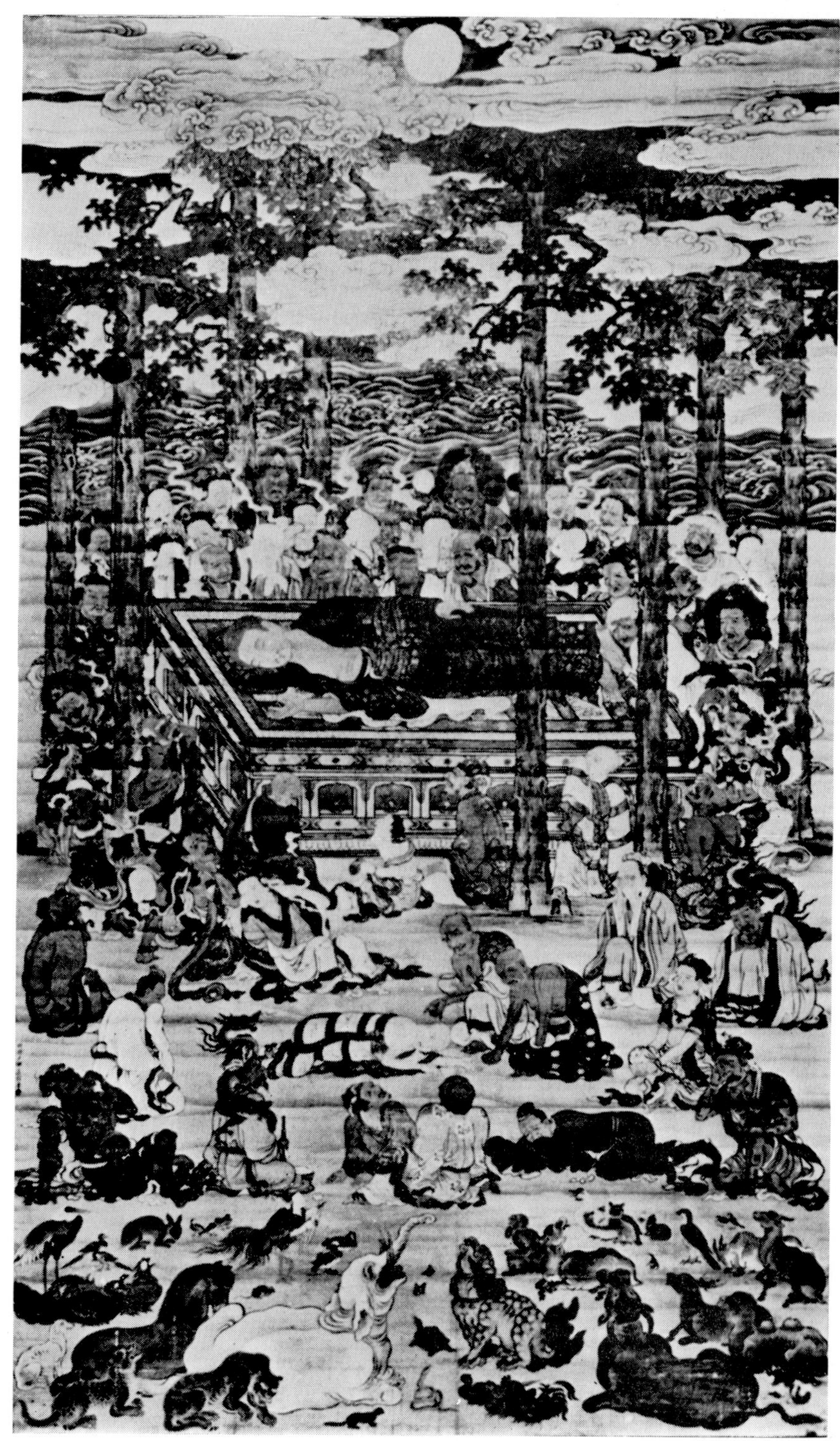

122. *Kano Shoei:* The Nirvana of the Buddha. *Hanging scroll, colors on paper; 588 × 348.5 cm. 1563. Daitoku-ji, Kyoto.*

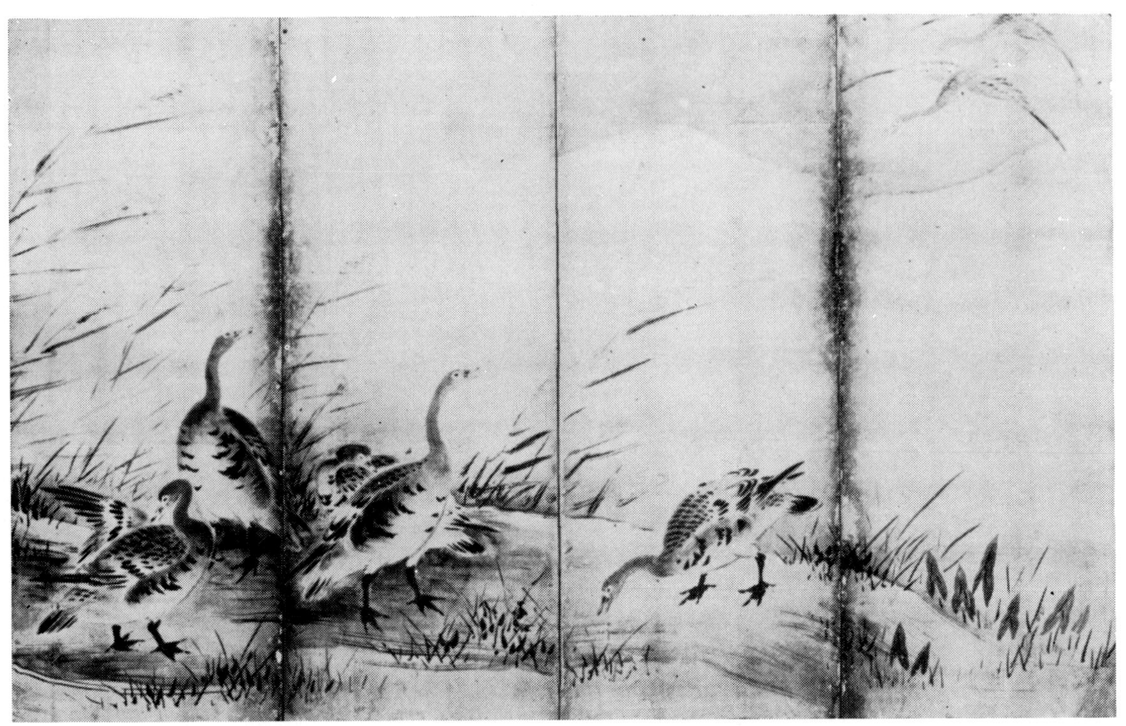

123 (above). Attributed to Kano Eitoku: detail from Wild Geese and Reeds. *One of a pair of sixfold screens (the other is* Pine Tree and Cranes), *ink on paper; 160 × 358.5 cm. Late sixteenth century. Wanaka Collection, Wakayama Prefecture.*

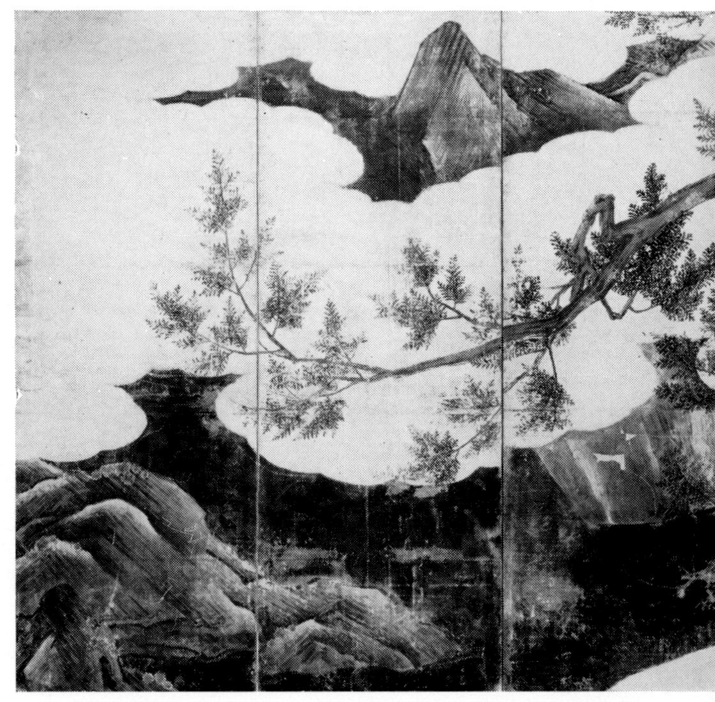

124. Attributed to Kano Eitoku: Japanese Cypress. *Eightfold screen, colors and gold on paper; 170 × 462.5 cm. Late sixteenth century. Tokyo National Museum.*

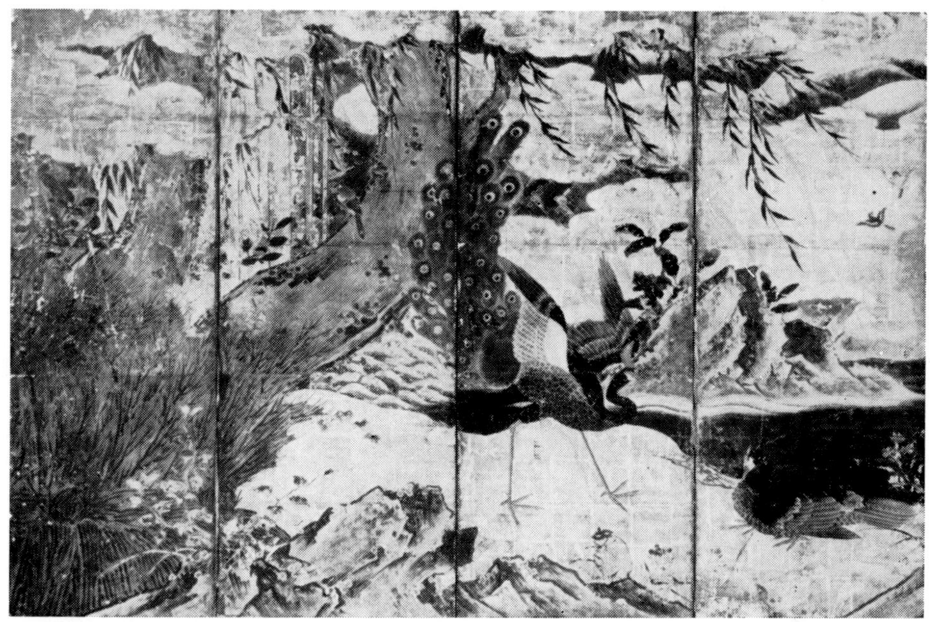

125. Kano Soshu: detail from Flowers and Birds. *One of a pair of sixfold screens, colors and gold on paper; 161 × 355.5 cm. Late sixteenth century. Taman Collection, Osaka.*

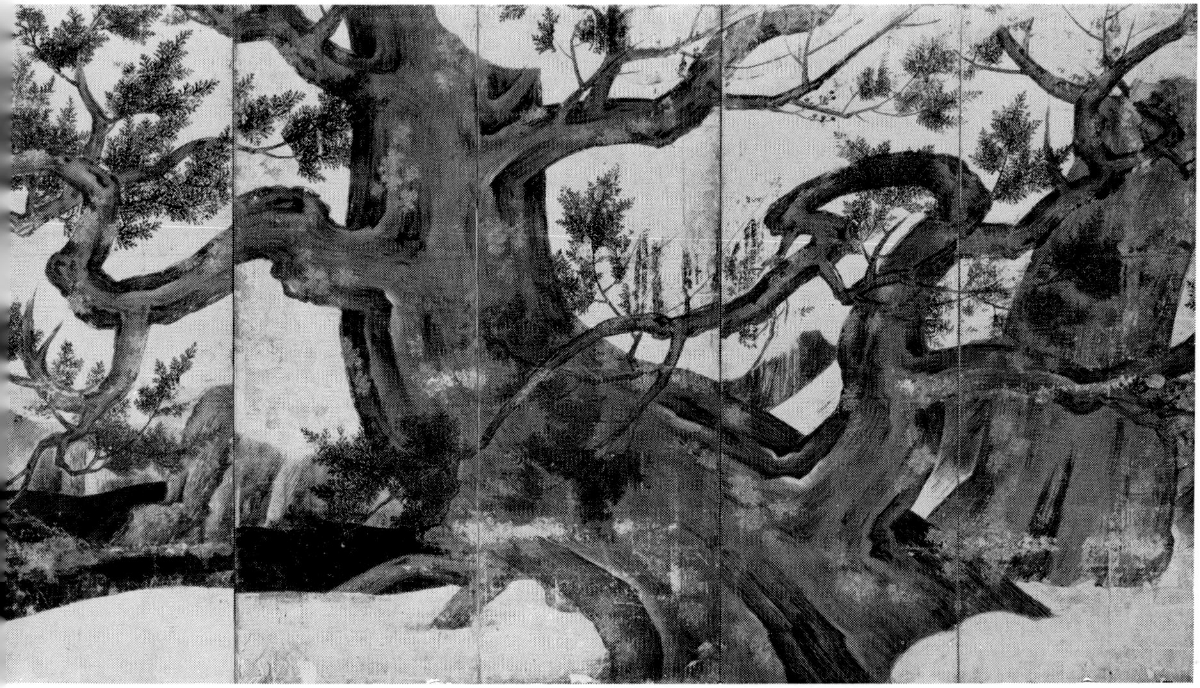

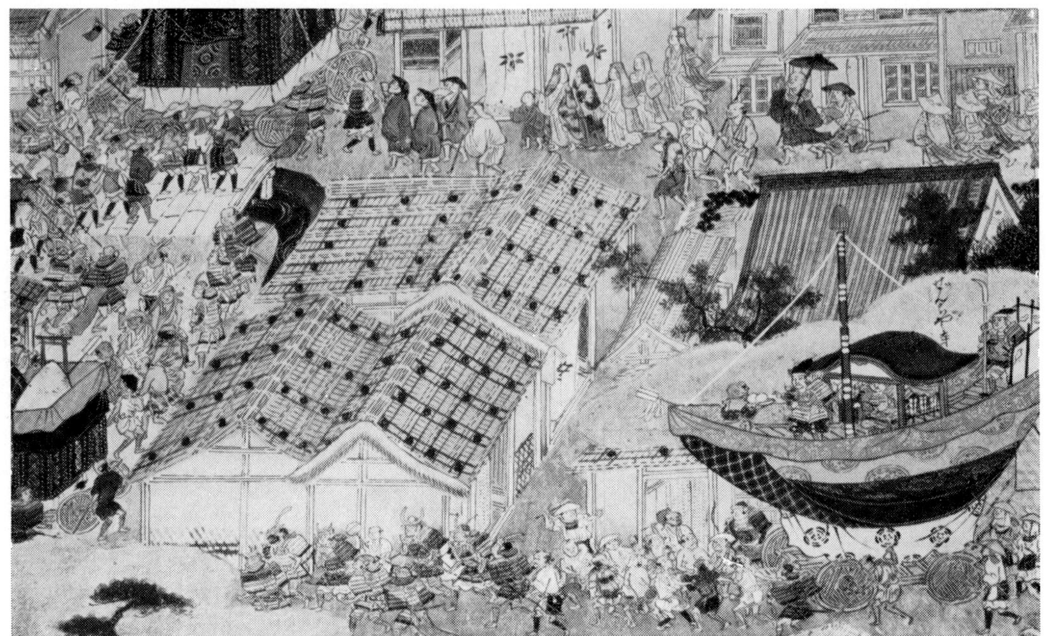

126. *Kano Eitoku: detail from* Rakuchu Rakugai *(Scenes In and Around Kyoto). One of a pair of sixfold screens, colors on paper; 159.5 × 363.5 cm. 1574. Uesugi Collection, Yamagata Prefecture.*

to-e influence, while the latter, a *kimpeki* painting showing clearly the bold, vigorous style of the early Momoyama period, is an indispensable standard work for the study of Eitoku's large-scale paintings. In addition, a pair of ink folding screens, *Pine Trees and Cranes* and *Wild Geese and Reeds* (Fig. 123), are useful reference sources. Yasunobu, a younger brother of Tan'yu, certified these paintings as works by Eitoku, so that they are useful at least for grasping what Yasunobu understood to be the characteristics of Eitoku's style.

EITOKU'S SHOHEKI-GA   As discussed in chapter four, there are numerous *shoheki-ga* attributed to Eitoku. However, of all these paintings, only the ink *Flowers and Birds* (Figs. 1, 12–14, 38, 39) and *Landscape and Figures* (Fig. 11), illustrating the traditional Chinese "four gentlemanly accomplishments" (calligraphy, painting, music, and chess), both in the main hall of the Juko-in, are generally acknowledged to have

been painted by him. An examination of these paintings in connection with Shoei's *fusuma* paintings in the Juko-in indicates that their traditional attribution to Eitoku is reliable; the paintings present no conflict with Yasunobu's concept of Eitoku's painting. The Juko-in works are believed to have been painted in 1566, when Eitoku was twenty-three years old, and are valuable as indications of the character of a gifted young artist.

Because *Flowers and Birds* and *Landscape and Figures* differ in subject, composition, and style, some may consider that they must be the work of different artists. Although *Flowers and Birds* features the close-up method of composition, *Landscape and Figures* is characterized by the panoramic landscape composition method. In addition, while *Landscape and Figures* is drawn precisely, with the shape of each object delineated clearly and in detail in dark ink, *Flowers and Birds* is drawn more boldly, objects depicted in a simplified form with broad, flowing brush strokes and using lighter shades of ink. These

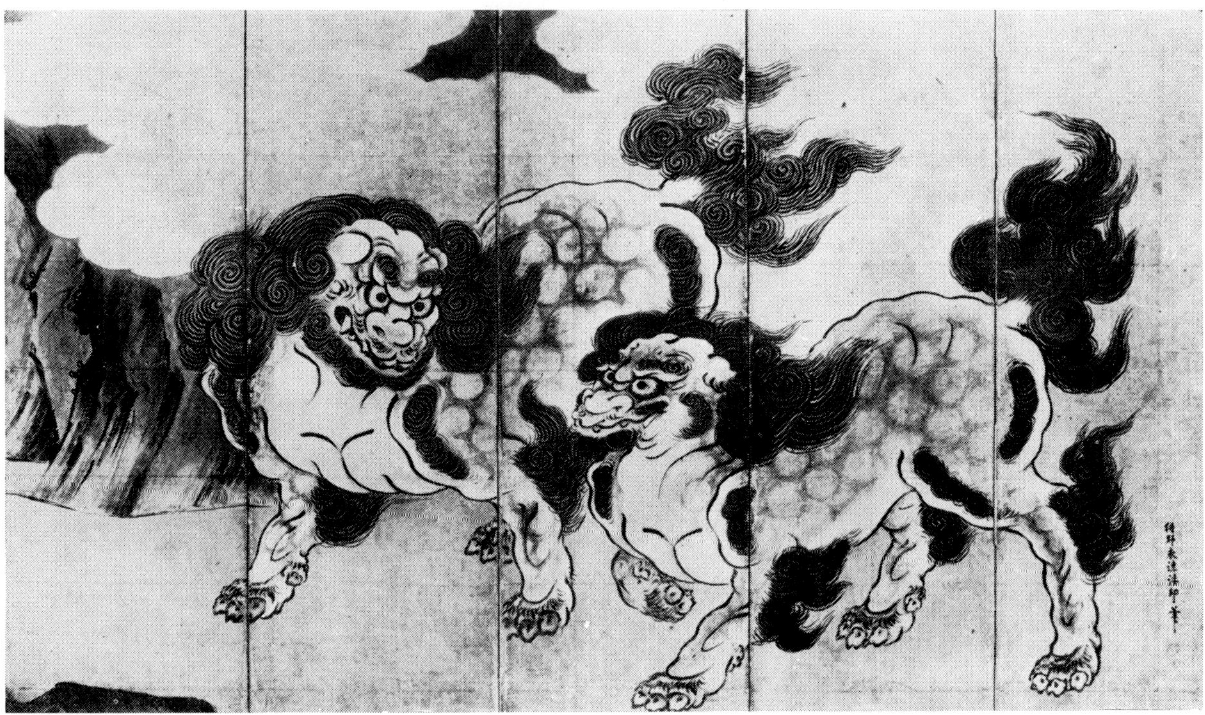

127. *Kano Eitoku: detail from* Chinese Lions. *Sixfold screen, colors and gold on paper; 225 × 459.5 cm. Late sixteenth century. Imperial Household Collection, Tokyo.*

differences in composition and style do, in fact, cause the two paintings to make quite different impressions on the viewer, but a common basic style can be seen clearly when the works are compared closely. For example, a comparison of the rocks in both paintings reveals that the sense of stability and weight seen in the conical arrangements of rocks is common to both works in spite of the difference in painting style (see foldout opposite this page). The free and forceful brush strokes rendering tree branches and other details in both paintings also show undisputably the touch of the same artist.

While both *Flowers and Birds* and *Landscape and Figures* can be regarded as works by Eitoku, it is the former that marks a new departure in composition. The unified method of composition, with its majestic feeling, became the typical composition method of Momoyama *shoheki-ga*.

EITOKU'S KIMPEKI PAINTINGS

Despite the large number of decorative *kimpeki*-style *shoheki-ga* painted by Eitoku following the construction of Azuchi Castle, none known to be definitely his work exist today. There are, however, a few surviving works that give at least a hint of the style of Eitoku's huge *kimpeki* paintings. One of the best is *Japanese Cypress* (Figs. 9, 124). Originally this was a *fusuma* painting in the household of Prince Katsura, but it has been remounted as an eightfold screen. It is painted in *kimpeki* style and features a unified composition centered on a huge Japanese cypress. The boldness and majesty of this work enable the viewer to imagine what Eitoku's paintings in the early Momoyama period must have been like.

Kano Eino states in his biography of Eitoku that Eitoku painted "landscapes, figures, and flowers and birds in detail," indicating that he painted

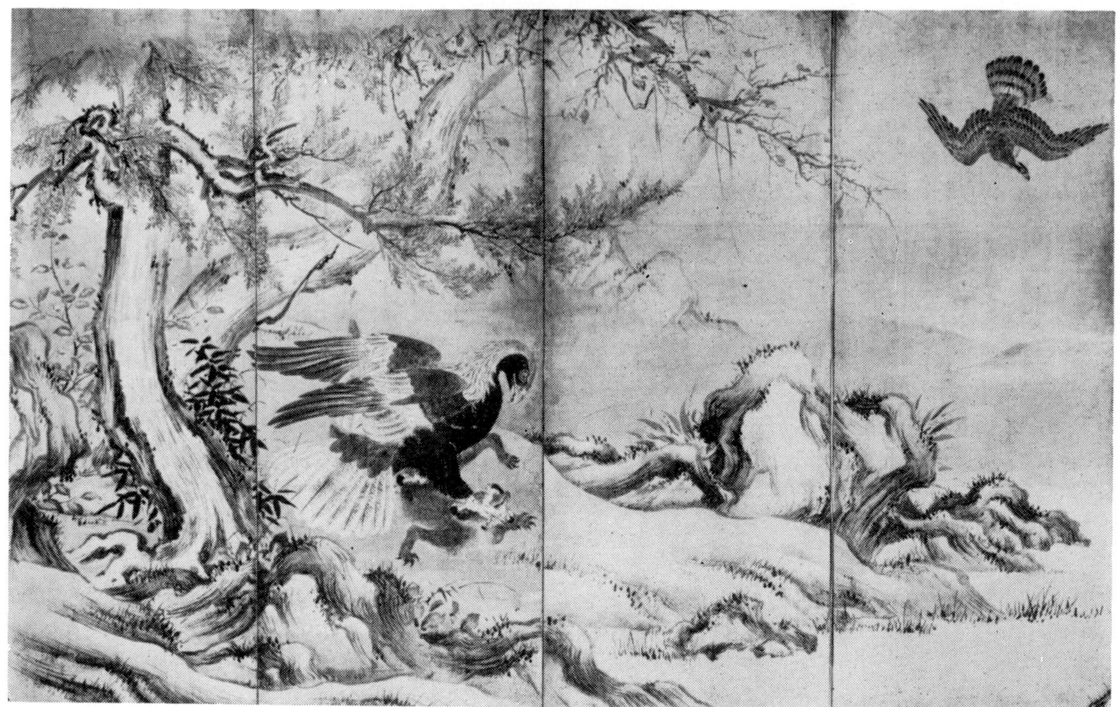

128. *Kano Sanraku: detail from* Birds of Prey. *One of a pair of sixfold screens, ink on paper; 152 × 354.5 cm. Early seventeenth century. Nishimura Collection, Shiga Prefecture.*

many pictures characterized by detailed delineation in addition to large-scale paintings with bold brush strokes and sweeping compositions. However, little progress has been made in research into Eitoku's detailed paintings. The *Rakuchu Rakugai* folding screens in the Uesugi Collection show the elaborate delineation that would allow them to be classified as detailed painting, and Eitoku may have painted *shoheki-ga* using the same technique. In this connection, some of the *shoheki-ga* in the *ohojo* (large *hojo*) of the Nanzen-ji in Kyoto merit study. The *ohojo* was an old building of the Kyoto Imperial Palace given to the temple in 1611. One opinion considers the building to have been originally the Seiryoden, while another view holds that it was the Nyoin Gosho, the palace of the emperor's mother; in any case, the interior of the *ohojo,* containing many *fusuma* paintings, is a treasure house for the study of Momoyama *shoheki-ga.* The poly-

chrome *Flowers and Birds* (Fig. 37), attributed to Kano Motonobu, has the oldest style; probably it was painted by one of Motonobu's talented pupils. It certainly was painted at least a generation before Eitoku's time, for it still shows the rigid and stiff use of the brush characteristic of the Muromachi period. The *kimpeki*-style *Twenty-four Paragons of Filial Piety* (Figs. 15, 40) and *Hermits and Noble Characters,* with their detailed delineation, present a problem. While the temple claims that they are by Eitoku, and while they clearly show his style in the strong brush strokes used to render clothing and in the facial expressions of the figures, more evidence must be presented and evaluated before they can be definitively authenticated. However, since the many *kimpeki* hermits and noble characters Eitoku painted in the donjon of Azuchi Castle no longer exist, these two paintings are important as works of the same type.

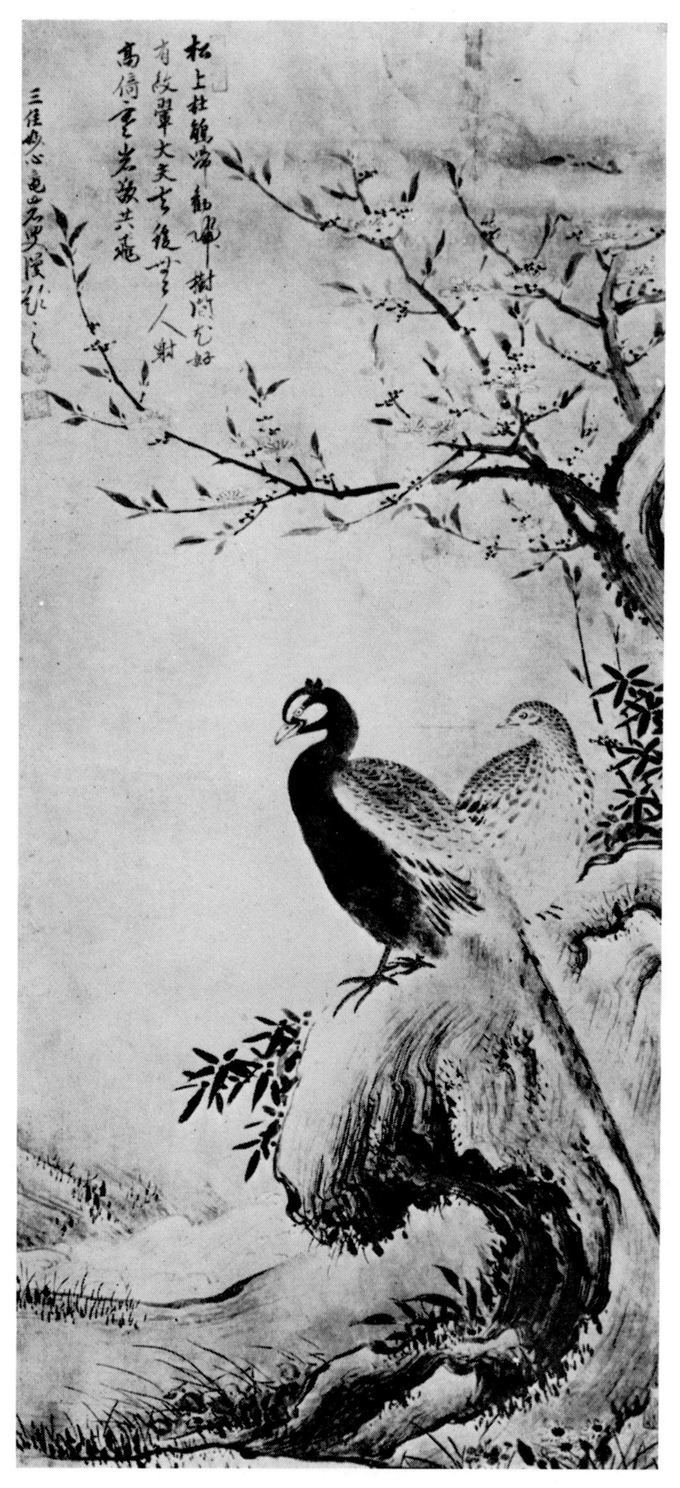

129. *Kano Sanraku:* Peach Blossoms and Pheasants. *Hanging scroll, ink on paper; 113 × 50.5 cm. Early seventeenth century. Formerly in the Moriwaki Collection, Shimane Prefecture.*

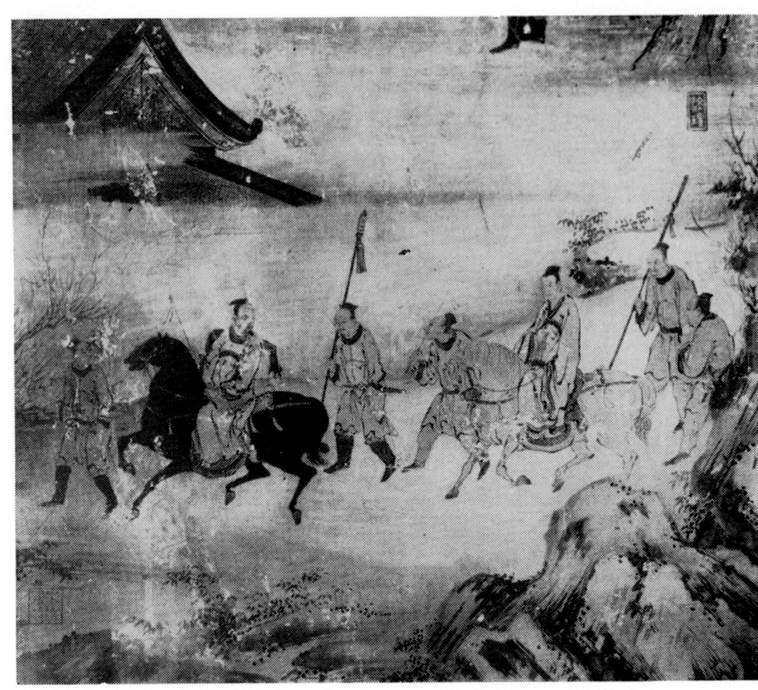

130. *Kano Sanraku: detail from* Teikan, *a scene from a Chinese illustrated book on things emperors should guard against. One of a pair of sixfold screens, ink on paper; 129.5 × 309 cm. Early seventeenth century. Formerly in the Nishida Collection, Toyama Prefecture.*

WORKS IN EITOKU'S STYLE   Among the numerous paintings attributed to Eitoku in temples in the Kyoto area, it is not unusual to find works that cannot be authenticated as being by him but were probably painted by artists who were greatly influenced by his work and followed his style. The *kimpeki*-style *Pine Trees and Mountain Birds* (Fig. 42) in the *genkan* (front entrance) of the Daikaku-ji and the *kimpeki* paintings centered on *Pine and Rocks* in the *genkan* of the Myoho-in are examples. The *kimpeki*-style *Flowers and Birds* (Fig. 41) in the *daishoin* (large *shoin*) of the Myoho-in must also have been painted by an artist associated with Eitoku. The composition is busier than Eitoku's and has a more sensuous beauty, suggesting a younger artist.

SOSHU   Soshu (1551–1601), a younger brother of Eitoku, is among the noteworthy artists surrounding Eitoku. According to the *Honcho Gashi*, "Soshu learned painting techniques prima-

rily from his brother Eitoku. He followed the rules carefully, but his skill did not match that of his father or older brother. He was given the title of *hogen* [a title awarded to artists, physicians, and others]." There are a number of problems connected with him and his works, especially those stamped with the seal reading "Genshu." According to the *Honcho Gashi*, both he and his son Jinnojo used this seal. So the question arises whether a painting stamped "Genshu" was painted by the father or the son. For various reasons, I would attribute to Soshu the *Portrait of Oda Nobunaga* owned by the Choko-ji, Aichi Prefecture; the *Ippen Shonin Emaki,* a picture scroll depicting the life of Saint Ippen, owned by the Komyo-ji, Yamagata City, Yamagata Prefecture; the framed painting *The Thirty-six Poets,* belonging to the Hokoku Shrine, Kyoto; the *kimpeki* folding screen *Flowers and Birds* (Fig. 125) belonging to the Taman Collection, Osaka; and the *Namban-ji* fan (*namban-ji,* "European temple," referred to a Christian

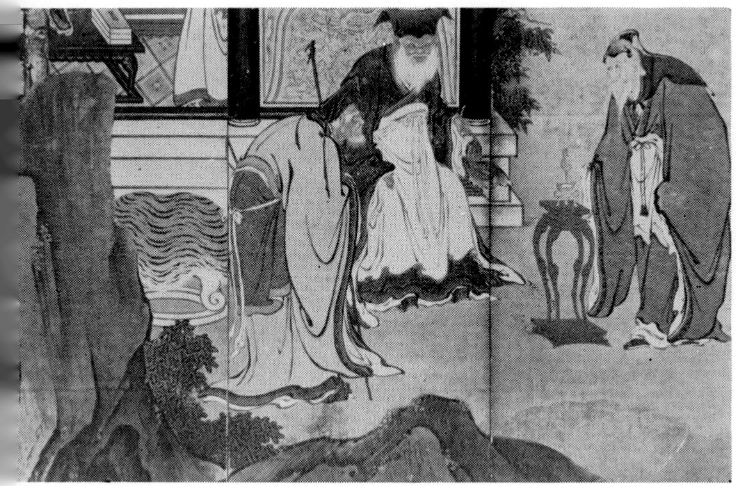

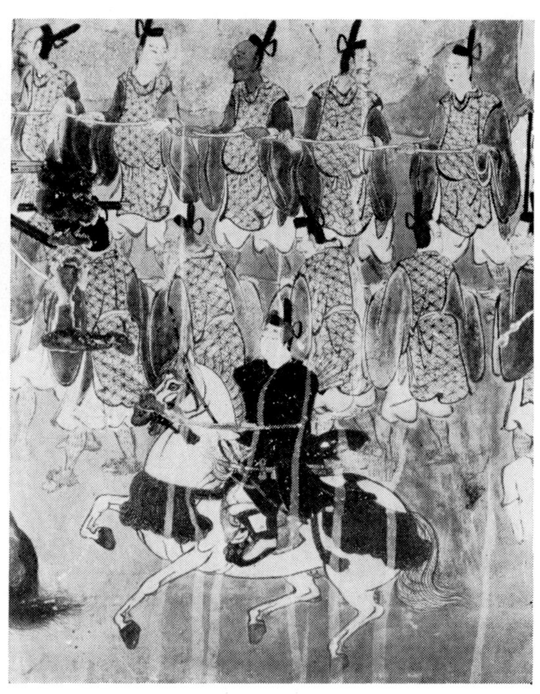

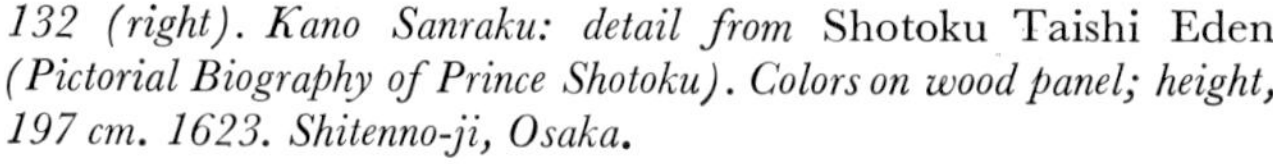

131 (above). *Kano Sanraku: detail from* Four Sages of Mount Shang. *One of a pair of sixfold screens, colors on paper; 177 × 362 cm. Early seventeenth century. Myoshin-ji, Kyoto.*

132 (right). *Kano Sanraku: detail from* Shotoku Taishi Eden (*Pictorial Biography of Prince Shotoku*). *Colors on wood panel; height, 197 cm. 1623. Shitenno-ji, Osaka.*

church) in the Kobe Art Museum. All bear the seal "Genshu." Because *Flowers and Birds* (Figs. 16, 43), a *kimpeki*-style *fusuma* painting in the Shinden of the Emman-in, Otsu City, attributed to Kano Eitoku, has a style similar to that of the *Flowers and Birds* folding screen in the Taman Collection, I believe the Emman-in work was also painted by Soshu. His paintings lack the magnificence of Eitoku's but are still filled with the splendor and vitality unique to the Momoyama period. Soshu's younger brother Kyuhaku, or Naganobu (1577–1654), is famous as a genre painter because of his folding screen *Merrymaking Under the Cherry Blossoms* in the Tokyo National Museum, but his achievements in *shoheki-ga* are unknown and await future study.

SANRAKU   After Eitoku's death his leading disciple, Sanraku (1559–1635), distinguished himself in the painting of *shoheki-ga*. Like Eitoku, Sanraku was favored by the Toyotomi clan, and he served as an artist of the clan until its collapse. After the fall of Osaka Castle, the Toyotomi stronghold, in 1615 and the death by suicide there of Hideyoshi's son Hideyori, Sanraku received the patronage of the victorious Tokugawa, who established a hereditary shogunate in Edo and ruled Japan for the next 253 years. Subsequent generations seem to have been more familiar with his name than that of his teacher, Eitoku. An amazing number of folding screens and *shoheki-ga* are attributed to Sanraku. However, when these are compared with his standard works, the number of paintings that can be firmly identified as his is not as great as claimed. Nevertheless, many more paintings by Sanraku than by Eitoku survive.

Sanraku's standard works include a pair of folding screens in ink, *Birds of Prey* (Fig. 128); a pair of folding screens in ink titled *Teikan,* depicting a scene from a Chinese illustrated book on things emperors should guard against; the ink hanging

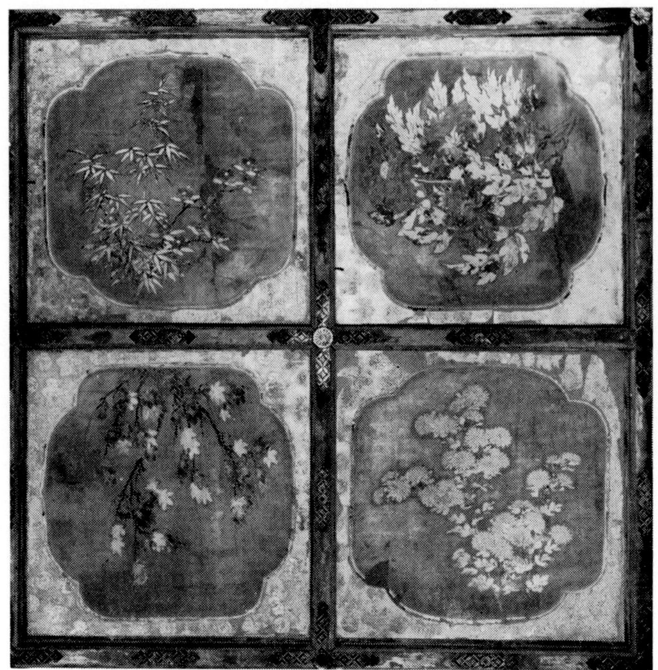

133. *Kano Mitsunobu:* Flowers and Trees. *Ceiling painting, colors. Early seventeenth century.* Honden, *Tsukubusuma Shrine, Shiga Prefecture.*

scroll *Peach Blossoms and Pheasants* (Fig. 129); and a few other hanging scrolls in ink. There are also several more folding screens considered to be his work. It is most interesting that three pairs of *kimpeki* screens belonging to the Myoshin-ji in Kyoto, *King Wen and Lu Shang* and *Four Sages of Mount Shang* (Fig. 131), *Yen Tzu-ling* and *The Three Laughers at Tiger Stream,* and *Dragon* and *Tiger,* which were formerly believed to have been painted by Kaiho Yusho, a master artist who was San-raku's contemporary, are now recognized as the work of Sanraku. *Shoheki-ga* that can be attributed to Sanraku include the following:

Peonies, colors and gold (Figs. 7, 44, 45); Dai-kaku-ji, Kyoto
Red Plum Blossoms, colors and gold (Figs. 46, 47); Daikaku-ji
Pine Tree and Hawk, ink (Fig. 17); Daikaku-ji
Landscape, ink (Fig. 20); Daikaku-ji
Landscape, ink and light colors (Figs. 19, 48); Shoden-ji, Kyoto

Chinese Lions, colors and gold (Figs. 22, 49); Yogen-in, Kyoto
Landscape, ink (Fig. 18); Daitsu-ji, Shiga Prefecture
Battle of the Carriages, colors (Fig. 21; remounted as a folding screen); Tokyo National Museum

The very best *shoheki-ga* are in the Shinden of the Daikaku-ji: *Peonies* (Figs. 7, 44, 45) and *Red Plum Blossoms* (Figs. 46, 47). These are among the best *kimpeki* paintings of the Momoyama period. I would like to add that a typical ink *shoheki-ga* of this period, *Pine Tree and Hawk* (Fig. 17), in the Shoshinden of the Daikaku-ji, shows an especially close relationship to one of the standard works, *Birds of Prey.* There is also a painting similar to the ink landscapes in the Daikaku-ji and the Daitsu-ji in the *shoin* of the Uraku-en in Inuyama, Aichi Prefecture. *Chinese Lions* (Figs. 22, 49) in the Yogen-in, depicting six Chinese lions, is mounted on wood panels in front of a Buddhist altar. These paintings had been eclipsed by the *shoheki-ga* of

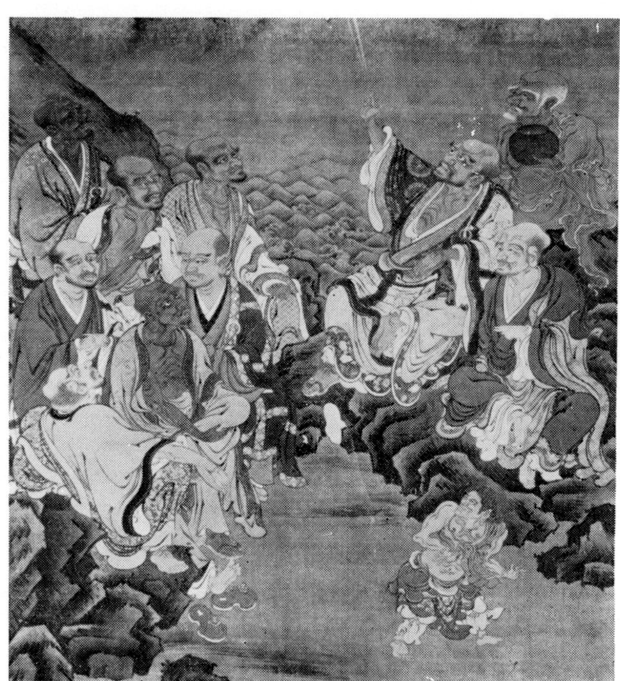

134. *Kano Takanobu: detail from* Five Hundred Arhats *(one of two paintings replacing* Five Hundred Arhats *by Mincho). Hanging scroll, colors on paper; 173 × 88.5 cm. Early seventeenth century. Tofuku-ji, Kyoto.*

Tawaraya Sotatsu (Figs. 119, 141), attracting relatively little attention. The *Shotoku Taishi Eden* (Pictorial Biography of Prince Shotoku; Fig. 132) painted on a wood panel and *Battle of the Carriages* (Fig. 21), an important *shoheki-ga* by Sanraku of a *yamato-e* subject, indicate the depth of his study of *yamato-e.*

MITSUNOBU As mentioned earlier, Kano Mitsunobu, Eitoku's heir, painted several unique *shoheki-ga* in the late Momoyama period. Unfortunately, in contrast to Sanraku, standard works by Mitsunobu are rare. Mitsunobu's works in the reception hall of the Kangaku-in, Onjo-ji, Otsu City (Figs. 8, 23, 98), and the painting in the *reioku* (a building, within the precincts of a Buddhist temple, enshrining the spirit of a dead person) in the Kodai-ji, Kyoto (Fig. 82), are therefore vital to the study of his *shoheki-ga.*

From the inscription written when repairs were made in 1799, we know that the *shoheki-ga* in the Kangaku-in reception hall were at that time at-tributed to Kano Mitsunobu. And we know from the *Kodai-ji Koki,* a record of the Kodai-ji written in about 1679, and the *Sanshu Meiseki Shi,* a compendium of famous places in Kyoto compiled by the Buddhist priest Byakue in 1702, that the Kodai-ji painting was also held to be by Mitsunobu. The attributions would seem to be fairly trustworthy, for these *shoheki-ga* have a number of common characteristics. Because the construction date for the Kangaku-in inscribed at the time of repairs matches the date of 1600 later found written in ink on another part of the building, the evidence of the 1799 inscription concerning the artist of the *shoheki-ga* is also believed to be reliable.

Therefore, although it is not possible to compare Mitsunobu's *shoheki-ga* with any standard works, we may reasonably treat his *shoheki-ga* in the Kangaku-in and the Kodai-ji as equivalent criteria. Some other extant *shoheki-ga* have the same style as these paintings and are also judged to be his work. These include the *kimpeki* flower-and-bird paintings (Figs. 24, 25, 85) in the *hojo* of the Honen-in,

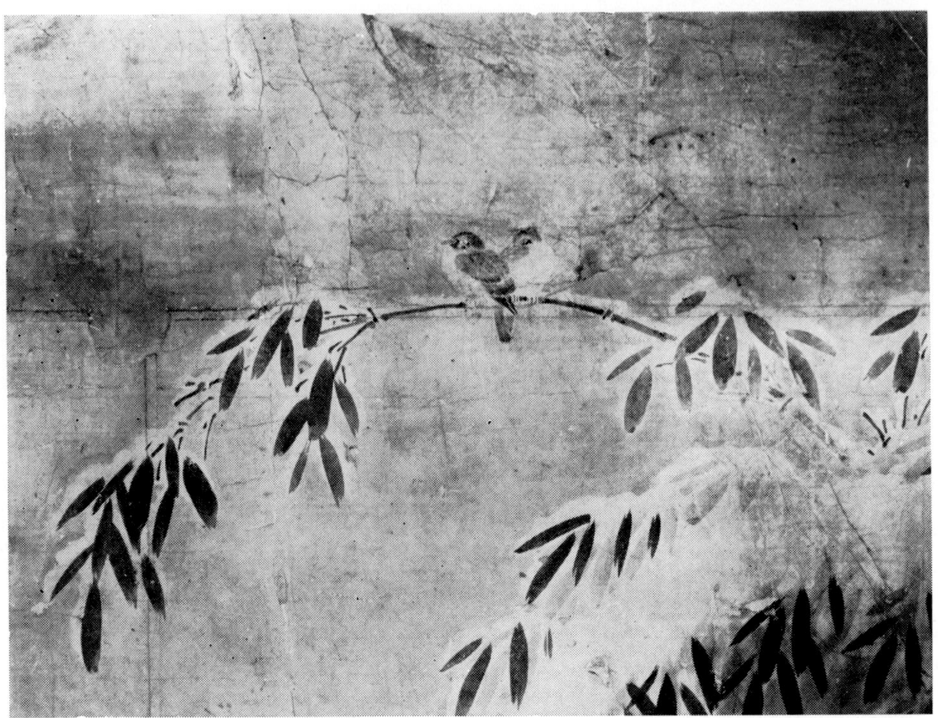

135. *Kano Koi: detail from* Bamboo and Sparrows in the Snow. *Ink and light colors on paper mounted on a wall. Early seventeenth century.* Shiroshoin, *Nijo Castle, Kyoto.*

Kyoto, a section of which has been made into a pair of twofold screens; the *kimpeki* painting *Hermits and Noble Characters* (Fig. 83) in the *daishoin* of the Myoho-in; the *kimpeki* painting *Flowers* (Fig. 84) in the *honden,* or main building, of the Tsukubusuma Shrine in Shiga Prefecture; and the ceiling painting *Flowers and Trees* (Fig. 133), also in the Tsukubusuma Shrine *honden.*

The paintings in the reception hall of the Kangaku-in include the *kimpeki*-style *Flowers and Birds* in the Ichi-no-ma, *Flowers and Birds* in colors in the Ni-no-ma, and *Peonies and Cat* and *Chinese Lions* in colors on cedar sliding doors in a hall. The *kimpeki* paintings in the Kodai-ji *reioku* include *Scattered Flowers and Birds* in the *gejin,* or outer chamber, and *Pine Trees by the Shore* (Fig. 82) in the *naijin,* or inner sanctum.

While Mitsunobu's *shoheki-ga* lack the overwhelming grandeur and power of the works of his father, Eitoku, they have a fresh realism and a quiet, inviting mood unique to Mitsunobu. With his refined and elegant style, he stands out among the painters of the Momoyama period. In his commentary on Mitsunobu in the *Honcho Gashi,* Kano Eino remarks, "The soft and light air of the *yamato-e* flowers and birds painted [by Mitsunobu] is enchanting." This seems a just evaluation.

TAKANOBU AND
SADANOBU

Kano Takanobu (d. 1618), a younger brother of Mitsunobu, executed important works on commission for the imperial household. In 1612 he painted the *Kenjo Shoji* (Fig. 87), a *shoji* painting depicting Chinese sages, in the Kyoto

136. *Hasegawa Tohaku:* Landscape. Fusuma, *ink on paper; 183.5 × 121 cm. 1589. Hojo, Entoku-in, Kyoto.*

144 · WORKS OF THE KANO SCHOOL

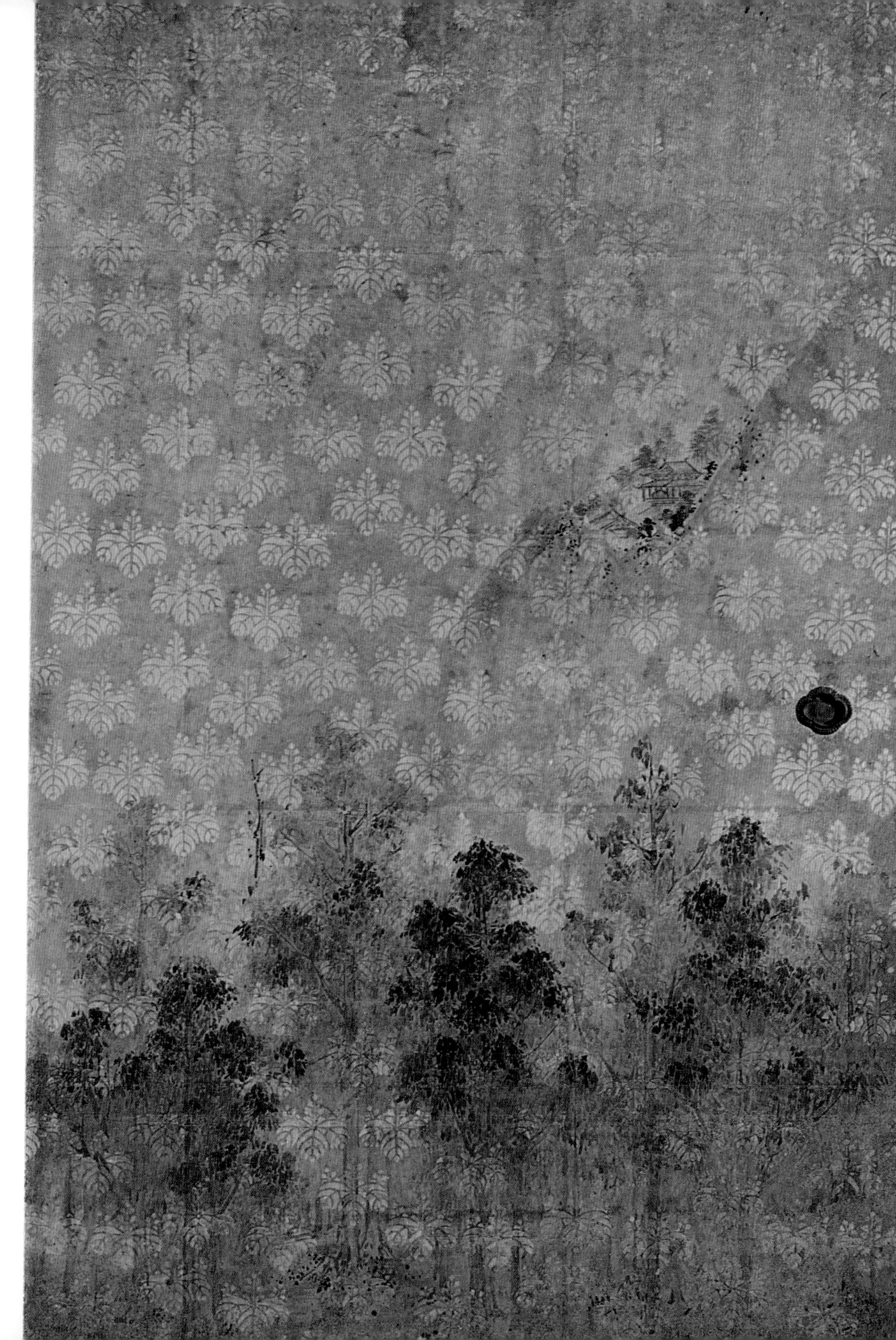

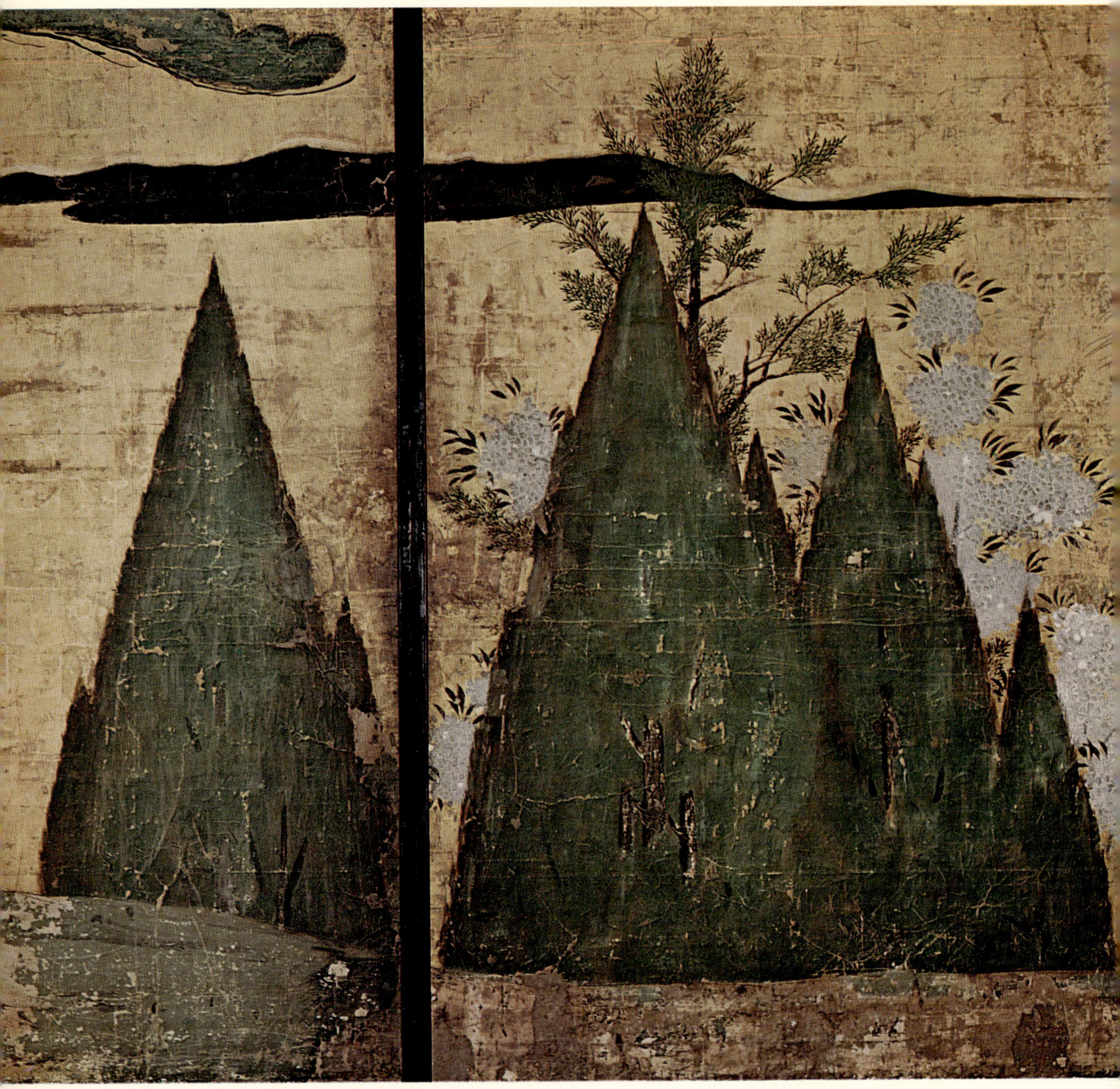

137. Attributed to Hasegawa Tohaku: Pines and Cedars. Fusuma, *colors and gold on paper; 184 × 143 cm. Early seventeenth* century. Shoin, *Myoren-ji, Kyoto.*

138. Attributed to Hasegawa Tohaku: Pine Tree and Cherry Blossoms. Fusuma, *colors* ▷ *and gold on paper; 184 × 142.5 cm. Early seventeenth century.* Shoin, *Myoren-in, Kyoto.*

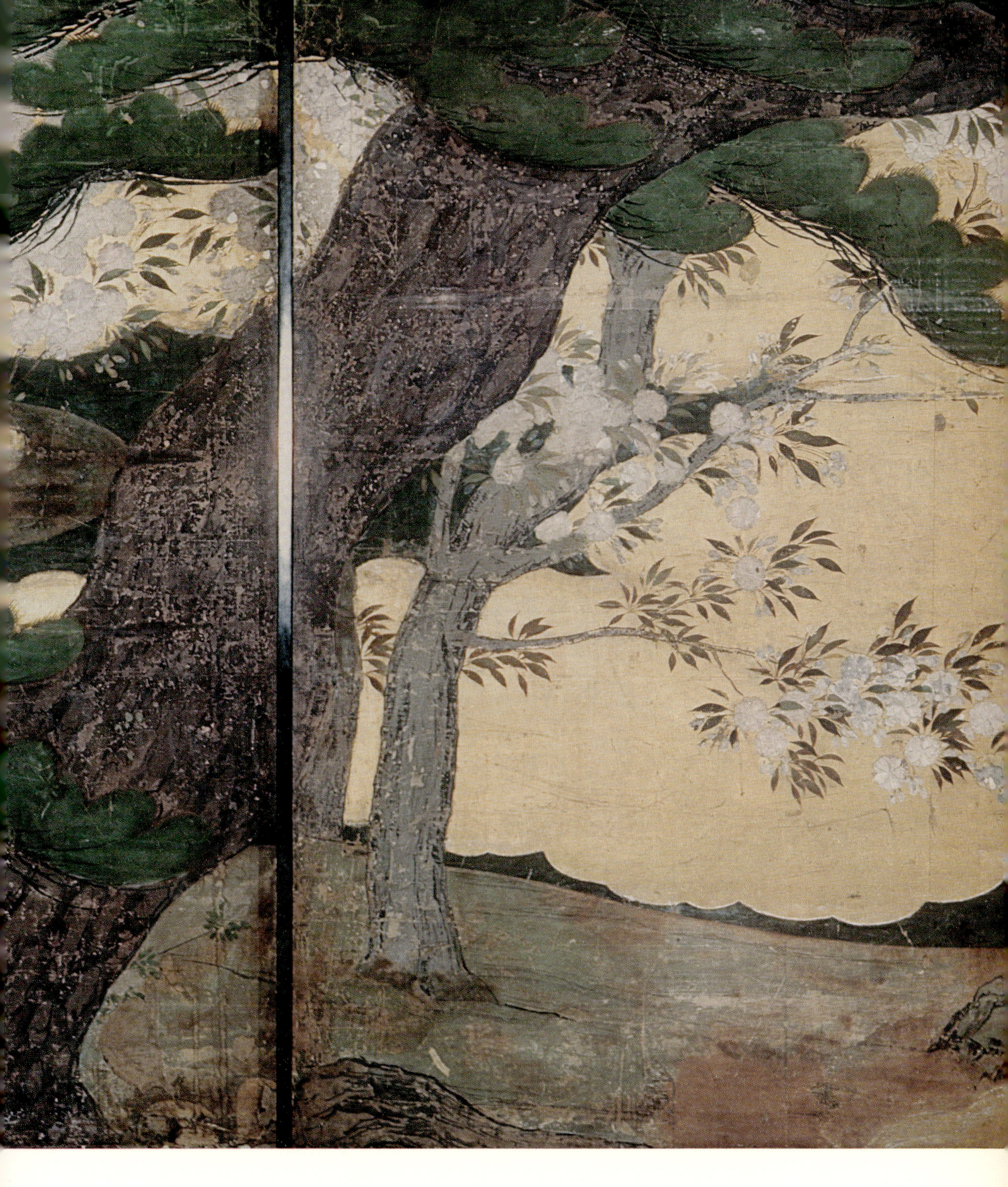

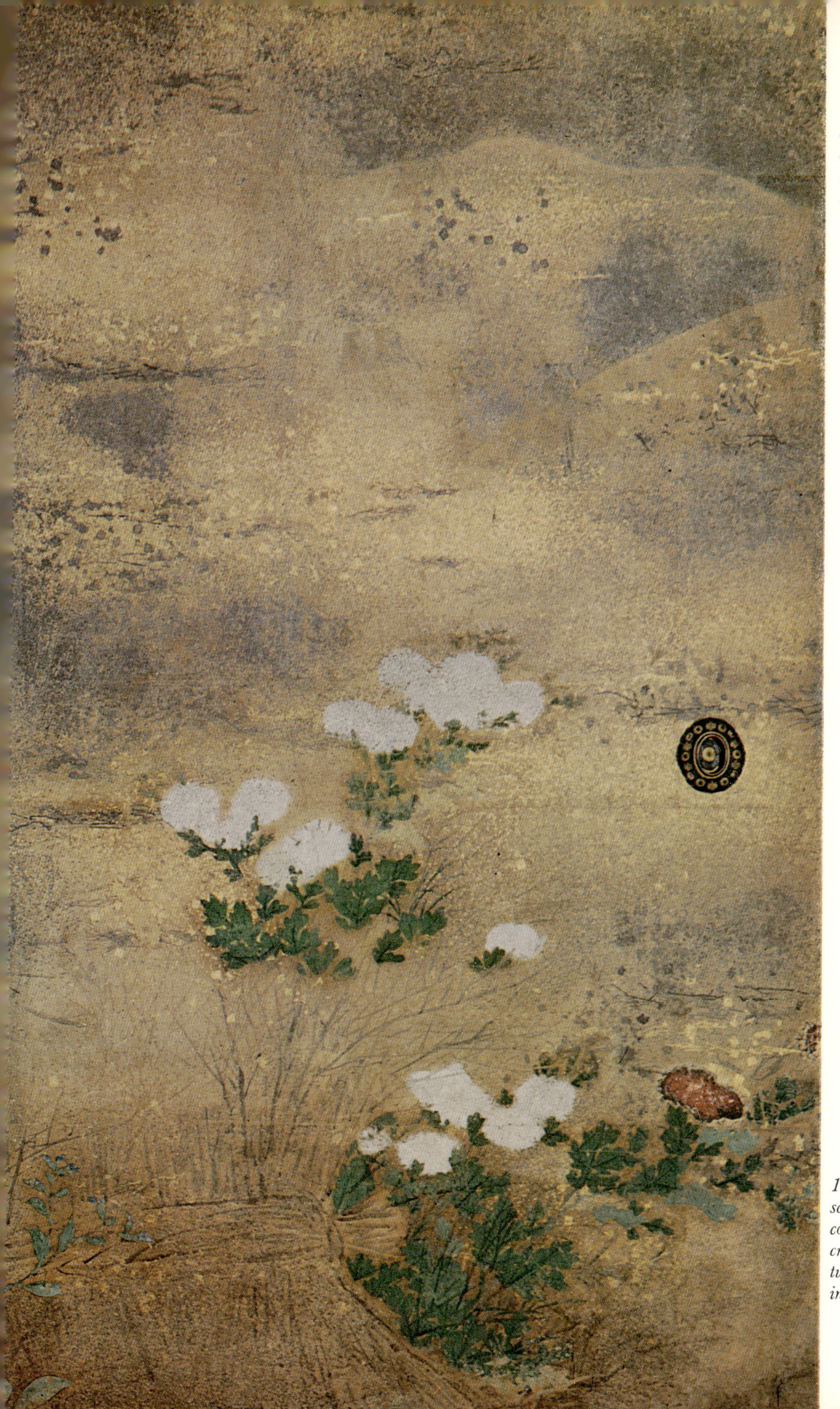

139. *Hasegawa school:* Autumn Flowers. Fusuma, *colors on paper; 176 × 117 cm. Early seventeenth century. Akigusa-no-ma, Sambo-in, Daigo-ji, Kyoto.*

140 *(overleaf). Hasegawa* ▷ *school:* Willow. Fusuma, *colors on paper; 179 × 142 cm. Early seventeenth century.* Omoteshoin, *Sambo-in, Daigo-ji, Kyoto.*

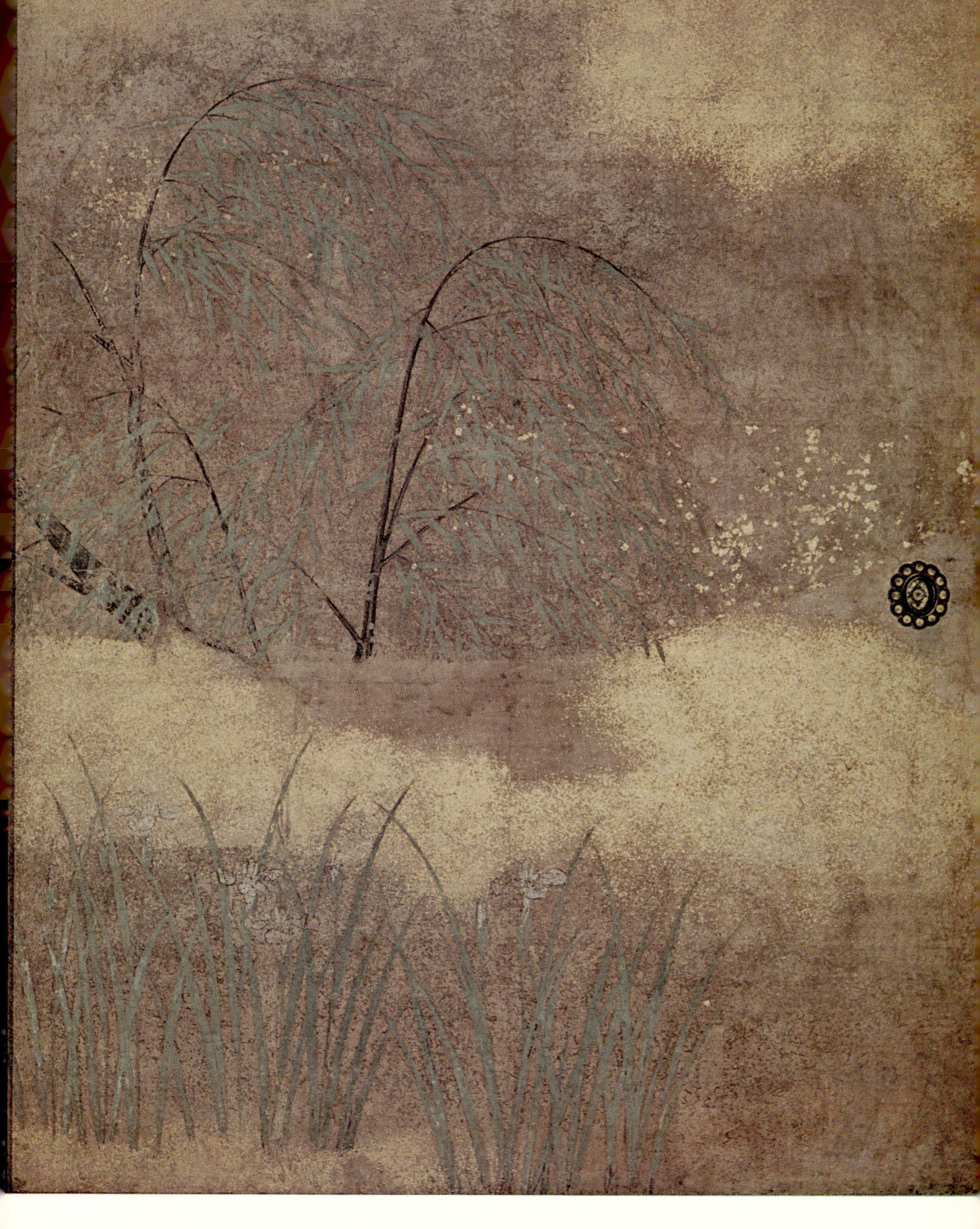

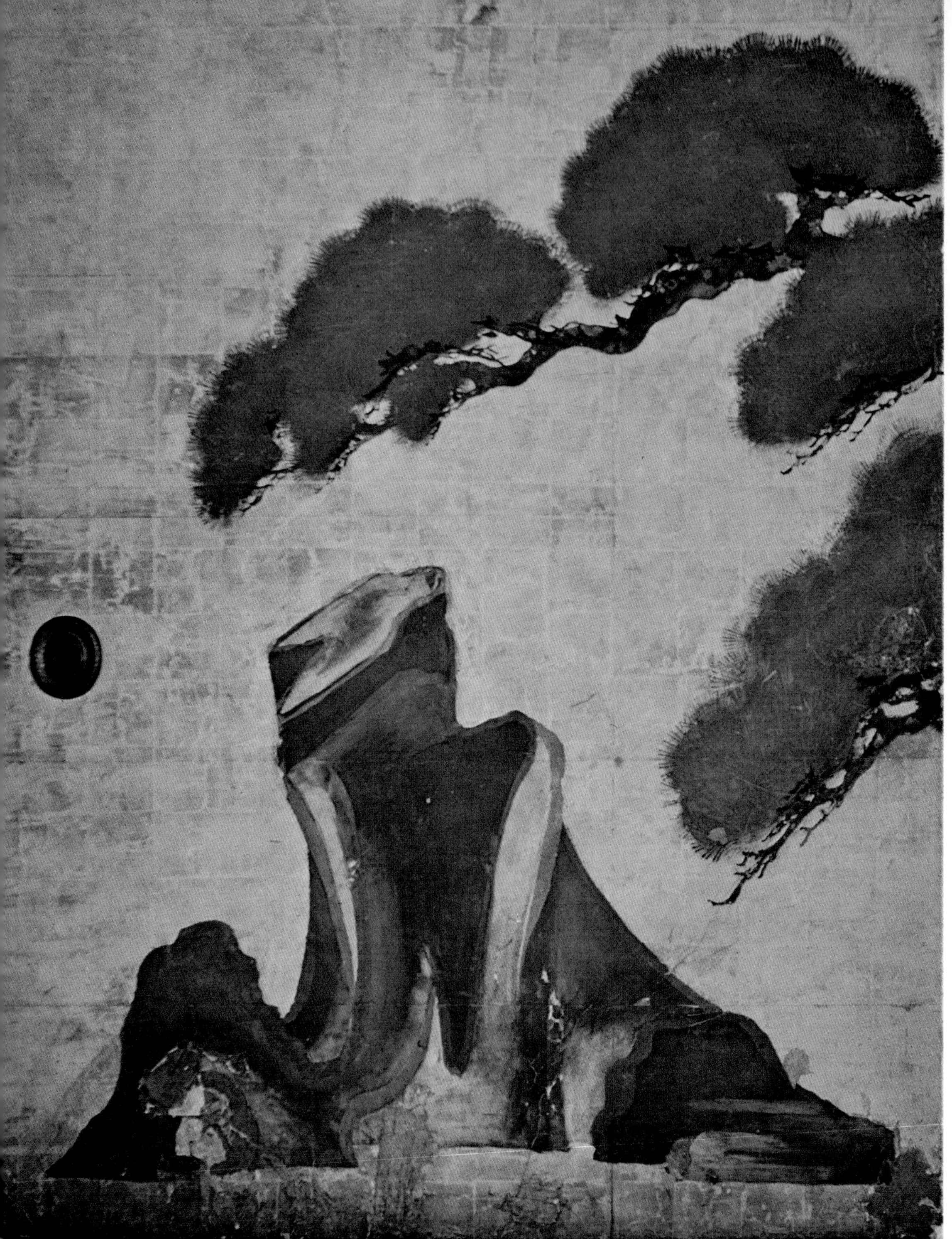

141. *Tawaraya Sotatsu:* Pine Tree and Rock. Fusuma, *colors and gold on paper; 184 × 141 cm. 1621.* Hondo, Yogen-in, Kyoto.

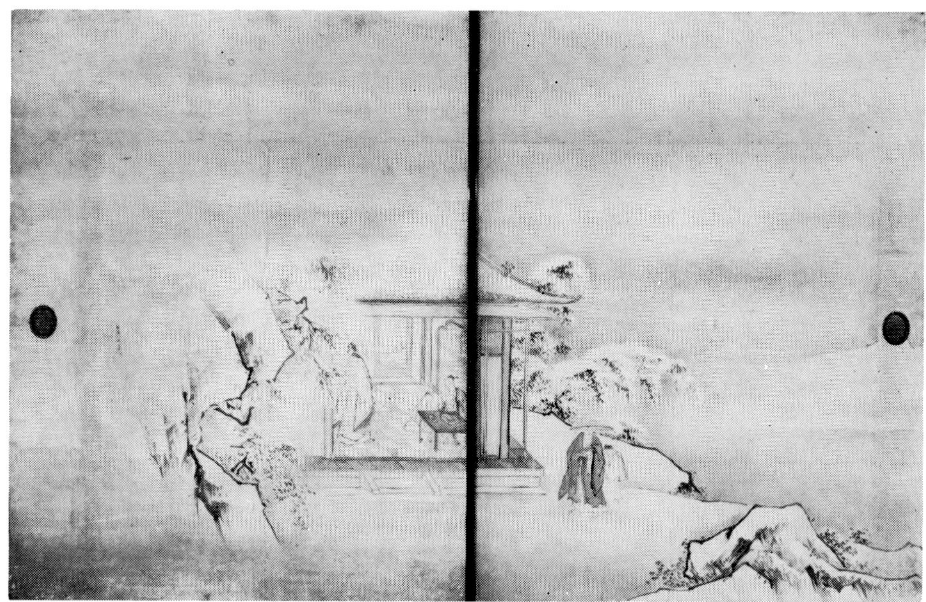

142. Kano Tan'yu: Landscape and Figures, *illustrating the four gentlemanly accomplishments.* Fusuma, *ink on paper; 187×140 cm. Early seventeenth century.* Shoin, Rinshunkaku, Sankei-en, Yokohama.

Imperial Palace. Early in the Edo period the painting was given to the Ninna-ji in Kyoto, where it remains today. The technique of drawing facial features and the use of strong shading in the *Kenjo Shoji* are characteristics also seen in his other paintings, such as the *Portrait of Emperor Goyozei,* owned by the Sennyu-ji, Kyoto. For some time I had maintained that there was a strong possibility that the *Kenjo Shoji* was the work of Takanobu, and recently this has been confirmed by documentary evidence (see *Kyoto Gosho* [The Kyoto Imperial Palace] by Michio Fujioka). No other *shoheki-ga* by Takanobu have been identified, but I believe that more of his works may be discovered in the future.

It is not surprising that hardly any paintings by Mitsunobu's son Sadanobu (1597–1623) remain today, because he died when only twenty-six. According to the genealogy of the Kano family listed in the *Koga Biko,* a dictionary of painters compiled in the Kaei era (1848–54), Sadanobu executed paintings in Nagoya Castle. Consequently, the existing *shoheki-ga* from Nagoya Castle should be ex-

amined with Sadanobu in mind, but because no standard works survive, they cannot be definitely confirmed as his work. Recently, however, attribution to Sadanobu of the *kimpeki*-style *shoheki-ga* formerly in the Shinden of the Emman-in in Otsu City (Figs. 26, 27, 86) has been suggested (see *Kyoto Gosho*). Other works by Sadanobu may eventually come to light.

KOI AND RYOKEI   Kano Koi (d. 1636), one of the ablest pupils of Mitsunobu, is well known as the teacher of Takanobu's three sons, Tan'yu, Naonobu, and Yasunobu. Extant paintings by Koi include *shoheki-ga* in the *shiroshoin* of the Ni-no-maru compound of Nijo Castle in Kyoto (Figs. 28, 135) and in the *hojo* of the Toji-in in Kyoto (Fig. 29). Some of the *shoheki-ga* in the Chion-in in Kyoto and in Nagoya Castle are also attributed to him, but these have not been definitely confirmed. Most of the *shoheki-ga* in the Nijo Castle *shiroshoin* are landscapes painted in ink and light colors. They include *Bamboo and Sparrows in the Snow* in ink and light colors and *Japanese Bush*

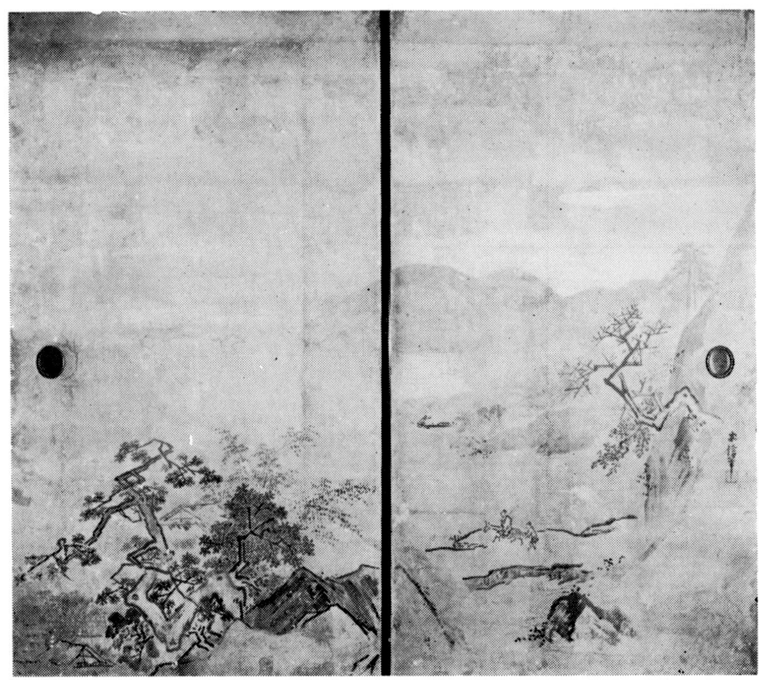

143. Kano Yasunobu: Landscape. Fusuma, *ink on paper; 170 × 92 cm. Early seventeenth century.* Shoin, *Rinshunkaku, Sankei-en, Yokohama.*

Clover by a Brushwood Fence in *kimpeki* style. All Koi's works are painted in a clean and elegant style allied to the style of Mitsunobu. Koi's painting in the *hojo* of the Toji-in, *Cattle in a Pasture* (Fig. 29), was originally in the Kaifuku-in, Myoshin-ji. Before World War II it was one of several *fusuma* paintings, along with *Chinese Children at Play, Landscape, Twenty-four Paragons of Filial Piety,* and *Autumn Flowers.* Perhaps because they had badly deteriorated, many of them were removed after the war; it is unfortunate that they no longer retain their original format.

Watanabe Ryokei (d. 1645), also a pupil of Mitsunobu and a contemporary of Koi, went unnoticed for a long time because he was eclipsed by his more famous fellow pupil. However, his works have gradually become better known in recent years, and it has been discovered that a surprisingly large number of his *shoheki-ga* are extant. The most important, all *kimpeki* paintings, are in the reception hall (Fig. 111), *shiroshoin* (Fig. 30),

Kiku-no-ma, and Gan-no-ma (Fig. 31) of the Nishi Hongan-ji in Kyoto. He also painted *shoheki-ga* in the Taizo-in of the Myoshin-ji (Fig. 32), the Daiho-in of the same temple, and the Shiga-in, Otsu City. It is highly probable that Ryokei also executed the *kimpeki* painting in the *hojo* of the Fumon-in, To-fuku-ji, Kyoto (Fig. 113). The painting in the *shoin* of the Daian-ji, Sakai (Fig. 112; mostly *kimpeki*), is the work of a Kano-school artist of the early Edo period, probably one who was closely associated with Ryokei.

TAN'YU, NAONOBU, AND YASUNOBU

The leading artists of the Kano school in the early Edo period, Tan'yu (1602–74), Naonobu (1607–50), and Yasunobu (1613–85), painted many *shoheki-ga.* Of the three, Tan'yu's achievements are the most remarkable, and more of his works have survived than in the case of the other two. The *shoheki-ga* in the *kohojo* (small *hojo*) of the Nanzen-ji in Kyoto, well known

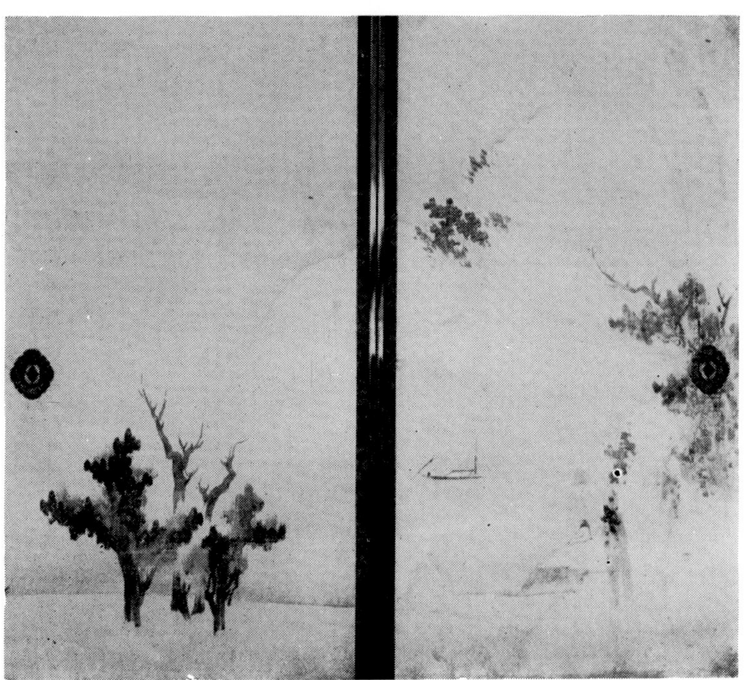

144. Kano Sansetsu: Landscape. Fusuma, ink on paper; 164 × 86.5 cm. Early seventeenth century. Shoin, Izumi-no-bo, Kyoto Prefecture.

as *Tiger and Bamboo* or *Tiger Drinking* (Fig. 118), is painted in a style even more decorative than usual for the Momoyama period, while attempting detailed delineation of the tiger. The *Landscape* in the Daitoku-ji *hombo* (main temple) *hojo* and *Dragon and Tiger* and *Landscape* (Fig. 34) in the reception hall of the Shojuraigo-ji in Otsu City are representative of Tan'yu's free-and-easy ink-painting style. Of the many other extant *shoheki-ga* by Tan'yu, those in the Jorakuden of Nagoya Castle (Fig. 33) are important works. *Landscape and Figures* (Fig. 142), illustrating the four gentlemanly accomplishments, and *Flowers and Birds* in ink on *fusuma* in the *shoin* of the Rinshunkaku in the Sankei-en, Yokohama, are *shoheki-ga* in the Kanto area worth seeing.

Perhaps because he died relatively young, there are not as many *shoheki-ga* by Naonobu as by Tan'yu. *Four Sages of Mount Shang* and *The Seven Sages of the Bamboo Grove* (Fig. 35), both painted in ink in the reception hall of the Shojuraigo-ji,

are authenticated representative works. Because its style is similar, *The Seven Sages of the Bamboo Grove* in ink in the *nakashoin* (middle *shoin*) of the Katsura Detached Palace, Kyoto, should also be considered Naonobu's work. Yasunobu was a much less skillful artist than either Tan'yu or Naonobu. Though none of his paintings is considered a masterpiece, the ink *Landscape* (Fig. 143) in the *shoin* of the Rinshunkaku, Sankei-en, is one of his best works.

SANSETSU   Sansetsu (1590–1651), the heir of Sanraku, was a distinctive Kano-school artist of the early Edo period. He developed Sanraku's style into one more decorative and charming, creating unique paintings in both ink and *kimpeki* style. The *kimpeki*-style *Flowers and Birds* (Figs. 50, 114), *Tiger and Bamboo,* and *Morning-glories and Clematis* (Figs. 51, 116) in the *hojo* of the Tenkyu-in, Myoshin-ji, are generally thought of as works by Sanraku, but it is reasonable to attribute them to Sansetsu along with the ink painting

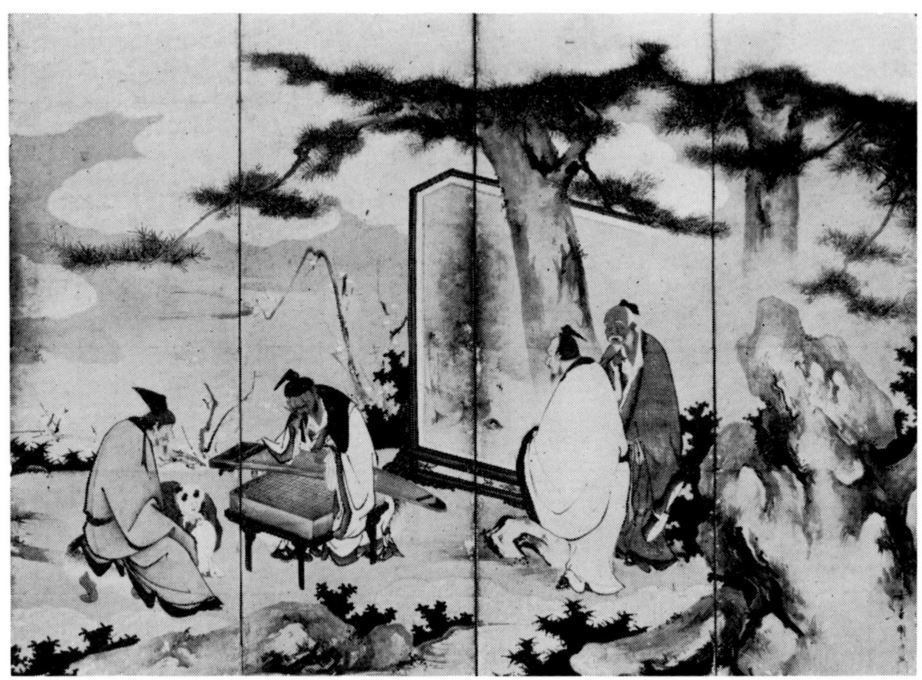

145. *Kaiho Yusho: detail from* Landscape and Figures, *illustrating the four gentlemanly accomplishments. One of a pair of sixfold screens, colors on paper; 177 × 364 cm. Late sixteenth century. Myoshin-ji, Kyoto.*

Landscape and Figures (Fig. 36) in the Seihoku-no-ma of the same *hojo.* Though some declare these *kimpeki* paintings to be the work of Sanraku in his later years, I disagree, for there are distinct differences in the painting of Sanraku and Sansetsu. Among Sansetsu's works are *Landscape* (Fig. 54) in ink in the *shoin* of the Jinno-ji, Yawata-cho, Kyoto Prefecture; *Tiger and Bamboo* and other paintings in colors on cedar sliding doors of the same *shoin;* the ink *Landscape* (Fig. 144) in the *shoin* of the Izumi-no-bo temple, also in Yawata-cho; *Flowers and Birds* (Fig. 117) in colors on cedar sliding doors in the *shoin* of the Myoki-an, Kyoto Prefecture; *Two Doves in an Old Tree* (Figs. 52, 115) in the *shoin* of the Ganzanken, Daitsu-ji, Shiga Prefecture; and *Landscape* (Fig. 53) in the *shoin* of the Daitsu-ji. In addition, there is the ink *fusuma* painting *Landscape and Figures,* with no signature or seal, in the *shoin* of the Uraku-en in Inuyama. These ink paintings show a style unique to Sansetsu.

OTHER WORKS OF THE KANO SCHOOL

The artists of many of the extant Momoyama *shoheki-ga* are unknown. Among these works, Kano-school paintings are most numerous. The paintings in the *hondo* and the Kanrantei of the Zuigan-ji in Matsushima, Miyagi Prefecture, are good examples. The *hondo,* built in 1609 by Datè Masamune, the powerful feudal lord who controlled the area including Matsushima, contains many *shoheki-ga* and paintings on sliding cedar doors. Some of these were painted by artists of the Hasegawa school, but there are also works of the Kano school. The highly decorative *kimpeki* paintings in the Kujaku-no-ma (Fig. 88) and the Taka-no-ma are by the same unknown artist of the Kano school, probably the artist who painted *Chinese Black Pine and Japanese Cypress* in the *shoin* of the Kanrantei. A comparison of the way the rocks are delineated in both paintings strengthens this impression.

CHAPTER SEVEN

Works of Other Schools

KAIHO SCHOOL There were many *kanga* schools besides the Kano in the Momoyama period. Among these was the Kaiho school, founded by Kaiho Yusho (1533–1615). Although Yusho was born into a prestigious warrior family, he wanted to become an artist and studied under Kano Motonobu. Later he founded his own school, leaving a major imprint on Japanese art history. His unique style, with its warrior-like forcefulness, is marked by strong individuality. Many of Yusho's paintings have survived, adding luster to the memory of his long life of eighty-two years. In fact, there are so many paintings by him that even his standard works, those that are clearly signed or stamped with his seal, are almost too numerous to list. Three pairs of folding screens owned by the Myoshin-ji are considered representative works: *Landscape and Figures* (Fig. 145), illustrating the four gentlemanly accomplishments; *San Suan* and *Han Shan and Shih Te;* and *Peonies* (Fig. 146) and *Plum Blossoms.* A general survey of Yusho's works reveals ink paintings to be the most numerous, but he also painted in the *kimpeki* style. His paintings vary widely in subject.

The Myoshin-ji used to have many *shoheki-ga* by Yusho, but now the Kennin-ji has the largest collection, with works found in the temple's *hombo hojo,* Zenkyo-an, Reito-in, and Daichu-in.

Though Yusho had contacts with Kokan Jikei and Baisen Toho of the Kennin-ji, it is thought that the reason this temple owns an especially large number of his paintings is his close friendship with the priest Ekei of the Ankoku-ji in Hiroshima Prefecture, who aided so much in rebuilding Kennin-ji following its devastation during the hundred years of civil strife preceding the Momoyama period. The *hombo hojo* of the Kennin-ji was transported from Ankoku-ji by Ekei in 1599. Its interior *shoheki-ga* were heavily damaged by a severe storm in 1934. Since then, these *shoheki-ga* have been remade into hanging scrolls and placed in the care of the Kyoto National Museum. The paintings include *Landscape* (Fig. 55), *Landscape and Figures* (Fig. 56), *The Seven Sages of the Bamboo Grove* (Fig. 57), *Flowers and Birds* (Fig. 58), and *Dragon in Clouds* (Fig. 59). All are ink paintings except *Landscape and Figures,* which is painted in ink and light colors. If these were painted in 1599, Yusho was then sixty-six years old. They are truly powerful works in which one senses the magnanimity befitting a master artist of the Momoyama period.

One of Yusho's strengths was painting clouds and dragons. Their tremendous forcefulness overwhelms the viewer. The detail from *Flowers and Birds* showing a pine tree and peacocks conveys a majestic feeling, while *The Seven Sages of the Bamboo Grove,* executed in the *fukuro jimbutsu* method and painted with simple delineation, is filled with grandeur. *Landscape and Figures* shows traces of the Kano school in the brush strokes, eloquently reminding us that Yusho studied under Kano Motonobu. Along with these paintings from the *hombo hojo,*

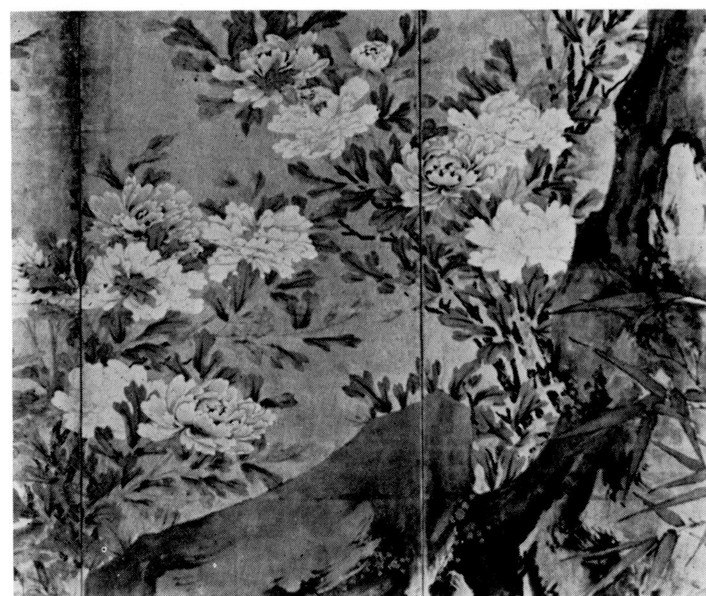

146. *Kaiho Yusho: detail from* Peonies. *One of a pair of sixfold screens (the other is* Plum Blossoms*), colors and gold on paper; 177 × 362 cm. Late sixteenth century. Myoshin-ji, Kyoto.*

147 (opposite page, left). Attributed to Hasegawa ▷
Toin: detail from Sixteen Arhats. Colors on cedar
door. Early seventeenth century. Hondo, Zuigan-ji,
Matsushima, Miyagi Prefecture.

148 (opposite page, right). Hasegawa Tohaku: ▷
detail from Sixteen Arhats. One of a pair of sixfold screens, colors on paper. 1609. Chishaku-in,
Kyoto.

Yusho's paintings in the *shoin* of the Zenkyo-an, Kennin-ji, clearly show the characteristics of his mature style. These are ink paintings of pine trees (Figs. 61–63), bamboo, and a plum tree (Fig. 60). The clean use of ink and vigorous brushwork illustrate features peculiar to this artist. The picture of a huge pine tree with birds sleeping in it is an outstanding masterpiece of ink painting.

Judging from their style, the *shoheki-ga* in the Reito-in and Daichu-in were painted earlier than the *fusuma* paintings in the *hombo hojo* and the Zenkyo-an, before Yusho reached his mature period. The *shoheki-ga* in the Reito-in are *Noble Characters* (Fig. 67) in ink, *Flowers and Landscape,* and *Flowers and Birds* (Figs. 10, 64) in colors. *Noble Characters* features a drunken Li Po, the great Chinese poet of the T'ang dynasty, as its central figure. The *fukuro jimbutsu* method of figure painting is also seen here. *Flowers and Birds,* the most outstanding *shoheki-ga* in the Reito-in, has a clean, elegant beauty, with superb harmony between the ink and colored portions.

Yusho's *shoheki-ga* in the *shoin* of the Daichu-in include *Landscape* (Fig. 68) in ink and light colors and *Heron and Reeds* (Figs. 65, 66) in ink. *Landscape* contains more detail than his later paintings, yet on careful observation his characteristic brush strokes and way of applying ink are apparent. *Heron and Reeds* has a clean and simple feeling, showing another aspect of his style.

Yusetsu (1598–1677), who was active as the central figure of the Kaiho school in the early Edo period, was much influenced by the Kano school. Although he painted a number of *shoheki-ga,* few survive. The only ones known are *Dragon in Clouds* (Fig. 69) and *Landscape* in the Rinsho-in, Myoshin-ji. The former is especially good.

HASEGAWA SCHOOL   The Hasegawa school, another *kanga* school of the Momoyama period, made surprisingly colorful contributions in the area of *shoheki-ga.* The achievements of Tohaku (1539–1610), the founder, are especially noteworthy. Tohaku is said to have been hostile to the Kano school, the predominant force in the artistic world at that time. Tohaku the artist

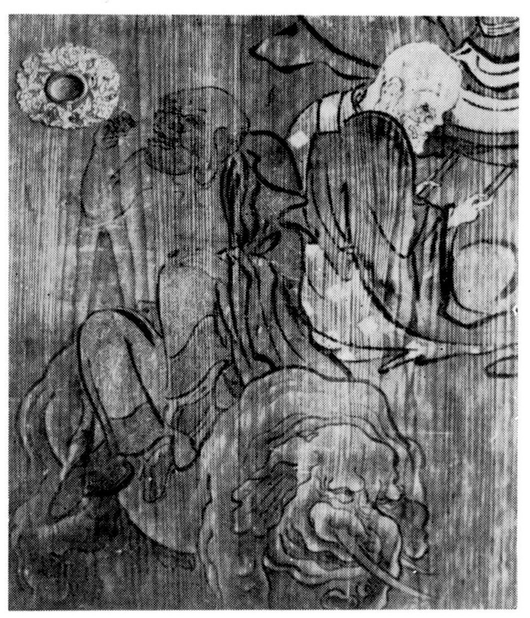
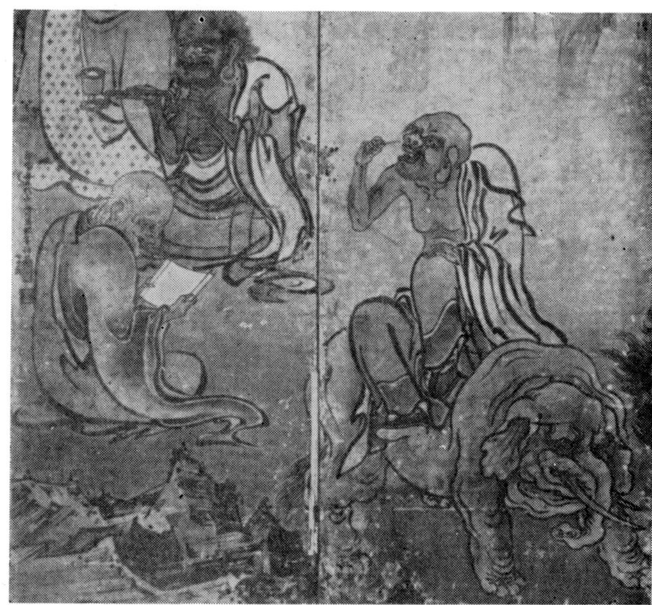

resembled a man out of office; he was unusual, and his art clearly showed his individuality. Recently it was learned that he was known as Shinshun in his youth. As Shinshun he used to be identified with his son Kyuzo, but now it is clear that Shinshun was not another name for Kyuzo but was Tohaku himself as a youth.

As with Kaiho Yusho, his contemporary, there are many confirmed standard works by Tohaku. The Tokyo National Museum's folding screen *Pine Trees* (Fig. 149), one of his standard works, is recognized as one of the finest ink paintings of the Momoyama period. *Monkeys in an Old Tree* (Fig. 150), ink paintings owned by the Ryosen-an, Myoshin-ji; the folding screens *Monkeys* and *The Seven Sages of the Bamboo Grove,* also in ink and owned by the Shokoku-ji; and a huge scroll owned by the Hompo-ji, *The Nirvana of the Buddha,* are also among his standard works. Tohaku's extant *shoheki-ga* exceed those of Yusho in number. Most are in the Kyoto area, and none have been found in the area of Nanao on the Noto Peninsula, where he spent his youth. Except for one *kimpeki*-style

painting in the Chishaku-in, most of Tohaku's representative *shoheki-ga* were painted either in ink or in ink and light colors. His ink *shoheki-ga* include the Entoku-in *Landscape* (Figs. 81, 136); the *Landscape* in the Rinka-in, Myoshin-ji; *Four Sages of Mount Shang* and *Hsien Tzu and Chu T'ou* (Figs. 71, 72) in the Shinju-an, Daitoku-ji; *Four Sages of Mount Shang, Zen Patriarchs* (Fig. 70), and *Pine Tree and Cranes* in the Tenju-an, Nanzen-ji; and *Old Pine Tree* and *Monkey Trying to Catch the Reflection of the Moon* (Figs. 77, 78) in the Konchi-in, Nanzen-ji. Recently, his *Four Beloved Flowers* (Figs. 73–76) was discovered in the Uraku-en, Inuyama. The dates when these *shoheki-ga* were painted, their subjects, and their styles vary, but a refreshing and forceful style characteristic of Tohaku's painting is common to all of them, indicating his versatility in painting landscapes, figures, animals, and other subjects.

Tohaku's early works, painted while he was known as Shinshun, show that he was also gifted in polychrome painting. Therefore it is believed that he painted a considerable number of *kimpeki-*

style *shoheki-ga*. It is known that until the great fire of Temmei (1788), his *kimpeki*-style *fusuma* paintings *Paulownia and Phoenix, Cherry Blossoms,* and *Pine Tree and Bamboo* were in the Hompo-ji, Kyoto. The only *kimpeki*-style *shoheki-ga* by Tohaku remaining today are those in the Chishaku-in, which are recognized as among the best *kimpeki* paintings of the Momoyama period.

The *shoheki-ga* in the Chishaku-in originally belonged to the Shoun-ji, which was built by Toyotomi Hideyoshi in memory of his beloved son Sutegimi, who died in early childhood. During the Meiji (1868–1912) and Taisho (1912–26) eras, these *shoheki-ga* were attributed to Kano Eitoku and Sanraku, but now they are recognized as works of the school led by Tohaku. The only exception is the *kimpeki* painting *Pine Tree and Plum Blossoms,* which has been remade into a twofold screen. This is believed to be a work of the Kano school. All the Chishaku-in *shoheki-ga* are paintings of flowers, flowering grasses, and trees in the *kimpeki* style, unquestionably representing the style of the Momoyama period, gorgeous yet fresh and vigorous. The Shoun-ji is thought to have been built in 1591–92. The style of these *shoheki-ga* presents no conflict with this date, for they are typical of the works of that time.

As mentioned earlier, it is recognized that these *shoheki-ga* were painted by the Hasegawa school, but there are varying opinions on the attributions of the individual paintings. I choose to divide the paintings roughly into two groups, one attributed to Tohaku and the other to Kyuzo. Tohaku's works center on the famous *Maple Tree* (Figs. 6, 79) and *Pine Tree and Flowers* (Fig. 4; this has been made into a pair of twofold screens); Kyuzo's paintings center on *Cherry Tree* (Figs. 5, 90, 91), which is as well known as *Maple Tree,* and *Pine Tree and Flowering Grasses* in the tokonoma of the large *shoin*. Tohaku's works are opulent, with a bracing and magnanimous air, while Kyuzo's are somewhat more delicate, conveying a sense of fresh elegance. Even as a youth, when he was called Shinshun, Tohaku had a special talent for painting in color, and he gave full play to this ability in painting *Maple Tree* and the other *shoheki-ga* around it. In

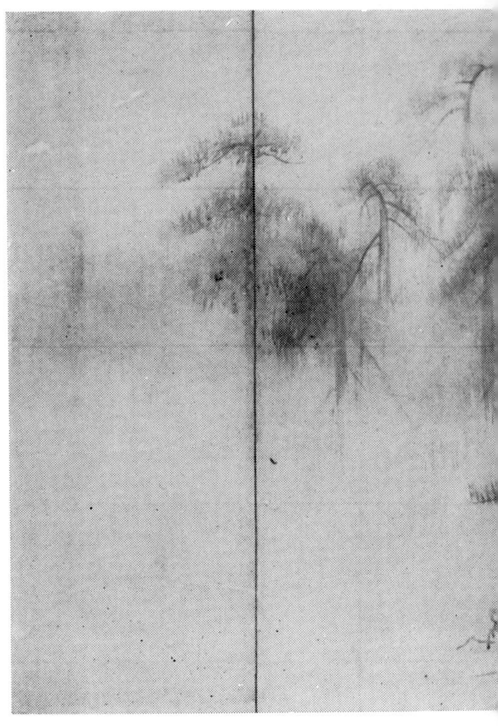

short, Tohaku was both an outstanding artist in ink and a superb *kimpeki* painter.

Kyuzo (1568–93), a son of Tohaku, died at the age of twenty-five while his father was still living. If he painted the *shoheki-ga* in the Shoun-ji, as I believe he did, he must have done so when he was twenty-four years old. Since there are not as many standard works by Kyuzo as by Tohaku, little material is available for comparison with the *shoheki-ga* in the Chishaku-in. However, records of the temple entered in 1705 and in the An'ei era (1772–81) list Kyuzo as one of the painters of these *shoheki-ga*. He probably joined his father in painting them.

Sotaku (d. 1611), Sakon, and Soya (1590–1677), the three younger brothers of Kyuzo, were also professional artists. Sakon and Soya should be considered artists of the Edo period, however. A few

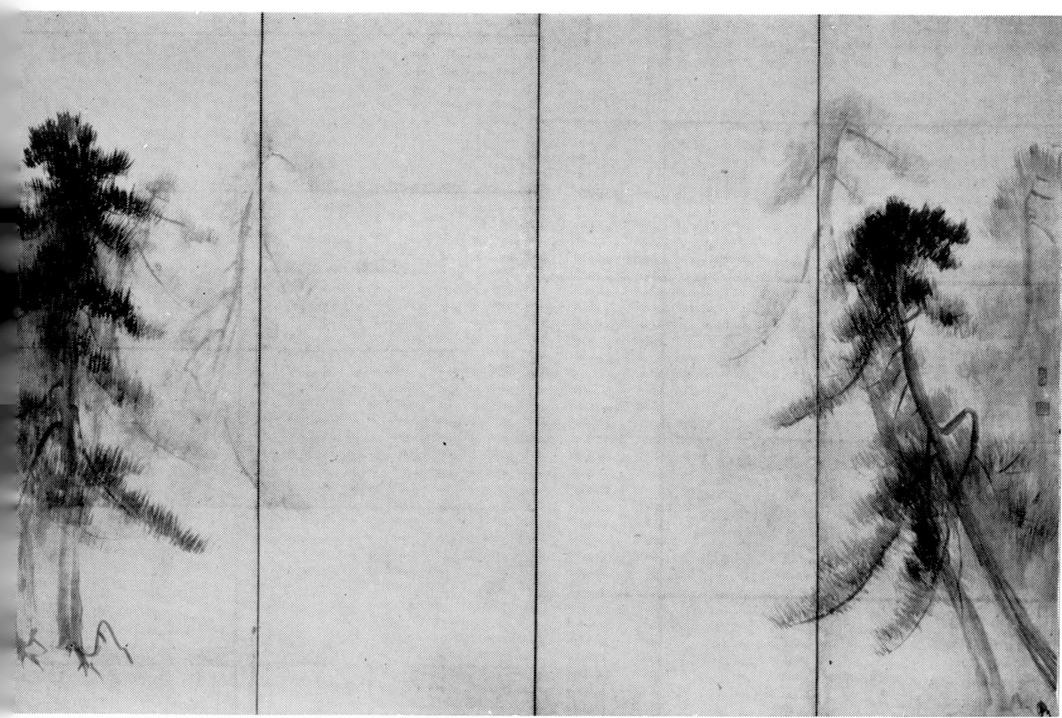

149. Hasegawa Tohaku: Pine Trees. *One of a pair of sixfold screens, ink on paper; 155.5 × 347 cm. Late sixteenth century. Tokyo National Museum.*

paintings by Sotaku remain, but no *shoheki-ga* have been discovered.

Among the extant Momoyama *shoheki-ga* in the Kyoto area, quite a number are thought to have been painted by artists of the Hasegawa school. The best are the paintings in colors and gold on paper of such subjects as pine trees, cherry blossoms, and cedars in the *shoin* of the Myoren-ji (Figs. 80, 137, 138); *Tiger and Bamboo* in colors and gold on paper (Fig. 92), *Autumn Flowers,* and *Rocks and Waves* in ink and light colors (Fig. 89; this can be regarded as Tohaku's work), which has been remounted as a hanging scroll, in the Zenrin-ji; and *Autumn Flowers* (Fig. 139), *Flowers and Birds,* and *Willow* (Fig. 140) in the Sambo-in of the Daigo-ji. Some of the *shoheki-ga* in the *hondo* of the Zuigan-ji are also attributed to Hasegawa Toin. They are recognized as works of the Ha-

segawa school from their style. The paintings on the cedar doors of this temple appear to have been painted by the same artist. It is interesting that the form and pose of each arhat in the *Sixteen Arhats* on the cedar doors (Fig. 147) and in Tohaku's screen painting of the same subject (Fig. 148; painted when Tohaku was seventy years old), owned by the Chishaku-in, are almost identical.

UNKOKU SCHOOL   The Unkoku school professed to be the legitimate successor of Sesshu, a priest who was an outstanding artist of the Muromachi period. A considerable number of works by its founder, Unkoku Togan (1547–1618), many bearing his signature and seal, are extant. He painted various subjects—landscapes, flowers and birds, animals, and figures—

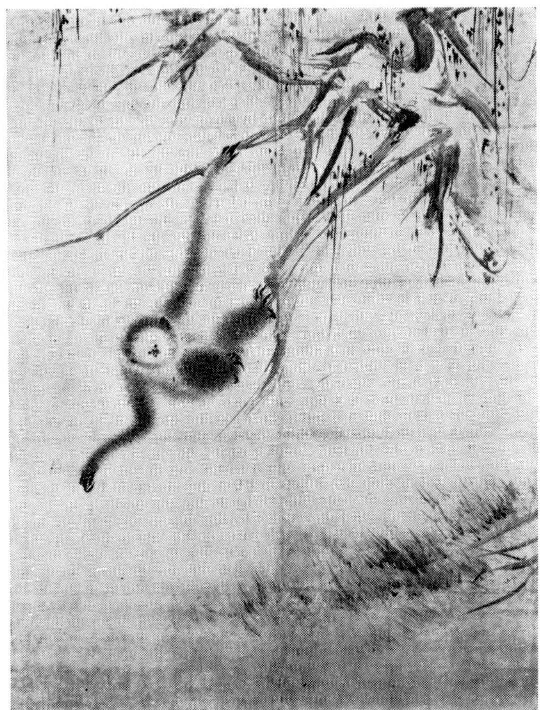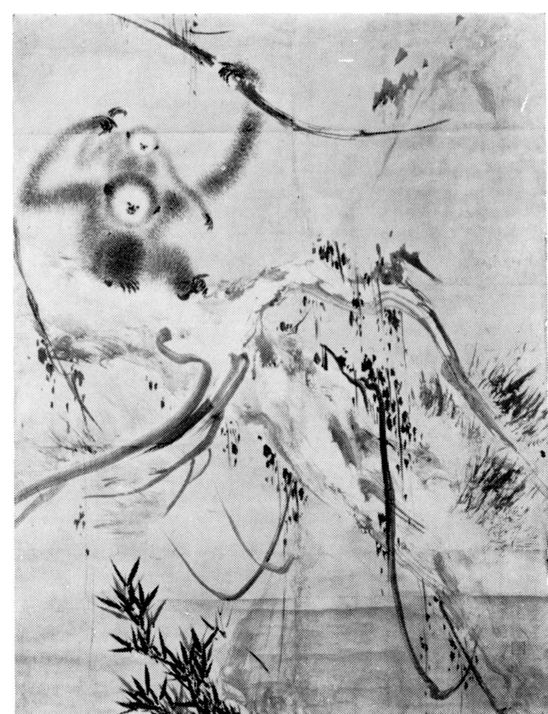

150. *Hasegawa Tohaku:* Monkeys in an Old Tree. *A pair of hanging scrolls, ink on paper; 154.5 × 114.5 cm. Late sixteenth century. Ryosen-an, Myoshin-ji, Kyoto.*

mostly in ink or ink and light colors. Compared to those of other leading artists of the time, his paintings in rich colors are few. As might be surmised from this, Togan was the most conservative master artist of the Momoyama period. In contrast to the gorgeous and colorful works of other artists, his paintings tend to be rather dark and austere.

Even so, like the Momoyama artist that he was, Togan also painted large *shoheki-ga* in an appropriate Momoyama style. His most famous works are in the main hall of the Obai-in, Daitoku-ji. He also painted *shoheki-ga* in other buildings of the Daitoku-ji, but only those in the Obai-in remain today. The Obai-in was built in 1588. If Togan painted the *shoheki-ga* at that time, he was forty-one years old. All are in ink and are found in three rooms. Their subjects are *Wild Geese and Reeds* (Fig. 151), *The Seven Sages of the Bamboo Grove,* and *Land-*

scape (Fig. 94). Each is a different type of painting, but generally they present a quiet mood. Especially in his *Landscape,* Togan has depicted a tranquil scene in the tradition of Sesshu.

The *shoheki-ga* in the *hojo* of the Fumon-in, To-fuku-ji, Kyoto, are also identified as Togan's work because their style is similar to that of the *shoheki-ga* in the Obai-in. There is a strong possibility that the *kimpeki*-style *Flowers and Birds* in the rooms in the front part of the *hojo* in the Fumon-in were painted by Watanabe Ryokei, as mentioned earlier. The *shoheki-ga* identified as Togan's work are in the rooms at the back and comprise *Landscape and Figures* in ink and light colors (Fig. 95), *Noble Characters* in ink (Fig. 96), and *Wild Geese and Reeds* in ink. The style of these ink paintings is completely in keeping with that of the works in the Obai-in. Also, the details of *Landscape and Figures*

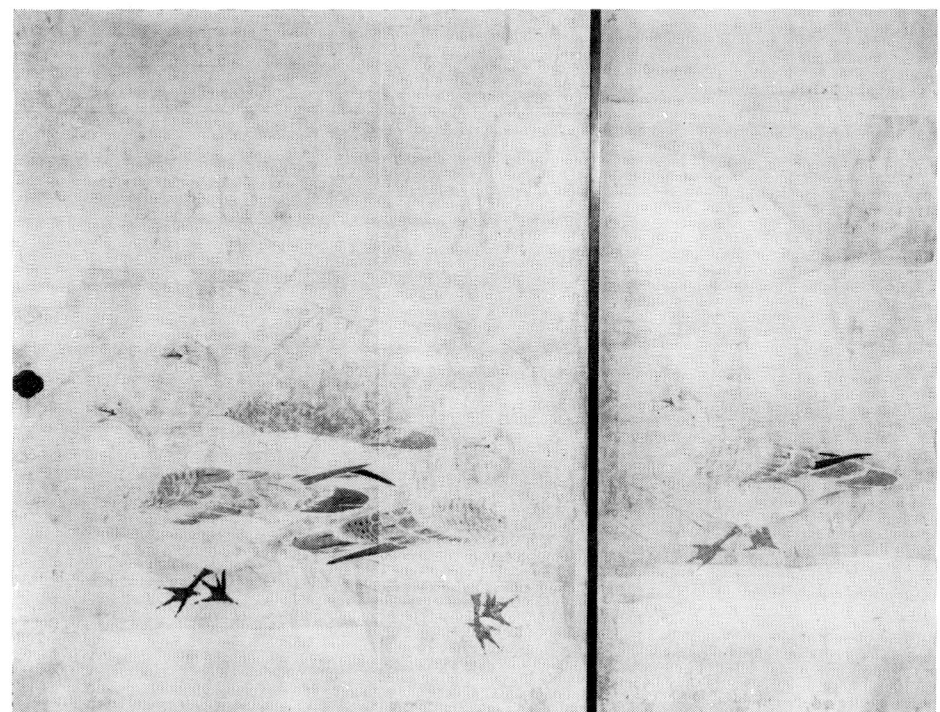

151. *Unkoku Togan: detail from* Wild Geese and Reeds. Fusuma, *ink on paper, 181 × 142 cm.* *1588. Main hall, Obai-in, Daitoku-ji, Kyoto.*

are precisely delineated, and the trees and rocks have characteristics identical to those in his *Land-scape* in the Obai-in. The temple claims that these were painted by Kaiho Yusho, but there is no ques-tion that they should be considered works of Togan.

Plum Tree and Crows (Fig. 97), painted on six *fusuma,* in the Kyoto National Museum, is a *shoheki-ga* with a mood quite different from that of Togan's works in the Obai-in and the Fumon-in. It is painted in ink and light colors on a gold back-ground. We are told that originally this painting was in Kobayakawa Takakage's Najima Castle in Kyushu. The painting depicts a flock of crows gathered in a plum tree in the snow; its composi-tion is sweeping and richly expressive, rendering it unique among Togan's extant works.

Toeki (1591–1644), Togan's second son, suc-ceeded him as the head of the family. Calling himself Sesshu IV, he was important as the leading artist of the Unkoku school in the early Edo period. He painted many *shoheki-ga,* including the fine works *Flowers and Landscape* in ink and *Landscape and Figures* in the main hall of the Juko-in. They lack the force of Togan's works, but the style of a new period is seen in their candor.

SOGA SCHOOL   Neither the birth nor the death date of Chokuan of the Soga school is known, but it is certain that he was living around 1610, for a framed picture of a *shimme* (a horse dedicated to a shrine to be used by a god) belonging to the Kitano Temman-gu shrine in Kyoto was painted by him and dedicated in that year. Using Sakai as his home base, he painted in the Kinki district centered on Kyoto. Although we

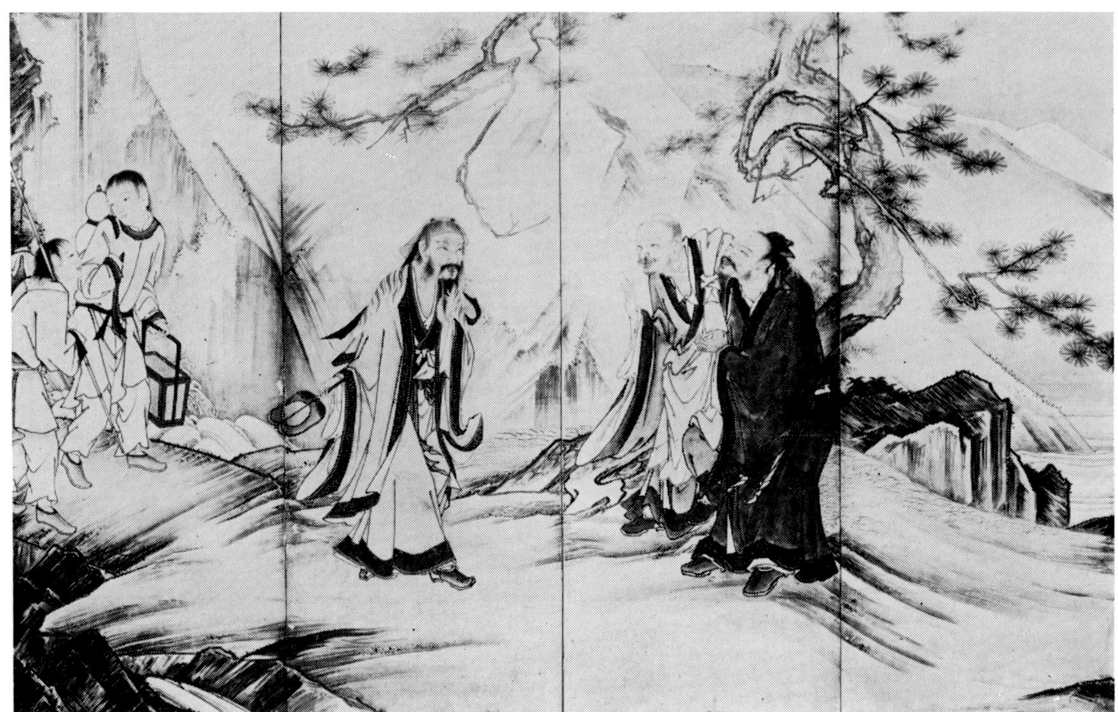

152. *Soga Chokuan: detail from* The Three Laughers at Tiger Bridge. *One of a pair of sixfold screens, colors on paper; 160.5 × 365 cm. Late sixteenth century. Henjoko-in, Wakayama Prefecture.*

have a considerable number of his paintings in the form of folding screens (Fig. 152) and scrolls, unfortunately no *shoheki-ga* by Chokuan are extant. Still, since he was a Momoyama-period artist, it is unlikely that he painted no *shoheki-ga*. In fact, Tani Buncho (1763–1840), an artist of the Edo period, noted in his memoirs that there was a *fusuma* painting, *Pine Tree and Hawk,* based on Chokuan's favorite subject, hawks, in the *shoin* of the Kensho-in of Nara's famous Kofuku-ji. The connection between the Soga school and the Kofuku-ji seems to have continued through the time of Chokuan's son, Nichokuan, as the Kofuku-ji possesses a folding screen by Nichokuan. (This screen is of a small type called a *furosaki byobu*.) It is believed that Chokuan painted *shoheki-ga* not only in the Nara area but also in Osaka and Kyoto, but none have yet been found.

Nichokuan lived in Sakai with his father, and

the dates of his birth and death are similarly unknown. However, the date of March 1656 appears in the inscription accompanying his *Hawk,* a hanging scroll donated to the Horyu-ji, Nara. Therefore we know that he was living at that time. Fortunately, several *shoheki-ga* by Nichokuan survive. His best works are in the *shoin* of the Taima-dera temple in Nara Prefecture. In the Goko-no-ma are *Landscape* in ink and light colors, *Fishing Boats by the Reeds* (Fig. 93) in ink and light colors, and *Flowers and Landscape* painted in ink on a small *fusuma* in the *chigaidana,* ornamental shelves adjoining the tokonoma. A seal of authentication reading "Nichokuan" is stamped on one of the small *fusuma*. Still other paintings are in the Sagi-no-ma: *Plum Tree and Hawk* in colors, mounted on a wall, and *Herons in the Reeds*. On *Plum Tree and Hawk* appear the inscription "Soga Chokuan-ni" and one seal. Among the relatively large number of extant paint-

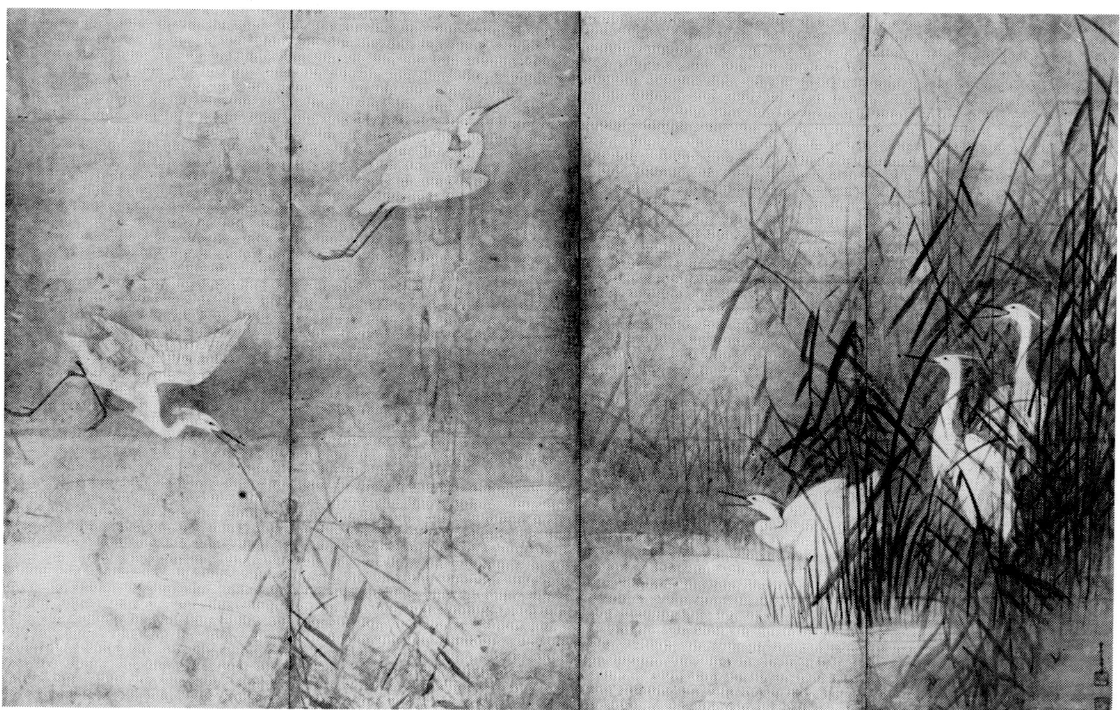

153. *Soga Nichokuan: detail from* Herons and Reeds. *One of a pair of sixfold screens, ink on paper; 151 × 355 cm. Early seventeenth century. Daitoku-ji, Kyoto.*

ings by Nichokuan, these *shoheki-ga* are painted with particular care, especially his favored subjects of hawks and herons. The hawks are sharply delineated, and the various poses of the herons are vividly rendered.

TAWARAYA SOTATSU   The Tosa school followed the tradition of *yamato-e.* Mitsunori (1583–1638) succeeded Mitsuyoshi as head of the Tosa family. Sumiyoshi Jokei (1598–1670) branched off from the Tosa school and restored the Sumiyoshi household. Both Mitsunori and Jokei are important artists in the *yamato-e* tradition in the early Edo period. However, it was Tawaraya Sotatsu who truly revived *yamato-e,* leaving a great imprint on the history of *shoheki-ga.* He was active in the late Momoyama and early Edo periods, but the particulars of his life, including the dates of his birth and death, are not known. There

are several stories concerning his background. One asserts that he was from a merchant family who were proprietors of a store named Tawaraya, dealing in brocades. Another says his family painted pictures on fans for sale. In any case, it is not difficult to imagine that his decorative style of painting may have been closely related to a family trade.

There are many masterpieces by Sotatsu in the form of folding screens, but the *shoheki-ga* in Kyoto's Yogen-in temple are among his rare works in this format. The *Miyako Rinsen Meisho Zue,* a collection of pictures of famous places in Kyoto by Akizato Rito, contains comments on the *shoheki-ga* in the Yogen-in. According to this source, Sotatsu painted those in the Shuro-no-ma and Matsu-no-ma in the main reception hall and also painted both sides of two cedar sliding doors in a room under the south eaves. These last were pictures of elephants, Chinese lions, and a rhinoceros. He also painted pictures in the rooms of the small reception hall. It is clear that in the Kansei era (1789–1801), when the *Miyako Rinsen Meisho Zue* was published, many paintings considered to be Sotatsu's work existed. However, only the *fusuma* painting in the Matsu-no-ma of the *hondo* (Fig. 141) and the cedar-door paintings *Elephant, Rhinoceros,* and *Chinese Lion* (Fig. 119) survive. The *shoheki-ga* in the Yogen-in appear to have been famous for a long time, for the *Gashi Kaiyo* by Ooka Shumboku, published in 1753, contains a miniature copy of the *Elephant* and credits it to Sotatsu.

Of course there are no signatures or other writing by the artist on these *shoheki-ga,* but their remarkably individualistic style indicates that they are indeed the work of Sotatsu, as has been generally believed. The *fusuma* painting in the Matsu-no-ma is executed in rich colors on a gold background.

Its strong and simple composition, consisting of only a pine tree and rock painted in soft thick lines, and the use of *horinuri* coloring (a method of coloring that keeps clear of the outlines) show a decorative style quite different from that of the *kimpeki* paintings done by the artists of the *kanga* school in the Momoyama period. Sotatsu skillfully used the techniques and style of the classical *yamato-e,* blending them into a new style. All the paintings on the cedar doors are in deep rich colors. He appears to have obtained ideas for the subjects of these paintings from the *Choju Emaki,* a picture scroll of birds and animals belonging to the Kozan-ji in Kyoto, but his rendition of the animals is highly original. The dynamic presentation of the Chinese lion in particular is superb. From the history of the Yogen-in, it is estimated that these *shoheki-ga* were painted around 1621.

TITLES IN THE SERIES

Although the individual books in the series are designed as self-contained units, so that readers may choose subjects according to their personal interests, the series itself constitutes a full survey of Japanese art and will be of increasing reference value as it progresses. The following titles are listed in the same order, roughly chronological, as those of the original Japanese editions. Those marked with an asterisk (*) have already been published or will appear shortly. It is planned to complete the English-language series in 1977.